12 y

SUCCESSFUL SCHOOL COMMUNICATIONS:

A Manual and Guide for Administrators

William Goldstein

Joseph C. DeVita

PARKER PUBLISHING COMPANY, INC.   West Nyack, NY

Dedication

We dedicate this book to our families
with affection, gratitude, and pride.

Library of Congress Cataloging in Publication Data

Goldstein, William
    Successful school communications.

    Includes index.
    1. Communication in education--Handbooks, manuals,
etc. I. DeVita, Joseph C.   joint author.
II. Title.
LB2806.G55   371.2   77-24679
ISBN 0-13-872036-3

Printed in the United States of America

THE MANY PRACTICAL WAYS
THIS BOOK WILL HELP
ADMINISTRATORS

Most school administrators are aware of the enormous amount of time it takes to inform, enlighten, and persuade students, faculty, parents, and members of the community. This book will save you invaluable time *at once* and increase your effectiveness by freeing you from much of the trivia and drudgery that stem from correspondence and other communications. Supervision as well as teaching performance often depends on how skillfully and clearly the administrator communicates. Developing written observations of the work of teachers, for example, setting and achieving objectives, and preparing *realistic* evaluations of the faculty performance are among the central issues that need to be dealt with effectively.

This book provides *hundreds* of *proven, successfully tested* ways for strengthening and polishing your ability to communicate skillfully, and this is frequently the key to superior administrative performance. Case studies, sample forms, checklists, specific techniques are provided—all dealing with *real* problems. You will find quick, dependable guidelines to clear communications in such important areas as:

- Designating specific responsibilities for everything connected with graduation ceremonies—all in easy, accessible form

- Responding to the letter of an angry parent
- Establishing *with* teachers the objectives on which they will be evaluated
- Writing a message for the school yearbook that says what *you want it to say*—with force and clarity
- Congratulating performing groups such as athletic teams and musical organizations in ways that not only express appreciation, but add to the school's positive public relations and help pave the way for future programs
- Suspending a student with full regard to his rights and "due process"
- Recommending changes in curriculum with *full justification* for your proposals
- Presenting arguments supporting your recommendation to a board of education
- Preparing speeches that *get results*
- Dealing with accusations against the school which appear in the local press
- Orienting students and parents to new scheduling procedures (e.g., "arena" scheduling), eliminating much of the anxiety and frustration which accompany major changes in long-established methods and procedures.
- Guiding faculty to a smooth, well-organized opening day of school—and later on throughout the school year
- Closing the school in June with ease and dispatch
- Setting tone and philosophy in school publications prepared for student *and* adult consumption and enlightenment
- Profiling the school through sensible use of vital data
- Sharing your new, *workable* ideas on educational matters with the rest of the academic community through publications

Clear communications are vital to the general success of an administrator; never have greater demands been placed on you to explain, account, clarify, and inform everyone connected with your school of what is *really* happening to, and with, your students. This book will enable you to simplify the process of communicating with faculty, students, administrative colleagues, and the public. It will help you avoid the needlessly overwhelming traps of detail and tedium, and give you the assurance that comes with the knowledge that you are communicating *clearly, promptly, and above all successfully.*

William Goldstein
Joseph C. DeVita

Acknowledgments

The authors are grateful to a number of people without whose cooperation and help this project would have been infinitely more difficult. We thank the school systems of Norwalk, Trumbull, and Weston, Connecticut where we developed and used many of the materials and methods which appear in this book.

CONTENTS

The Many Practical Ways This Book Will Help Administrators . 9

1 Bringing It Home—Establishing School and Community Rapport . 17

Communications That Prevent Misunderstandings . Dynamic Models for Elementary School Communications . Effective Methods for Expanding Public Relations in Secondary Schools . Handling Parental Complaints

2 Communicating with and for the World of Students . 37

Your Guide to "Instant" Communications . You and the School Paper . Policy on School Newspapers . Yearbooks, Memories, and Stuff . Toward "Snappier" Student Handbooks . Letters of Recommendation That Make a Difference . Correspondence That Shows You Really Care . Guidelines for Correspondence . Summary

3 Examining Key Factors Affecting Communications with Students . 62

Involving Student Leadership "For Real" . Responding to Petitions of Students . Dynamic Methods of Stifling Rumor and Hysteria . The Law and the Student . Sensible Approaches to Suspension and the Community . Student Handbooks Ride Again . Selling Your Courses of Study Well . Self-Scheduling Made Easy . Graduation—The Final Touch . Conclusion

4 Communicating Effectively with the Faculty . 99

"Good to Have You With Us" . Daily Bulletins . Here's Our Policy . Practical Guidelines for Communicating Well with Faculty . Do Teacher Handbooks Matter? . Intriguing Methods of Communicating Board

13

4   Communicating Effectively with the Faculty (Cont.)

Policy . Introducing and Analyzing the Community to New Faculty . Letters of Reference Can Make a Difference . Correspondence with the "Chiefs". Reporting and Evaluating Instructional Data . Survey of Computerized Guidance System . Structuring Departmental and Faculty Meetings . Welcome Back! It's September and We're Ready! . Have a Nice Summer, But Before You Do... . Next Year, Your Assignment Is... . Good Feelings Through Congratulatory Notes . Issuing Individual and School-Wide Directives . Delicate Handling of Reprimands and Other Negative Correspondence . Guidelines for Development of Budgets . Overcoming Resistance to Change . "So Long—It's Been Good to Know You" . Conclusion

5   Constructing and Communicating Supervisory and Evaluative Systems with Sensitivity and Skill . 132

Organizing the System . Procedures for Supervision and Evaluation . Assumptions Lay Groundwork for Durability . Certain Assumptions . Observation Reports: Their Nature, Use, and Function . Making "Objectives" Come Alive . Evaluating Your Secretary . Evaluating Services of Chairmen and Administrators . Evaluations for "In the Meantime, in Between Time" . Accountability Forms for Supervisors . Establishing Supervisory and Administrative Calendars . Preparation of Materials for Nonrenewal of Contract and Dismissal . Summarizing Supervisory Conferences . Administrative and Appeal Procedures . Conclusion

6   Communications That Will Help You Cope with the Unexpected . 171

Situation . Situation . Conclusion . Student Press—What They Say and Write About . Viewpoint . Evaluating Communications Endeavors

7   How to Accomplish More with Central Office Communications . 199

Human Relations . Field Trips and Their Legal Implications . Situation and Questions . Student Suspension Policies and Due Process . Disciplinary Procedures and the Need for Well-Defined Board Policies . Now You See Them Now You Don't

8   Successful Communications with the Public and Press: "Volcanic Partnerships" . 225

Handling the Angry Letter . Press Credibility or Perish . Improving Public and Press Relations . Getting Proper News Coverage . Three Often Overlooked Groups of Positive Public Communications . Being Aware . Twenty-five Typical Questions of Concern

9 Making Speeches That Get Results . 243

Preparing a Presentation for the Board of Education . The "Service Club" Delivery . Addressing Professional Groups . So You're a Panelist Now . Speaking to Student Groups . What P.T.A.'s, Boosters' Clubs, and Other Parent Groups Want to Hear . Introductory Remarks at School Functions . Contributing from an Audience . Speaking to "Pressure" Groups . Planning the "Big" Speech . Conclusion

10 Writing for Professional Journals—With a Purpose . 257

What is There Really Left to Say? . Association Survey . Gallup Poll . Public Perception of a "Good" School . Twenty-five Typical Questions of Concern . Student Concerns . Gauging the Reading Audience . Finding Outlets for Your Writings . Introducing Yourself to an Editor . When Should You Hear from the Editor? . How Much Should You Expect? . What Does the Contract Include? . What Happens After You Have Completed the Manuscript? . Examination of Some Sample Correspondence . Checklist for Supervisory Observation of ESL and Mainstream Teachers . Self-Evaluation Checklist for Mainstream Teachers of ESL Pupils

Index . 276

1

BRINGING IT HOME—
ESTABLISHING SCHOOL
AND COMMUNITY RAPPORT

Communications between the school and community are a vital part of today's educational scene. This chapter will spell out hundreds of dynamic and innovative ideas for preventing communication gaps and for encouraging harmonious school-community relationships.

One of the first tasks the communications-conscious principal must accomplish is to solicit the support and understanding of the superintendent of schools as to the necessity for improving school-community relations. Once his imprimatur and encouragement are received, the principal may start out on a multipronged attack which may be designed to accomplish his primary goal as stated.

Logically, several crucial events have to happen simultaneously. Some review of the literature by the principal would be helpful. Rallying the support of the staff and emphasizing both the importance and the benefits to be derived has to be accomplished carefully and tactfully.

Figure 1-1

Here's an idea to improve Brien McMahon High School. . .

_____

_____

_____

_____

_____

Please reply to: Name _____

Address _____

? I have a question about Brien McMahon High School. . .

_____

_____

_____

_____

_____

Please reply to: Name _____

Address _____

I heard a rumor that. . .

_____

_____

_____

_____

_____

Please reply to: Name _____

                   Address _____

Place
Stamp
Here

Joseph C. DeVita, Principal
Brien McMahon High School
Norwalk, Conn. 06854

847-0481

Once these initial steps are achieved, the principal may wish to identify and survey the several publics[1] within the school district. It may be interesting to note that preconceived notions as to how many identifiable publics are served by your school may be expanded once you "zero in" on this type of survey.

- Keep in mind that the school should listen to what the publics want to know.

- Remember that communications are a two-way street.

COMMUNICATIONS THAT PREVENT MISUNDERSTANDINGS

Preaddressed card systems do wonders for improving school-community communications. In addition to answering personal concerns, they reinforce the concept of "the school is really interested in what I have to say." (Figure 1-1)

The principal is an educational leader in the community and is directly responsible to the superintendent for the management of the school to which he is assigned.

In this capacity, he is expected to consult with the superintendent and/or his designee as often as necessary concerning the best interest of his school. He is expected to study the problems of the school and seek to develop the school to the point of highest effectiveness.

He must maintain a close relationship with the community served by his school, and encourage and make possible a free exchange of ideas and concerns between the community and the school system.

We all recognize the above responsibilities and problems of administrators. Now let's look at some proven solutions on the elementary level.

DYNAMIC MODELS FOR
ELEMENTARY SCHOOL COMMUNICATIONS

The principal must be a key element in any communications program. Even though a well defined school-community public relations program is not mandated from the central office, much of a positive school atmosphere has to be the responsibility of the prin-

---

[1]Publics, as used in this text, are the numerous pressure groups, organizations, and segments of a community that express an interest in schools and attempt to influence their direction.

cipal. Thus, it is his primary responsibility to know the school community and collect data and information which will provide insights into the needs of his school-community public relations program.

Workable Public Relations Activities

Key: Unique activities for principals are indicated by "P."
Activities specifically designed to be used by the faculty are marked "F."
Combined efforts are designated by "P-F."

P. The principal must be personally committed to an open, honest, on-going two-way flow of communications between the school and community.

P. The principal must provide the leadership to organize in-school education of staff members as to their role in the school-community public relations program.

P-F. A faculty committee may be assigned the task to plan for the involvement of parents and community resources in the program.

F. Perhaps a selected teacher and a group of youngsters may be interested in developing a newsletter.

P-F. It is advantageous to utilize parent volunteers in school affairs, thus developing a cadre of parent supporters for school activities.

P-F. Encourage news releases by all staff members. A sample format may be:

Figure 1-2

All Personnel
John C. Gold

GUEST SPEAKERS, VOLUNTEERS, FORMAT

Through the school year you will invite many guest speakers, volunteers to escort or assist you during a field trip or activity, and parents and friends who will participate in one way or another to help us provide a rich educational experience. It is important that I know who these people are and what kind of service they will be providing. *Please* keep me informed before you make a final decision by completing this form. This will also provide us with the necessary information so that we may properly recognize these valuable contributions.

Many thanks.

Who? (Name)_____

Organization (if he represents any)_____

What? (will he be doing)_____

When? (Date-Time)_____

Where? (Place)_____

Why? (how does it fit into the educational program/plan)_____
_____

How many students are involved?_____

Sponsoring and involved teachers?_____

P. Publish a school handbook which may include a historical brief, some pertinent concerns, rules and regulations, special study opportunities, reporting dates, staff names, and study tips which may aid the concerned parent.

P-F. Keep a steady flow of announcements going home regarding special events and interesting activities.

F. Send personal invitations to parents to attend special school day events.

P-F. Organize class picnics; trips for parents, teachers, and students.

P. Encourage a parent-teacher-student partnership in career day activities.

P-F. Invite community people into the classroom as guest speakers. Follow up the presentation with a certificate of appreciation, e.g.:

Figure 1-3

CERTIFICATE OF APPRECIATION

This certificate is presented to

MARY JANE O'DONNELL

In recognition of your valuable contribution to the youngsters of Mill Hill School. We hope this certificate will serve as a lasting memento of this pleasant experience.

_____   _____   _____
Principal   Teacher   Date

P-F. Have children sing, perform, demonstrate, throughout the community.

P-F. Display art work in local department stores, supermarkets, doctors' offices.

P-F. Utilize special days in the year as positive public relations vehicles:[1]

- Independence Day
- Flag Day
- Veteran's Day
- Memorial Day
- Citizenship Day
- Thanksgiving Day
- Benjamin Franklin's Birthday
- Lincoln's Birthday
- Dr. Martin Luther King's Birthday
- Black History Week
- Minority Groups in America
- Christmas
- Chanukah
- Passover
- United Nations Week
- Earth Day

P-F. Have youngsters participate in clean-up days on school property.

P. Provide coffee hours for parents to discuss programs, policies, and opportunities within the school.

P-F. Invite parents to witness reading, science, and math classes in action.

P. Publish a pocket-size calendar of events for the school.

P-F. Develop and utilize "Happy Messages" to be sent home.

---

[1]DeVita, Pumerantz, and Galano, *Teacher's Handbook of Classroom Programs For Special Days,* (West Nyack, New York: Parker Publishing Company, 1973).

P-F. Keep a steady information flow of supportive services being received by students of the school.

P-F. Provide for parent-teacher positive conferences.

P-F. Use interpreters for foreign-born parents and ESL students.

P-F. Recognize parents and adults who participate in school functions.

P. Develop and utilize a staff profile sheet, e.g.:

Figure 1-4

TO: All Staff Members

FROM: Albert J. Vann

RE: *Staff Profile*

CONFIDENTIAL

As part of our internal public relations program, I am going to develop a staff profile—this will be a composite and not identify individuals—for community distribution. With this objective in mind, would you please complete the following resume:

NAME_____

POSITION_____

DEPARTMENT_____ SUBJECTS_____

COLLEGE EDUCATION (Last college first—include special programs/degree or program)_____
_____

Please   check   highest   degree: AB_____
MA_____   MA+15_____   6th Yr._____
6th Yr. + 15_____   PhD_____
Travel _____
Unique Professional Experience Director of Upward Bound, Tutor in Boston Settlement House, Peace Corps, Vista, etc.)
_____
_____

*Any Professional Honors*_____
_____

Publications (title, publisher, book article)_____
_____

Any Other Pertinent Data (hobbies, etc.)_____
_____

If a Veteran: branch of service, medals, honors, any items of
human interest_____
_____

P. Encourage teachers and students to participate in public relations activities.

P. Provide leadership models for sending out news releases.

P-F. Have evening discussions of curriculum trends and offerings to keep parents informed.

P-F. Encourage home contacts and home visits (if invited).

F. Provide after school help for students and be sure the community is made aware of this added service.

P. Hold mini-tours for small groups of community people.

P-F. Encourage classroom teachers to publish classroom newspapers highlighting student accomplishments.

F. Utilize inside and outside bulletin boards to recognize student contributions.

P. Set up a listener's team of interested parents for feedback purposes.

P-F. Post a monthly birthday calendar where students and staff members may list their dates.

F. Create a slide presentation and have teachers and students show slides in and around the community.

P-F. Invite real estate people in to visit classrooms and discuss curriculum.

P. Institute a suggestions box.

P. Form a student-principal-teacher advisory group.

P-F. Arrange parent-teacher-student talent shows.

EFFECTIVE METHODS FOR EXPANDING PUBLIC RELATIONS IN SECONDARY SCHOOLS

A great deal of today's educational criticism is aimed directly at the heart of the secondary education division. Much of it is a "frustration backlash" of lost parental control over the youngster, the questioning of moral sexual standards, the new freedoms of "gays," and the uncensored publications usually found at the high school level. The school system is also blamed for not having a "tight ship" in terms of perceived disciplinary practices, allowing students to dress too casually, encouraging girls to be less than ladies by participating in boys' sports, and enticing boys to abdicate their masculinity by allowing them to participate in cooking and child development classes. Added to these are attacks by the intellectual professional writers on school organization, policies, and the reluctance of educators to change.

The principal must rally the forces of the school. All the multiethnic forces, all the staff members, all the students, and all personnel must feel his educational commitment to a sound, active public relations program. His leadership in this area may very well be the key to the survival of the local support base—budgetary as well as psychological support.

Workable Public Relations Activities

P-F.. Use the students as positive carriers of worthwhile educational offerings, i.e., open messages may include:

HUMANE ENVIRONMENTS

STAFF

COURSE OFFERINGS

ORGANIZATIONAL PATTERNS

ACTIVITIES

P-F. Establish a continuous telephone communications system to the home which expresses the theme "we care for your youngster."

P. Encourage teachers to make their subject matter dynamic and rewarding for all students.

P. Establish a newsletter to all members of the school community.

P-F. Use the school newspaper as a communications source.

P. Establish a school news article, written by students, in the local newspaper.

P. Establish a radio program, conducted by students, to highlight school happenings.

P. Cooperate with community groups in resolving local problems or distributing community information.

P-F. Encourage local, state, and national organizations to give student, school, and personnel awards and publicize the event.

P-F. Assist the community and provide educational experiences for the students by organizing day-care centers.

P-F. Invite elementary and middle school youngsters to musicals, sporting events, and plays held at the high school.

P. Establish small parent discussion groups within the school.

P. Encourage and publicize the professional publications of staff members.

P. Utilize the athletic accomplishments of the coaching staff and students to enhance *esprit de corps*.

P-F. Encourage the creation of jazz groups, marching bands, debating teams, and other school activities to get students involved.

P-F. Recognize National Honor Society members in ceremonies in which parents may participate or attend.

P-F. Use the American Field Service exchange students as local speakers.

P-F. Invite local dignitaries to sports and academic banquets.

P. Use the Open House approach to encourage community visitations to the school. A fine example of this may be illustrated by:

Format for Language Awareness Night

PURPOSE: To promote community involvement. To inform the community of the role the study of foreign languages plays in today's world. To demonstrate to the community what is actually taking place in the language classes. To allow teachers, parents, students, and friends to converse on an informal basis. To introduce and present cultural aspects of the foreign countries by way of skits, plays, displays, music, dance, costumes, and delicious dishes. To promote the study of foreign languages.

INVOLVEMENT:The affair is open to the public but special effort will be made to involve parents, students, and friends. Parents and students will be asked to prepare foreign dishes.

PUBLICITY: Open messages, newspaper, radio, students in classes, announcements and involvement of foreign language teachers in middle schools, morning announcements, notices on bulletin boards, phone calls to parents.

COMMITTEES: A. Newspaper articles
B. Radio
C. Middle Schools
D. Annex
E. Program
F. Typists

ROOM
ASSIGNMENTS: France, Canada
France, Africa, Caribbean
Italy
Spain I
Spain II
Latin America, Mexico
Germany
Rome, Greece (Latin)
French play
Movies, slides, displays, etc.

P. Follow-up special events with short notes of congratulations, making sure that copies are placed in the person's permanent record file.

P. Provide senior citizens with invitations and complimentary passes to all school events.

P-F. Bring the senior class play, interclass plays, and skits to the people, i.e., hospitals, community groups, elementary schools.

P. Provide and publicize scholarships, career information, and college day programs for all members of the community.

P. Communicate curriculum revisions and innovative methodologies to the community.

P-F. Encourage coach/sponsor personal communications to the parents of participating youngsters.

P. Establish and promote school-community related clubs, e.g., Key Club.

P-F. Use college tutors to assist students and communicate these arrangements to the parents.

P-F. Establish and recognize a school gospel choir as an excellent community performing group.

P. Disseminate articles and innovative subject materials to all school-community members.

F. Use the bulletin board effectively to advertise and promote appropriate messages. Some guidelines and rationale might include:

Bulletin boards can be wonderful tools for student-public relations. They can be valuable instructional aids and can help create a positive classroom image.

Uses of Bulletin Boards

1. As a decoration
2. As a means of keeping students posted
3. As a means of reviewing a unit of work
4. As an incentive to improve
5. As a means of rewarding pupil achievement
6. As an introduction to a unit of work
7. As an opportunity for creativity and self-expression

Bulletin Boards as Display Areas

1. The use of bulletin boards should be a pleasurable and educational experience.
2. Take down the display as soon as interest lags.
3. Use only pictures and other data that are up-to-date.
4. Use colors to create interest and add a professional touch to the board.
5. Keep the display down to the level of the viewer's comprehension.
6. Bulletin boards are most effective when they become student projects.
7. The display must be well planned and correlated with school work.
8. Provide for individual differences.
9. Bulletin boards should be changed at least once in a ten-week period.

F. Use business and community resource people in the classroom.

P-F. Recognize the contribution of community resource people with written commendation letters or appreciation awards.

P-F. Arrange for students to study and work in the community.

P. Distribute a profile sheet highlighting staff backgrounds, qualifications, and accomplishments.

P. Create a principal-staff-student-parent advisory council.

P-F. Use students as school volunteers.

P. Cooperate quickly, pleasantly, and willingly to assist community groups in renting school facilities, or to provide appropriate school data.

P-F. Recognize special days and events throughout the school year, e.g., Spanish Day, Flag Day.

P-F. Work cooperatively with colleges and universities in placement of student teachers.

P. Use "I heard a rumor," "I have a question," "I have an idea," cards for communication purposes.

F. Organize school-wide efforts to assist such groups as Save the Children Federation, Salvation Army, and so on.

P-F. Create mini-courses and special interest courses.

P. Provide easy, in-school procedures for voter registration, selective service, obtaining working papers, and other services for students.

P. Recognize teachers by commendation letters for involvement in extracurricular activities.

P. Organize college tours for minority and economically disadvantaged students.

P-F. Utilize community resources to supplement professional experiences in school.

P. Send commendations to teacher aides, custodians, secretarial and supportive staff members.

P-F. Participate in Father's Club and P.T.A. dinners, dances, and events.

P-F. Issue appreciation certificates for guest speakers.

P-F. Share information concerning the school's philosophy and objectives with the entire community.

P. Develop and use easy, informative, public relations format sheets for submitting news releases.

P-F. Develop and use Happy Notes for all students. Example:

Figure 1-5
Happy Notes

Date_____

Dear Mr. and Mrs._____

Just a short note to let you know how pleased I am that
_____

_____

_____

Sincerely yours,

_____
Teacher

P-F. Translate forms and messages into Spanish, Italian, Greek, etc., for foreign-born parents. Example:

Figure 1-6
Noticias Buenas

Estimados Senor y Senora:_____
Deseamos avisarles del progreso de su hijo(a)_____

_____	Esta majorando en su trabajo escrito.
_____	Demuestra mas confianza en su trabajo oral.
_____	Asiste a todas sus clases.
_____	Paso su ultimo examen con una nota alta.
_____	Es muy cooperador.
_____	Es muy creativo.
_____	Hizo un informe superior.
_____	Es muy punctual.
_____	Es muy respetuoso.
_____	Muy artistico.
_____	Trabajo es muy organizado.
_____	Muestra mucho entusiasmo y interes en su trabajo.
_____	Termina lo que empieza.
_____	Capta conceptos nuevos con facilidad.
_____	Otros comentarios:_____

_____

_____

_____

Muy atentamenta,

_____
Maestro(a)

P-F. Create an atmosphere of cooperativeness, mutual respect, and dignity by your philosophy.

P. Be sure students have access to the administrative staff.

P-F. Be courteous to all people entering the building or phoning for information by greeting them politely with expressions of friendliness, and by being patient with all concerned.

Daily Avalanche—Dealing With the Paper Problem

As principal, you have just returned to your desk following a three-day professional conference to be greeted by a ton of papers, letters, messages, and commercially prepared brochures. Many are pertinent and important, many may go directly into "file thirteen," and some can be considered at a more leisurely moment. This is a real life situation facing all of us. What can be done to resolve this avalanche?

Prevention and training are your best medicines. Your right arm—your personal secretary—must be astute enough to earmark and sort your incoming communications flow.

- A separate pile for emergency items.

- The name of the department chairman written in the upper corner of an academic brochure.

- The name of a club advisor concerning a fund raising possibility or your assistant who is responsible for this area.

- A separate pile of "junk mail."

HANDLING

- Your personal assessment of the emergency items sorted in priority order.

- Your perusal of the earmarked names with a quick check to the out basket.

- A glance at the junk mail—your decision to redirect it, to file it, or to throw it out.

Time is valuable. Split-second decisions can help you handle your communications flow and prevent the repeat items from stealing time—time which cannot be replaced.

HANDLING PARENTAL COMPLAINTS

Handling parental complaints can make or break you as an administrator. Your tactfulness in resolving their concerns will result in one of two reactions: "We have a great sensitive principal at the helm of that school," or, "The snobbish dumbbell doesn't even know what I'm talking about."

Administrator:

Listening shows respect but listening does not necessarily mean agreeing. This is especially true with the first generation parent, the minority group parent, and the parent from the less affluent members of your community. What's important?

- Greetings that are warm and friendly.
- Availability of a bilingual speaker if necessary.
- An on-staff representative of the minority group being present.
- Get out from behind your desk if possible.
- A cup of coffee.
- Having counselor, social worker, teacher, unit coordinator, or pertinent data available which may help eliminate the anxiety or answer the question.
- Be friendly but firm in your decision.
- Allow for the constitutional (due process) rights of appeal to your superiors with personal confidence.

Teacher:

It is vital that the teacher be guided in the "how to" of parent-teacher conferences. Thus, the following guide may be of extreme value in preventing negative feelings about the school, its staff's competency, and its concern for its young people.

Parent Conference Guide

Without forgetting that each parent is unique in his personality and his problems, it may be helpful to list a few guides to conferences in general.

1. Responsibility for the success or failure of a conference rests primarily with the teacher. It is good to remember that success is relative and each conference must be judged according to its own circumstances and results.

2. It is easier to build a cooperative relationship if the teacher is not seated behind the desk. Behind a desk the teacher is in the place of authority, not partnership.

3. The teacher's greeting should be friendly and relaxed. If he is hurried or tense, the parent will know it. It is difficult to discuss a problem with someone who looks as if he wishes you were not there, or would leave soon.

4. Listen and then listen some more. The teacher did not invite a parent to deliver a lecture to him. Encourage the parent to talk and then listen to what he has to say.

5. Find out what the parent is thinking and feeling about his child. This is important because the teacher cannot understand the child's behavior until he knows the parent's attitude.

6. If a parent says he is worried about his child's behavior, follow through. Find out why he is worried. The teacher should not assume that he knows why. He and the parent may not feel the same way about the child.

7. If a parent gives what he thinks is a reason for a child's behavior, accept it and lead the discussion to the possible causes. Behavior is the result of many factors, not just one.

8. If a parent suggests a plan of action, accept it if it is at all possible to do so. It is better for the parent to make a suggestion than for the teacher to force one of his own. One of the goals in parent counseling is to try to get the parent to take the initiative. If the parent's plan fails, it is always possible to suggest others that may strike nearer to the root of the difficulty.

9. If the parent cannot suggest reasons for a child's behavior, or plans of action to deal with it, the teacher might suggest

alternatives for joint consideration. This might be a possibility: "What do you think? You know all the factors of the situation better than I do." Or, "We might try this and see what happens. It may take us awhile to find the source of the difficulty." Such an approach makes the parent a participant in a final decision for a tentative plan and leads to discussion that helps him to accept the plan on his own.

10. It does not help to argue with a parent. Arguing will arouse resentment and resistance.

11. It is better not to assume that a parent wants help or advice. Such an assumption usually brings resistance because it implies a form of criticism.

12. Most parents cannot be objective about their own children. Therefore, do not criticize, either directly or indirectly. Criticism is fatal to guidance or a cooperative spirit.

13. Avoid giving direct advice when the parent states his problems and leans back saying, "Tell me what to do." Let any advice or suggestions grow out of mutual discussion and a growing insight on the part of the parent into the reasons for the behavior.

14. Try to be aware of sensitive spots and avoid embarrassing the parent by noting facial expressions, gestures, and voice. These all give a clue to the parent's emotions.

15. Accept anything the parent tells you without showing surprise or disapproval. If the teacher cannot do this he will not get an honest picture of the parent's attitudes and feelings.

16. The teacher should be ready to recognize problems that are so difficult as to prevent him from giving sufficient help to the parent.

17. It is helpful to try to close the conference on a constructive, a pleasant, or a forward-going note; such as a plan for a future consultation, a definite date for the next conference, a statement of encouragement or reassurance, or a statement of a plan for cooperative action.

Generally, parent conferences are arranged through the counselor. At the end of each conference, teachers will be requested to fill out a *Conference Evaluation Sheet* which should be routed to the unit coordinator for his information and to the counselor for filing. Example:

Figure 1-7

CONFERENCE EVALUATION SHEET

Pupil_____ Teacher_____

Date of Conference_____Length of Conference____

Who came to the conference?_____
_____.

Give a brief summary of outcome_____
_____
_____
_____
_____
_____
_____
_____

Route to: Unit Coordinator_____
           Counselor   _____

Conclusion:

As every practicing public educator knows, a tremendous amount of misinformation and one-sided information is generated by uninformed publics. Therefore, it behooves all of us to develop a systematic, two-way, public relations operation for preventing this problem and for coping with its related ramifications. This is precisely what the material in this chapter is intended to do for the on-line educator—provoke thought and provide some workable examples. Communicating with and for the world of students is designed and developed in Chapter 2.

2

COMMUNICATING WITH AND
FOR THE WORLD OF STUDENTS

Communicating with students has become increasingly important to school administrators. Demands for meetings, letters, policies, and clarification surround the practicing administrator daily. While elementary and middle school students require attention by way of written communication from the head of a school, high school students *insist* they not only have access to the school's administration, but also that a network of sophisticated written and oral "services" be available to them.

YOUR GUIDE TO "INSTANT" COMMUNICATIONS

Two central ways exist by which administrators and teachers communicate with the student body at large, notwithstanding the sometime device of assemblies which are becoming increasingly rare except on a "drop-in," voluntary basis. They are: (1) the public address system which, while it is quick, tends to disrupt the instructional

37

program; and (2) the daily bulletin which, while silent, depends heavily on the fidelity of faculty for its oral delivery.

Public Address System:

Announcements have a self-deluding way of causing administrators to feel that they have communicated effectively with large groups of students. The public address system *can* be a first-rate method of conveying information quickly. Unfortunately, many oral deliveries fail conspicuously to reach their audiences because of rudeness and inattention in the classrooms. Furthermore, irritation with its abrasive interruptions often subtracts from its value as a transmitter of vital and useful information. Here are several key guidelines for its effective use:

- Never use the public address system during class time except for extreme emergencies such as fire drills, evacuations because of genuine bomb threats, or the like.

- Insist that faculty members complete and sign a simple form (see sample) which contains a *very brief,* factual message or special request of students or colleagues. No announcement will be made until this has been done.

- All P.A. announcements will be made either *prior* to the start of classes or between periods.

- Items which may be placed on the school's daily bulletin *will not* be read over the public address system.

- All skits, humorous exhortations to attend dances, plays, or other student activities are restricted to early morning, preclass times.

- Whenever possible, have *students* who are responsible and intelligent make all announcements. Voices of administrators have a way of becoming unheard and unheeded, especially if there is no variation of speakers.

- In larger schools, it might prove beneficial to place a faculty member in charge of the morning P.A. announcements. Conceivably, this responsibility might be assigned to the advisor to the Student Council since the actual announcing chores are well handled by members of that group. During the balance of the school day, a secretary, well versed in policy regarding its use, would be detailed to superintend its use, and, for that matter, its nonuse.

A simple, effective form to be completed by individuals or organizations needing to communicate via the public address system follows:

Figure 2-1

P.A. REQUEST FORM

DATE(S) TO BE READ:_____
Morning_____or afternoon_____

MESSAGE:

AUTHORIZATION:__._____
Advisor

_____
Administrator

****Note: Proper authorization
        must appear on this form
        or message will not be read.

Daily Bulletins

In order to reduce the amount of annoying "air time" saturating schools, the device of the "daily bulletin" has proved almost uniformly successful. Such announcements are read daily by teachers in *homeroom* or during *first period* in schools where no homeroom organization exists. Not infrequently, teachers will delegate this duty to a responsible student or an alternate if the main reader is absent. Good daily bulletins have the following characteristics:

- Each item is short, well written, but *not* literary in style.

- Order of presentation of items should be viewed as irrelevant. Sequence of entries should be as each arrives, for ease of typing by the secretary assigned to the task.

- Deadline times should be assigned for daily submittal of items so that the secretary may type, run, and distribute the completed bulletins to mailboxes of teachers prior to their departure from work that day

- Homeroom or first period teachers must be *required* to read or to have someone else read the bulletin each morning. Substitute teachers must also be oriented to this procedure. Frequently, complaints are lodged that teachers are failing to read the announcements, and students, as a result, are not "getting the word." Such accusations, if true, must be corrected immediately, or else the whole idea of well-organized communication on a large scale collapses.

- Bulletins, after having been read, should be posted for that day on a specially dedicated spot on the bulletin board of the room in which they were read so that late arrivals can check items which may pertain to them.

- If a "Faculty Bulletin" is also used, it should be produced as a *separate* document. Such a bulletin is excellent as an intrafaculty device or for the administration to use to communicate with teachers outside the framework of meetings. Such bulletins (using the same format as the one designed for students) should be destroyed after reading, since "sensitive", semi-personal items frequently appear thereon. While they usually do not consist of confidential information, such items are really not the concern of the student body.

- Items written for such bulletins, especially those concerned with meetings of one kind or another, should contain the following: (1) date, (2) time, (3) place, (4) purpose, and (5) name of sponsor or person to contact.

- All submittals for bulletins must allow sufficient "lead time" for recipients of the notice to plan their participation. Usually, twenty-four hours is adequate.

- Items having a special significance (such as major changes in policy or practice) or a long-range nature to them (such as scheduling a series of half-days of school to accommodate workshops for faculty) might well be "run" on the bulletin for several consecutive days.

No system of mass communication is perfect; malfunctions can, do, and will occur. Nonetheless, since one communicates only orally and in writing, sorting the "best of all possible worlds" becomes an administrative task of critical order. Experience shows that a combination of approaches similar to those suggested works effectively and lessens the abrasions caused either by communicating sporadically and poorly or not communicating at all.

YOU AND THE SCHOOL PAPER

Administrators have had, over the recent past, less and less contact with school newspapers. Freedom of expression and the electric dimensions of our times have caused mature students, especially in high schools, to speak out on aspects of their schools which, for one reason or another, they find unsatisfactory. Administrators may no longer act as censors or "clearinghouses" for what students ought to think and say. In short, school newspapers are no longer benign, slick little public relations devices, nor may they be viewed as anesthesia for a disbelieving parental clientele. Students can, should, and do speak out. Indeed, many student newspapers have taken on the prevailing philosophy of the American press at large—that of adversary, a kind of "loyal opposition."

In general, the role of administration in dealing with its indigenous student press consists of: (1) recommending to a board of education policy guidelines for student journalism within the context of the most recent court decisions governing such publications, (2) writing an occasional "message" or request for the paper, (3) appointing the advisor for the enterprise, and (4) meeting as needs arise on reviews of frequency of publication, nature of the tone of the paper, and a general review of its content and philosophy.

With this in mind, it might be good to point out that administrators, when asked to contribute something of pertinence and value to a student publication should neither rant nor be inane. Each message should be short, crisp, well-phrased, and deal with a current problem in which students appear to have a compelling interest or even passing fascination. For example, the issue of "freedom with responsibility" appears to be a persistent, highly fashionable theme today. The "guest editorial" which follows is the response of the author, then principal of Trumbull High School, to a community concern over the issue of "freedom" for high school students. The editorial appeared in *Aquila,* the high school newspaper:

Figure 2-2

How Much   Freedom   Is Enough?

Most high schools have done away with what many students used to call a suppressive atmosphere. Trumbull High School seems to be a place where students can learn in an environment uncluttered by useless rules but which still maintains a rather rigorous atmosphere of control with reason, and freedom with responsibility.

To be sure, there are students at the high school who cannot cope with the notion of privilege; fortunately, this group is in a rather conspicuous minority. Nonetheless, their numbers are sufficient to deprive the school periodically of the very special comfortable climate which we have tried to build here. But our society is affected, as we all know, in the same way by people who somehow cannot or will not adjust to reasonableness.

The vast majority of our students understand that in order to get, one must give. To maintain an adult, mature environment, **requires** adult, mature contribution from every student. "Freedom" demands that we understand the purpose of a school—which is to grow and learn; these purposes carry with them pleasure in **limited** ways. The high school whose students experience profit from their years there can only function well when students are given over to helping to make the place academically, vocationally, and socially suitable. **Never confuse the purpose of a school with that of an organization which is purely social and riveted to fun alone.** To do that undercuts the very foundations of privilege, and can only lead to a return to the dim days so characteristic of the sterile places nobody ever wanted. Fortunately, the vast majority of our students understand and accept that, and that is what makes us what we are in Trumbull High School.

Messages, however, are almost incidental; they are expectations each administrator has in carrying out his central functions in "relating" to large groups of students. The following is a reasonable policy under which any school newspaper can function essentially unfettered, yet within the moral and legal strictures of responsible journalism:

POLICY ON SCHOOL NEWSPAPERS

Here are the recommendations on the amount of control or lack of it which is appropriate for a responsible student newspaper:

1. No form of censorship should be placed upon a student newspaper so long as it adheres to the following conditions:
   (a) Anything published in a school newspaper *must not* be libelous and/or attack any individual.
   (b) Responsible journalism makes accuracy of reportage mandatory.
   (c) Under no conditions should a school newspaper resort to obscenity in expressing its point of view.
   (d) All articles published in school newspapers should reflect good taste and propriety at all times.

2. The responsibility for proper guidance in regard to any school publication rests in the main with its appointed advisor and, of course, the school administration by extension.

3. The secondary principals recognize that school publications at the junior high school level will need more careful scrutiny and supervision because of lesser maturity of junior high school students.

4. Appropriate supervision and guidance must never be construed as censorship which is abhorrent to responsible journalism.

No policy legislates fully. Administrators cannot reasonably expect regulations to provide total insurance against attacks and criticisms of rules which students, in their system of values, find "suppressive," "unenforceable," or "anachronistic"—favorite pejoratives of pupils in the twentieth-century climate of fault-finding, second-guessing, and chronic dissatisfaction. About the best one may expect from policy is that it establish guidelines which have moral vigor, vibrance, and rational parameters within which intelligent young people can and will work.

YEARBOOKS, MEMORIES, AND STUFF

Probably one of the most driving, almost instinctively emotional experiences young people have is their overwhelming sense of togetherness. As is true of student newspapers, the yearbook or "annual" has undergone vast metamorphosis since the practice of having such publications was first established. Where administrators have a role is when they are featured as "factors" in the school and, accordingly, are asked to "say something" to this year's graduates. Such messages are very special and form a kind of eternal farewell, dispensing hopefully a non-sterile, consummate wisdom to which the reader may cling and which is, if nothing else, reflective of decent, breathing sentiment.

Such messages should carry with them not a bland "fare-thee-well" flavor, but should rather be a well-thought-out, balanced, literate statement whose essence ought to linger as years slip by.

Examples of what one might say follow:

Figure 2-3

Principal's Message

Whatever years are allotted to each of us, no one ever knows ahead of time; that is one of the "sweet mysteries" of life. One thing is certain, however. When a moment passes by it is gone forever, and nothing can recall it. So it is with the years in high school, which for our seniors, are only memories now.

For some, these remembrances are tender and warm; for others they are bland, neutral, perhaps even colorless. In Shakespeare's words, however, "What's done cannot be undone." Nonetheless, there is a large-looming future awaiting all of you which ought to be seized aggressively so that your lives will be filled with time well spent and years well lived. Take the future and let it be yours; make the world and your place in it what they ought to be.

Fondly and with best wishes always,

William Lonsdale
19___   Principal

Principal's Message

Too often, like Gatsby, we tend to spend so much of our lives "in between time;" a foot in the past, a glance to the future. Others will say, sometimes cynically, that there are really only two good places—where we've been and where we're going.

I would like to think that somehow your years at Elmtown High School provided a striking three-year moment where, in a sense, time stood still, clocks froze, past and future blended somehow, but only to heighten the bittersweet things one lives through at *that* time, in *that* place If we, the faculty, and you, our graduates, have touched each other, even slightly, with a little sentiment and a bit of intellect and a lot of wisdom, then all our lives are ever so enriched by just having known one another.

As you leave high school, try to remember the feeling of friendship which drifts out of that sensitive little allegory, *Jonathan Livingston Seagull:*

> *But overcome space, and all we have left is Here. Overcome time, and all we have left is Now. And in the middle of Here and Now, don't you think that we might see each other once or twice?*

Fondly and with best wishes always,

Thomas Packer
Principal

19___

Principal's Message

Nothing is as empty as lives filled with consuming loneliness and gnawing regrets about what might have been. The poetry and songs of centuries echo in many ways the human calamity of unfulfilled hopes and smashed dreams. No such despair characterizes the Class of 19 .

Your class, the first to complete its entire high school sequence in our new building, recognized from the beginning that high school is, in a sense, the last stop of your young years, and your experiences here seem to overflow with friendship, laughter, and the unforgettably gentle pleasure of familiarity. You have respected each other; you have found and cemented lasting relationships; above all, you have enjoyed yourselves, blending academic seriousness with a light, sensitive social scene.

Milton once called time "the subtle thief of youth." Do not let this clockwork larceny destroy your zest; life is too short to tamper with the sweetness of moments well lived!

Fondly and with best wishes always,

Robert Rhodes
Principal

19___

From the examples given, the reader may note that a central theme—that of universal feeling on saying "farewell"—pervades. In addition, the ambivalence of departure and memory, as well as heightened anticipation, round out the general impact of each message. Variations on such central themes are legion and eminently useable. Congratulatory drivel has no place in a sound, sensible message; neither is there room for the ultimate trap—sermonizing; each is left, if needed at all, for other less lasting times.

TOWARD "SNAPPIER" STUDENT HANDBOOKS

Variations on student handbooks are very widespread; every school worthy of the name distributes some set of rules, advice, and calls for participation in its life. Like the teacher's lesson plan or the district's curriculum guide, such little booklets go either ignored after their initial distribution or are referred to so seldom that their publication altogether seems to be a tragic waste. This is not quite true, however, of some of the material contained in worthwhile publications.

A major attention-getter can and should be the *first* communication a reader sees on opening the pamphlet, whether the handbook is mimeographed and very short or professionally printed and very detailed. To be sure, principals tire of writing advice, exhorting students to achieve or extolling the virtues of the place; nonetheless such "words" have become standard "literary" fare. Parents and students expect them, and, having said that, one can clearly see that the psychological climate for communicating with impact has been historically set. Knowing that a principal's message, in all likelihood, will be read, he should seize that opportunity to: (1) say something of value, (2) transmit some sort of enthusiastic feeling about the school, and, more subtly, (3) transmit his own image of caring and administrative substance.

Following, the reader will find three messages of varying lengths dealing with one theme, but which carry slightly different emphases:

Figure 2-4

Principal's Message

Every now and again some people are given a special opportunity to build something lasting, something which will contribute not only to themselves, but perhaps even to generations which will follow. In opening our new high school, each of you in the student body, each of us on the faculty has this chance.

Our new school plant is a handsome building; its facilities are modern and imaginative; it reflects the pride and commitment of a community to its youth—*and it is empty and void of meaning without* **you** *and what you give it in exchange for what it will try to give you.*

Our new organization, into so-called "houses" (schools-within-a-school), highlights our attempt to create for you a warm, hospitable place of learning with the kinds of human relationships which give each of you a feeling of belonging, a feeling of being a genuine part of what school and real education are supposed to be all about.

Be aware of what is available to you: *support your school* and take advantage of what it offers; cement relationships with teachers and classmates which matter; above all do not let your high school years pass you by, for they are really "golden" years and should form the fabric of many grand memories. If these years do slip by in humdrum ways, you have lost irreplaceable moments; you have lost that magical sense of being part of something words cannot really describe; you have lost, beyond recall, part of what it means to be young.

To all of us at this high school, 19___ is unique in all of time. Let us make the most of it...together.

S. Ralph Stanton
Principal

Principal's Message

Rules are for "the greatest good of the greatest number"; they stand only so that you can proceed with the very serious business of learning with as few needless problems and interruptions as possible. Know and do what is expected of you here, so that the spirit and substance of high school will be with you always. You see, there is really no escape from childhood, friendship, ideas, and school years; they become a strong blend of past, present, and future...no matter what.

To the end of avoiding broken dreams participate *now,* in the present, and take pride in the place to which you will some day refer with affection and sentiment as *Alma Mater.* Let none of you leave high school without a sense of having shared in what it stands for, because if you remain on the margins of these central years, irreplaceable moments will dissolve having passed you by unnoticed. Study, learn, participate, contribute, make a difference! High school and the "stuff" of its existence is not for phantom strangers...it is for *you*...*everyone of you!*

> Joseph Berenson
> Principal

Principal's Message

Thomas Wolfe believed, and people seem to agree, that "you can't go home again." When something is over, somehow it seems unable to be recaptured at least in the way in which we would like to recall "the way we were" or what might have been.

Try to remember that high school is not a place for regrets, not a spot where life slides us by; it is a place where students are not just a part of its vitality; they *are* its life. Be involved with your classmates—participate in the school's many, varied activities—never, never say that high school spirit is for someone else, because *you* and your companions are the only reasons why our high school stands.

Have a grand, spirited, and delightful year!

> Howard Framm
> Principal

Piquing one's curiosity on a handbook, however, creates only a momentary kind of interest. Handbooks must "be made of sterner stuff." Most reflect school policies rather well and provide broad as well as detailed perspectives on expectations of students, guides to conduct and achievement, rules and regulations, mechanical and organizational guidelines, as well as descriptions of activities. Almost none, however, provide a well planned, clearly laid out *year-long* calendar of the school's events whose dates do not conflict, and whose central organization permits both students and parents to make long-range plans of a social as well as financial type. Such a "master calendar" is not difficult to plan, nor is it impossible to hold inviolate with respect to the chronic shifting of dates and times which commonly occur when events of other schools come into collision with it. Quite obviously, no one would suggest complete inflexibility on dates and times, but a fairly rigid stance on maintaining the calendar's integrity will lend predictability and substance to one's planning system.

A pungent, pertinent message and a well-constructed master calendar *set tone;* they project an atmosphere of confidence, warmth, and efficiency; in short they establish an organized, substantial academic and social environment.

LETTERS OF RECOMMENDATION THAT MAKE A DIFFERENCE

Writing letters of recommendation has always been a staple of any administrative position; principals receive many and write many. Such communications seem to be eternal. With the destruction of confidentiality regarding such letters, however, writing them has become a whole "new ball game." At the same time, demands for letters are as ubiquitous and frequent as ever. Essentially, all administrators are trapped by the sterility of recommending "nice" young people for colleges or jobs in highly competitive academic and economic marketplaces. Letters of recommendation cannot be reduced to a series of rules or a set of "do's and don'ts." However, articulate as one may get about them, when all is said and done, the most powerful and persuasive ones are those which are: (1) colorful, (2) "different" in their approach, and (3) detailed in such a way as to make the subject of the letter truly an individual in the finest sense of that word.

For the most part, letters of recommendation are requested of administrators to assist students in gaining acceptances to colleges, securing employment, and supporting applications for scholarships. Obviously, after writing literally hundreds of letters for waves of students from year to year, any administrator would weary of the process and might even tend to slip into the web of writing a kind of generic, "catch-all" prose in each of his communiques. This, should it happen, would jeopardize the candidate considerably if his competitors become the beneficiaries of more lively, personalized documents. Problems in correspondence tend to arise not so much in *what* is said about an applicant (although that also might yield difficulties), but rather how and in what light things are presented.

Letter writing, especially these days, becomes a useful art unto itself. Each letter written about a student needs to be a sophisticated, supportive, highly individual document which not only *describes* the student, but in some sense places the writer "on the line" in predicting how the student will fare in his desired situation and how he might contribute to the receiving school or firm—a kind of reciprocal benefit theory.

Standard letters of recommendation pose no mystery and few problems; yet situations arise which vary ever so slightly from routine correspondence. The reader may find the following "scenarios" helpful:

Situation: As principal of Elmtown High School, you have been asked by Dahlia Spenser, a first-rate student, to be a reference for her in her quest for admission to Bates College. A standard form arrives which *you* complete, rather than delegating this task to her counselor. Somehow you feel, though, that added "power" might enhance her chances of acceptance. So, in addition to the form, you write a letter as a kind of insurance policy that the school is doing all it can for this young lady. The letter might look like this:

January 4, 19___

Director of Admissions
Bates College
Lewiston, Maine

Dear Sir:

I am returning the completed form given to me by Dahlia Spenser, a senior at Elmtown High School. I would like, however, to add some commentary with respect to this outstanding young lady in support of her application to Bates College.

As her records will indicate, Dahlia's rank-in-class establishes her academic credentials quite well. But while her scholarly achievements are quite good, these do not really yield the measure of Dahlia Spenser. She is, in my judgment, one of the finest young ladies and contributors to a high school whom I have seen in my career.

However, as you know especially well, there are many other fine students applying to first-rate colleges. What separates Dahlia from the others is her outstanding commitment to her high school, her companions, and the general tone of "civic" responsibility and pride she has manifested while a student with us.

I have found Dahlia to be an outstanding leader, organizer, and spirited young lady. She is articulate, clear thinking, and above all, mature and most responsible.

Were it not for students like Dahlia our high school would be a much poorer place. For she is one of those people who breathe life into an institution and cause it to perform insofar as it is possible—the way it is designed to perform.

Dahlia is an absolutely delightful young lady whom I would recommend to you for acceptance at Bates without reservation. I would add, furthermore, that I am quite convinced that she will contribute much to your college, to her associates, to her family, and to herself by being granted admission to your school.

I recommend her to you unequivocally.

Sincerely yours,

John F. Young
Principal

JFY/sd

Situation: Mr. and Mrs. Joseph Rogers, crushed by the failure of their daughter, Pam, to be accepted to the main campus of the University of Massachusetts, come to your office to see what assistance you might be able to give them. Recognizing that the likelihood of a decision reversal is far less than persuading for acceptance prior to a determination, you decide to try anyway, since the university's decision, in your judgment, may be unjust through no fault of theirs. You decide that the university may inadvertently have overlooked the "real" Pam. Such a letter may read as follows:

January 15, 19__

Dr. Martin West
Director of Admissions
University of Massachusetts
Amherst, Massachusetts

Dear Dr. West:

This morning Mr. and Mrs. Joseph Rogers, parents of Pam Rogers, a senior at Elmtown High School, visited with me to let me know that their daughter had not been accepted for study at the Amherst campus, but rather had been granted admission to one of the branches.

At their request, I am writing this letter with the hope that it might be possible for you to reexamine her candidacy for admission to the Amherst campus. Pam is a delightful young lady who has done well academically all along. Indeed, she stands 37th in a class of 536 students which is, by any standard, outstanding. Her test data (I.Q., achievement, etc.,) show her to be certainly of good quality and this is, of course, accentuated by her high rank-in-class standing. Where the problem seems to rest is in her SAT scores in which she quite obviously did not do well, our records indicating a total score of 780 in her latest one. However, her previous SAT scores, taken when she was a junior, yield an aggregate of 940—also not especially high, but certainly significantly higher than her last set which causes one to wonder about her performance on that particular day.

I am aware of the compelling issues which cause anyone to be denied admission to the main campus especially since the number of applications far exceeds the number of students that can be admitted. I do feel, however, that in this case perhaps some reconsideration might be given in light of Pam's long history of academic success. I might add that she is surely the kind of person whose intelligence, temperament, conscientiousness, and commitment would enable her to achieve academic success at the University.

In order to do the best we can for Pam, would you be kind enough to let me know if there is any chance at all that she might be accepted at this time at the main campus. I do hope you will give her favorable consideration and, in any event, I appreciate your attention.

Sincerely yours,

Bernard T. Rogers
Principal

BTR/sd

Situation: One of the school's fine young men began to generate enthusiasm for learning a little late in high school days. Nonetheless, you sense that he possesses sufficient intellectual raw material as well as contributory spirit to warrant an extra effort to gain his acceptance to a college appropriate to his background and interests. Such a letter might appear as follows:

December 9, 19__

Dr. John Harris
Director of Admissions
Southern Connecticut State College
New Haven, Connecticut

Dear Sir:

I am writing this letter for Jack Foster, a senior at Elmtown High School, in support of his application for admission to Southern Connecticut State College.

Jack is a reasonably bright young man who, during his early years of high school, did not achieve his potential. As a matter of fact, at the end of grade ten his rank-in-class, as reflected by his transcript, was 531 out of a class of 621. That statistic in and of itself is inadequate, since on the following rank-in-class calculation Jack went up to 460 out of 609. I would also like to point out that his SAT scores went from a composite of 880 to a more-than-respectable 1040. It would seem that this conspicuous improvement in Jack's rank-in-class and SAT scores indicate a student who may very well be finding himself or may indeed have found himself. Whatever statistical armament Jack may not have had prior to this year, he has made significant strides in providing proof of his academic capacity.

Jack Foster is a fine young man—he is polite, conscientious, and strikes me generally as being serious of purpose. Furthermore, he seems to have a reasonably mature insight into the kinds of things which interest him, and a realistic assessment of what he is truly able to do. In addition to these qualities, Jack is a fine athlete, having participated in varsity football as well as track.

All in all, I would say to you that Jack Foster is the kind of young man whom we are proud to have at Elmtown High School, and whom I can support rather readily for admission to do college work. I do hope you will find him acceptable for your school.

Sincerely yours,

John F. Young
Principal

JFY/sd

Situation: A fine young man visits you most anxious for acceptance to the state university. You realize that his chances are *at best* marginal. Nonetheless, you feel compelled to support him with full knowledge that, in all likelihood, the university will not waive its traditional standards for acceptance. After advising him candidly about this, you might write a letter such as the one which follows:

December 11, 19___

Dr. William Blanford
Director of Admissions
University of Connecticut
Storrs, Connecticut

Dear Dr. Blanford:

I am writing this letter in support of Stanley Corelli's application for acceptance to the University of Connecticut. As Stan's records will indicate, his SAT scores are not especially high, but his rank-in-class approaches the upper forty percent of the graduating class of 1973. With these data in mind, I am aware that undoubtedly his chances for acceptance to the Storrs campus are probably not good. At the same time, I would like to recommend him to you for acceptance there if that is at all possible and, if not, that he be given serious consideration for acceptance at the Stamford branch of the University.

I have found Stan to be a delightful young man, one who is an outstanding football player and also a very fine citizen in our school. He is the kind of individual who relates easily both to his peers and to the adults in the academic community. I feel quite strongly that one of Stan's major assets is his maturity. He adapts very well in a situation and tends to have a basically realistic grasp of the things which he is able to do and those things, of course, which he feels he is unable to do. Above all, though, I feel that he is an outstanding young man and, as such, would make a substantive contribution to the general university community.

I do appreciate your consideration. Thank you.

Sincerely yours,

Milton R. Worth
Principal

MRW/sd

Most problems in connection with written references come about as a result of students who either present marginal credentials for a *particular* school or who overreach conspicuously in their desire to attend so-called "status" schools. After honest counseling and frank assessment of the student's chances, letters of recommendation written with tasteful candor might do just enough now and again to "turn the corner" for some individuals, and that is frequently reward enough. On the other hand, every success of this kind is worth ten routine acceptances in human as well as public relations values, for in no way will such successes be kept silent by the recipients.

CORRESPONDENCE THAT SHOWS YOU REALLY CARE

Everyone needs gratitude, appreciation, and esteem, especially in the eyes and perception of his supervisors. Nothing is as shattering and asphyxiating to morale and building the *will* to work than having hard, successful work go unnoticed and treated cavalierly. In this respect students are no different from adults; they appreciate being appreciated.

Small schools tend to have an atmosphere of intimacy and visibility more conducive to close personal contacts. Large schools, of course, are characterized more frequently by detachment and anonymity. Whether a school is large or small, however, is classically irrelevant, for people are people and need recognition for their accomplishments. Winning teams, successful plays and concerts, outstanding publications, extraordinary scholarships, and the like require, indeed *demand,* acknowledgment of a written as well as oral kind.

Administrators in general are prompt to recognize individual performance and achievement; such courtesy stands as long-established expectation and practice. To congratulate groups, however, appears not to be quite so common, yet is every bit as critical. For it is *their* collective achievements which frequently generate the elusive, yet crucial atmosphere commonly referred to as "school spirit." To buoy the morale of performing groups of students burnishes not only their sense of themselves, but also of the image of the school they represent with such pride. Athletics, of course, present the least complicated illustrations of this concept.

Situation: After many losing seasons resulting in low morale of the student body and increasingly less participation of contenders for the football team, a remarkable reversal of the school's fortunes occurred—a winning team. Crowds began to pack the stands; cheerleaders had something tangible to yell about; a whole community came alive. No principal could ignore the contribution such a ball club made to the life and spirit of Elmtown High School. So, at season's end, amidst other accolades for the team members, the following letter seems appropriate:

ELMTOWN HIGH SCHOOL

November 27, 19__

To: The 19__ Elmtown High School Varsity Football Team
From: Edward W. Thompson
        Principal

Thanksgiving and its great football game has come and gone; in fact, that rather glorious victory is now just a momory, however pleasant that memory. You are the finest football team in the history of Elmtown High School, and that staus is extraordinarily well deserved. This whole season has been one about which, I suspect, each of you might very well be talking when you are into middle age and perhaps even beyond. This seems a bit remote for you right now, but some day, if you think back on these words, I think you will see that 19   may very well creep into whatever conversation you may be having at the time. *And that is as it should be.* For while athletics are not the reason for our existence, they certainly are a substantial part of any first-rate high school program.

By this time it has probably occurred to you that ranking fifteenth in the state is indeed a major achievement; that an outstanding 8-2 record is another major achievement; that good feeling and spirit go far beyond winning, and what your dedication to sport and the things that sport stands for has meant to Elmtown High School.

All the hours, all the thousands of pounds of weights that were lifted, all the sprints, all the sweaty palms before the ball games, all the uneasy evenings before the big ones have yielded to you the fruits of what can only be described as "bloody hard work." Now you know the meaning of what your coaches call *desire* and *pride*—and they were right, weren't they? It is a good feeling to win but it is a great feeling to win the right way—and you won the right way, which in my judgment, is the only way.

On a personal note, I would like to point out, as I have done on many occasions in the community, that you are not only fine athletes (for that would not be enough), but that you are superb young people with a sense of commitment and a feeling for the sport and your school. In short, you are the kind of young men for whom, when Tom and Matt led you onto the field each Saturday, people stood with respect and pride automatically. For at that precise moment, you stood for all the good things for which Elmtown High School stands. If I could freeze one such moment when the community looked at you with pride and affection on those Saturdays, I would present you each with a picture of that very emotional scene so that you could keep it and cherish it for all of time. Each of you has truly earned the powerful respect of all of us.

Never let us down and *never forget* 19___ for that was your year and it shall always be that way.

Situation: Not to be outdone, the following year's basketball team, while not winning the state championship, did indeed reach the final play-off game only to lose, advancing beyond any competitive stage reached by past teams. The championship, while eluding the team, seemed not to matter all that much. What mattered was the extraordinary togetherness those players were able to cement in the student body and community. An appropriate tribute sent to all players might read as follows:

ELMTOWN HIGH SCHOOL

March 19, 19___

To: The Elmtown High School Basketball Team

The 19X1-19X2 basketball season has come and gone now. With a season's record of 20-4, the Eastern Division championship won, and reaching the final of the "LL" state tournament, you have achieved something no other basketball team in the history of Elmtown High School has ever attained. But, as you know, statistics are never the measure of people or places that really matter.

The spirit which your season's performances breathed into our high school and our community is irreplaceable. I think you know that you are far more than simply a basketball team, you represent everything good for which people would like to think they stand. You represent spirit, hard work, dedication, and pride in self and school—things you have delivered in such abundance to your companions and community.

It is hard to imagine (unless one lives through a season like this one) the anxious moments, the delightful anticipations that are so much a part not only of sports, but of what high school life ought really to be like. I think each of you sensed the almost incredible affection that our student body and adult community had for you as your season continued to generate the wild enthusiasm with which it finished.

You have carved for yourself not only a magnificent record, but also a set of unforgettable memories which will remain with you (for that matter with us also) always. As the years will roll on, each of you will reflect over and over again on the greatness of your "championship" season—your moment! With your spirit and drive, you have unified our high school more than ever before.

No words can express how proud we are of you. You have done what you have done well. Above all, you have carried yourselves with grace and dignity and represented our school with honor.

Contratulations!

Sincerely yours,

Margaret R. Jackson
Principal

MRJ/sd

Situation: While not drawing huge crowds, girls' athletics do matter, and frequently significantly so. Elmtown High School's girls' basketball team achieved that school's first state championship, and in so doing, did indeed draw crowds rivalling those attending the boys' games. To these young ladies, a principal might write the following:

ELMTOWN HIGH SCHOOL

March 19, 19_____

To: The Elmtown High School Girls' Basketball Team

In the words of our cheerleaders, "Yes, we are the best!" *We're number one and you made it so!* You made it so with hours of hard work, with practicing until it hurt, with giving of yourself and your time, and most of all, with that magnificent spirit of unity and teamwork that you have shown all year.

As time goes on and the joy of the moment begins to fade, the sweetness of what you did for yourselves and your school will never leave you. In all of time you will be the only ball club to have given Elmtown High School its *first state championship*. Yes, you are a *state champion* and that may seem to say it all.

But it really does not say it all because you have carried your high school with you. You have brought our student body of over 2000 into a glorious togetherness which would not have been possible without your magnificent achievement. We are all so very proud of you; you are superb athletes and wonderful young people!

Congratulations on a splendid, memorable season!

Sincerely yours,

Leonard T. Irving
Principal

LTI/sd

Individual letters are deeply cherished by their recipients, and singularly appreciated by their parents. While they tend to be fairly standard, they signal an administrator who cares enough to act graciously. An example of the kind of letter about which people care and to which they respond with their own brand of gratitude follows:

March 18, 19___

Dear Max,

I guess this must be some kind of "first" when a student is a major editor of two award winning publications in the same year.

Flying Tiger, our newspaper, is first-rate and your enthusiasm and energy in bringing this about are well known. Your role as one of the senior editors of last year's *Twilight*, our literary magazine, also contributed greatly to its superb Medalist ranking.

With a first place award to *Flying Tiger* from the Columbia Scholastic Press and a Medalist ranking for *Twilight*, you have truly achieved excellence as a student journalist and we are very proud of you.

Contratulations and best wishes for continued journalistic success!

Sincerely yours,

James Osborne
Principal

JO/sd

GUIDELINES FOR CORRESPONDENCE

Writing to and for students is an art all its own when done well. It must not become a routine, sterile, *pro forma* ritual; for to allow that kind of deterioration in outlook places a school in imminent danger of not caring about its students. A few simple hints may prove useful:

- Always react in *writing* to individual students or performing groups who achieve beyond routine expectations.

- Mail such correspondence to pupils' homes; it has more flavor and personal quality when handled that way.

- Try to make letters unique, seeking that special "touch" to which that person or group can readily relate.

- Avoid meaningless words such as "great," "fine," "nice," and the like. Words such as "superb" or "outstanding" are similarly hackneyed, but for lack of appropriate substitutes or synonyms continue to have utility with young people.

- Depending on the volume of correspondence, try to sign each letter personally. This may not always be possible, but should be done when feasible.

- Address students by their *first* names; it gives the letter meaning and warmth.

- Do not "overwrite" or "overpraise," but do not inhibit your comments either. Be guided by the value of the moment and try to reflect on its emotional impact with appropriate use of language.

- Use school stationery to send all congratulatory notes or a first-rate mimeographed group letter. Spirit-duplicated material is too informal and fades with time.

- Always send letters out immediately following the termination of an event. A delay of a week or two can be lethal and counterproductive, engendering more hostility and charges of inefficiency and "afterthought" than appreciation.

- Try to be different in what you say and how you say it. Bland letters do little to enhance a school's vibrance or image of enthusiasm, togetherness, and energy.

- Be sure your correspondence is literally "letter perfect," since all good intentions are severely undercut by sloppy workmanship in matters of communicating. Proofreading carefully pays rich dividends.

- If there is a local press, release group congratulatory letters to it *after* they have been mailed to recipients; they tend to make good reading for the caring general public.

SUMMARY

Communicating with and for students is an endless activity, enriched mainly by the gratitude it forges from those who are appreciative of your efforts and sensitivity to *their* needs and concerns. Doing it well requires chronic attention to events, people, and detail. While it is not complicated, neither is it simple. It requires skill, understanding, organization, and, above all, an instinct for what matters and what does not. Not all correspondence or communication is pleasant. All, however, is vital and needs to be treated with maturity and sound judgment.

3

EXAMINING KEY FACTORS AFFECTING COMMUNICATIONS WITH STUDENTS

Ever since the late sixties, students have demanded an ever-increasing share of attention. Despite the contempt with which so-called "relevance" may now be viewed, students' voices are not very frequently left unheard—or if they are, vandalistic spasms surely follow and schools show the ugly pockmarks of deaf administrators and faculties. The question really becomes not *whether* to communicate (for that is a vital matter recognized by everyone), but with *whom*, how *often*, and to *what* ends. School administrators agree, however perplexing the timing and issues become, that student councils at all levels of schooling need to become central switchboards for sound relations and communications or be dissolved and replaced by democratic groups more representative and able. Unlike the aspirin commercial's pitch, all student councils are *not* alike—some are more effective than others and show it conspicuously. Effective or ineffective, student councils provide some form of peer guidance and must be reckoned with accordingly.

INVOLVING STUDENT LEADERSHIP "FOR REAL"

Probably the best way in which to communicate with large groups of students is through representative groups. The first thought which occurs to any administrator in a crisis, as well as in an organized planning situation when it comes to discussing issues with students in order to solicit their views and their counsel, is to turn, of course, to the group of elected representatives commonly called the Student Council. In recent years, however, student councils have fallen into some disrepute, usually as a result of their inertia coupled with the chronic accusation that those who are elected are sadly unrepresentative of the student body at large. Whether the council is appropriately representative of the entire student body becomes inconsequential, for its membership *was* elected by that very student body—elements of which will always accuse it of being unrepresentative.

How best might a school administrator communicate not only with the student council, but with other representative groups as well? Let us look at the kinds of action which a principal may take in dealing with an issue affecting student welfare and which, in his judgment, requires student participation in the formulation of a decision.

Who are the Student Leaders?

First, the administrator should turn to those elements of the student body who have the initiative, organizational skill, and above all the *influence* to direct collective student action in a positive direction. The following model of student leadership contacts may prove helpful:

STUDENT "MINI-CONGRESS"

- Officers of the student council
- Editor-in-Chief, school newspaper
- Class officers of each grade housed in that school
- President, each viable school club or organization

Second, students who are engaged in work-study programs may be unable to participate in any extracurricular activities. However, a group of students, hand selected either by the principal or by the students themselves, can represent that element of the student body with effectiveness, if given the opportunity and told in advance about the date and time of any contemplated meetings.

Frequently, it is imperative to understand that it is not so much the *issue* with which students are concerned (although that may very well be important also), but rather the *process* by which they are asked to participate in something of consequence and value. It is also important to have the members understand that their opinions will, if not heeded, at least be weighed by those in the roles of making decisions.

Decisions made in a "twilight zone," however, are seldom effectively implemented. It is important, therefore, to have members of the student press, literary magazine, or other kinds of publications available at all gatherings where *exploration of issues* takes place. It is essential that such student journalists report with accuracy not only the deliberations, but also the process of sifting alternatives prior to the administration's arrival at a reasonable decision affecting the welfare of everyone connected with the issue.

How Will Decisions Be Communicated?

It is one thing to meet and discuss; it is quite another to implement and *communicate* the results of such meetings. Good administration requires that decisions, mutually agreed upon, be communicated appropriately to the *entire* student body. Such communications must do the following in order to be effective:

1. Be put in writing and posted in all rooms, signed by the president of the student council or its secretary, and all other key elected officials of student groups having counseled in the process whereby the principal arrived at that decision.

2. The communiqué must include: (1) the issue as it arose, (2) the alternative proposed, (3) final student recommendations to the administration, (4) the administration's initial position, and (5) the decision and effective date of its implementation.

3. Copies must be sent not only to the student press, but to the local press as well, especially if an issue, such as an "open campus," is of sufficient magnitude to warrant the attention and support of parents.

4. A listing of follow-up activities or a tentative trial period during which the solution to the problem will be implemented.

5. A scheme for evaluating the ultimate impact of any decision.

If everyone connected with the school is clear on (1) what channels of communications exist, (2) how someone may avoid frustration in initiating communication, (3) how long it will take to get a response, and (4) how responsive and caring the school's faculty and administration are, a good deal of difficulty can be avoided. Clearly, however, accusations that school administrators fail to communicate will continue to exist. If, however, responsible administrators can point to the channels built for the hearing of grievances and for the initiation of responsible changes, then the charge becomes phantom and the good experiences students have will tend to drown the flimsy countercharges which simply generate sterile noise without much substance.

RESPONDING TO PETITIONS OF STUDENTS

Frequently, issues will become so incendiary that students will resort to the age-old method of petitioning in order to secure resolutions to problems which they consider serious. One must recognize that the petition is a device very much in the American grain of securing redress from grievances. It causes those in authority to come to grips with issues which perhaps have been delayed far too long and need immediate attention in order to quiet sources of irritation, especially among those who feel themselves chronically wronged as a result of not having this particular problem solved.

For example, let us assume that a school adopts a policy that any three class cuts will result in a student automatically failing that course. In the absence of an historical policy in this area, students become accustomed to individual treatment relative to class cuts, and the number of class cuts may have become irrelevant to a student completing the requirements for the course. With the demand of the public for a stricter accountability regarding student attendance, the school administration might respond by acquiescing in a very "tight" kind of policy, demanding that students attend class regularly with the threat of failure invoked for a certain number of so-called "illegal absences."

Frequently, a student petition will be brief, but will be garnished heavily by rows and rows of signatures attesting very quickly and very visually to the massive dissatisfaction with which the students view the new policy.

How one handles this kind öf communication is, of course, very seriously a matter of style. Nonetheless, the fact that it needs to be handled and quickly so goes without saying. Failure of the school's administration to come to grips with a student-generated issue of this magnitude will only cause students to go not only to the superintendent of schools, but probably to the board of education and the local press simultaneously. Should this kind of chronic malcontentedness seep into the community without administrative action, then one needs to *overcommunicate* on the issue, perhaps causing him to overreact to it as well. In any event, to attempt to ignore this kind of request is not only "bad communications," but will probably yield an inefficiency and counterproductivity in the daily activities of that school principal.

Perhaps some guidelines on the treatment of petitions may be of value:

- Whenever a principal receives a petition, he should immediately inquire as to who it was who delivered that petition so that immediate face-to-face communication can come about to determine the intensity of the request as well as its points of origin.

- Once determination has been made on who or what element of the school's population initiated that petition, the principal should call an immediate conference of the student leadership involved—prior to organizing the general leadership elements alluded to in the "Mini-Congress" model previously illustrated.

- After reading the petition and placing a reasonable degree of value on the merit of the request, the school's leader should begin to formulate some courses of action regarding the exploratory channels he will use in order to arrive at an analysis of all points of view regarding the problem.

- Copies of all petitions should immediately be sent to the superintendent of schools, so that he does not discover indirectly what is happening in one of the schools for which he has final responsibility.

- When forwarding the petition, a brief covering memorandum, indicating not so much the principal's outlook on the problem but rather his mode of attack on the issue, should be attached.

- If interim measures are required to "keep the pot from boiling," the principal should immediately call together his student leadership assemblage (the so-called "Mini-Congress") and his faculty advisory counsel in order to determine, very quickly, the kinds of stop-gap measures that may be required to keep things at a reasonably peaceful and harmonious level.

- If an interim solution is proposed, that solution should immediately be communicated through the student leadership called together to discuss the issue in the first place or, if the problem is a procedural one, through the public address system.

- Releases to the student press as well as to local newspapers will help to prevent exacerbation of serious issues. If nothing else, such releases, when handled delicately, will also yield the preception of responsiveness on the part of the school's administration to expressed student needs.

- In the absence of urgency, however, the usual route of a petition should conform to referral to the student council with a request that they react to its contents and propose alternative solutions to the problem as they see it. A meeting among the school's administration and the student council and its advisors would not be out of the question either and is probably an excellent idea—once again to signal an appropriate degree of responsiveness to what students see as a matter of some urgency.

- When the problem is finally resolved and appropriate releases to interested parties have been sent, then the superintendent of schools, assuming that he has not been involved in the solution to the problem, should receive a written memorandum outlining precisely what the ultimate resolution to the situation has been and the kind of process through which all parties yielding that resolution went.

- If the principal feels, however, that the petition is the work of cranks or fringe groups whose degree of influence might be at best marginal, and he senses that the issue is not a central one, then he should call that group together and, through careful and polite engineering, "pull the plug" on the entire issue or delay its hearing to such a degree that it tends to atrophy of its own weight. It is pointless to debate that about which no one really cares; it is a wise administrator who sees issues which are, indeed, issues: No principal should fight phantoms.

- It is good to recognize that frequently the petition is the height of student anger and resentment and its very creation may, itself, be the solution to the problem.

- If a petition carries with it serious implications, the solution for which is out of the hands of the principal (yet he sympathizes with its content), he should refer that request to the superintendent of schools in whose jurisdiction the solution to the problem may lie. If, on the other hand, the problem's amelioration rests in the area of policy, namely the role of the board of education, then the principal should recommend to the superintendent of schools that he place this on the agenda for the next board meeting and communicate his recommendations to the "aggrieved" party of students who initiated the request in the first place.

Certainly, the last things that responsible school people want to deal with are wild rumors about "what's going on in that place." Should rumors begin, however, there are ways to check and disspell them.

DYNAMIC METHODS OF STIFLING RUMOR AND HYSTERIA

No institution these days escapes the malignant business of rumors, hearsay, and sometimes the degeneration of both into hysteria. It has always been so when groups of people are frightened about one thing or another and the social climate at times breathes fear for a variety of reasons. Sometimes parents are afraid their children will not be able to attend the institution of higher education of their first choice. At other times, they fear for the safety of their children in the school environment for one reason or another. The spasms of vandalism, the fights and intimidations which occur on school grounds and enroute to and from school have sufficient magnitude to cause many parents a good deal of anxiety. Whatever the cause, one thing cannot be dismissed lightly—and that is that the adult community is afraid, not only of the young adults who are served by the public schools but also of the contemporary climate of violence.

Such concerns, exacerbated by the prying eyes and voices of the media, only serve to make matters worse in this regard. Hence, each school administrator must be prepared to communicate almost instantly on the business of unfounded charges and accusations by which his institution is frequently marred and labeled.

Since no institution is free from the wild fantasies of others and the customary distortions of situations which may be less than pleasant, it behooves every responsible educator to be aware of what is happening and of ways to handle such situations.

Let us examine what might conceivably by a typical situation in which a school principal will need to respond with wisdom, calm, and foresight:

Situation: A large surburban high school, in a very middle-class community composed largely of professional, semiprofessional, and well-paid skilled workers, has been afflicted by a series of negative press releases designed to cause all sorts of concern. Foremost among the charges was one promulgated by a local politician which stated, in effect, that the school was riddled with drub abuse and the school's administration and faculty were "turning the other cheek," blissfully unaware or uncaring about the rapidly deteriorating situation which allegedly was occurring. Recognizing that all schools at that time had been plagued with illicit drug traffic, sometime use of nonhard drugs even in the building's smoking area, and certainly wild abuse outside of school at parties, in cars, and out-of-the-way places, school authorities were quick to deny the charges in a low-keyed kind of way. They even branded them as "hysterical" because of the manner in which they were released preemptively to the press without ever being discussed with school administrators, either publicly or in private. Given this situation, and recognizing it to be rooted fundamentally in hysteria and in political adventurism, the school's principal decides on a course of action which is multi-pronged in its approach.

Proposed Solution: The principal, recognizing the forces at work for what they are, decides to use the following methods of communication in order to not only refute the charges but also, if possible, to dispell them:

1. When called by the press, he releases whatever facts and figures he has available and in no way hides these data from them.

2. Calling together a group of student leaders, he explains what the charges are and in very frank terms enlightens them on

what he sees as the central political motivation for the charges in the first place.

3. While not suggesting to students what they ought to do, he outlines for them alternative courses of action which they might be able to take in order to defend not only their reputations, but the reputation of the school as well.

4. Aware that too much "leadership" on his part could cause him to be accused of manipulating the student body for his own ends, the principal carefully withdraws from the situation, having said what he had to say to the sources which will print his words.

5. The students decide from among the alternatives proposed by the head of the school, and one of the school newspapers releases quick-hitting sheet which is distributed to the entire student body.

6. Aware that students will be arriving at a board meeting in order to state their views to the legal authorities heading the schools in that community, the principal insures that he is also there. He decides ahead of time that, unless specific questions are directed to him, he will remain silent and that his physical appearance will show sufficient support and alliance with elements of the student body who cared enough to deny the charges and also to point out the real motivation of the "trumped up" accusations with which the school must contend. Sensing a severe budget crisis in the making, members of the student body are very quick to connect a contemplated budget reduction to the lack of confidence in the school which surely follows wild accusations of a fear-inducing character.

7. Since the charges are of extreme gravity, the principal also decides that he will enlist the forces of parents he knows to be supportive of the school. Calling such a meeting prior to that of the board of education, he asks the group to make an appearance, not so much to counteract the charges, but to point out the *positive* things which occur in the school from which their children have profited and from which, of course, they will continue to profit as long as its reputation remains unblemished and not butchered by irresponsible accusations.

8. In order to apply the *coup de grace* to the entire affair, the principal also decides to preempt, if possible, future hysterical accusations by analyzing for the parents the nature of rumor

and hearsay, as well as the damage both can do if they go unchecked and unanalyzed. Using the school-to-home newsletter as a prime vehicle, he decides to let expedience govern his operation.

Having seen the kinds of action a prudent principal is able to take, given the situation as it developed, it might be wise at this time to point out some generally useful guidelines for dealing with rumor and hysteria:

- Always encourage parents at public meetings, as well as in any communications you send home, that if they hear something which appears to be seriously injurious to the reputation of the school or its students or which is a severe departure from what has customarily been policy, to call the school immediately to check it out.

- If the principal should be surprised by an accusation which appears in the local press or on the local radio station, he should in no way "blow his cool" and respond in anger or in the heat of the moment. Clearly, he should always respond in a calm, reasonable way with specifics which dissect and decimate the charges so as to not only determine the full truth of the situation as it exists, but also to destroy, once and for all, the credibility of those who would make irresponsible charges without regard to consequences.

- In order to communicate well, use all specialist personnel who might have access to information regarding the issue as it has been raised. For example, guidance counselors would make excellent resource people regarding charges involving widespread use of drugs by high school students. It is always necessary, however, when placing counselors before the public to caution them on how to deal not only with the anger of the community, but also the preservation of anonymity in any illustrative material that they may use.

- Never be defensive, even though you are defending. No one would believe an overly defensive head of a school, for his entire interest is vested in the protection of that institution. While most people probably do not realize it consciously, they nonetheless can sense when someone is masking the truth or clouding an issue in such a way as to attempt to dissipate a problem simply because it is unpleasant, not because it fails to exist.

- Invite people to visit the building. If random charges of lack of discipline or severe and ubiquitous use of drugs are true, then obviously visitors to the building will be able to see the scene as it unfolds. If you have nothing to hide, then hide nothing. Open the doors to the school you administer widely and with warm welcome. This will serve to dissipate very quickly the incipient charge that the doors are closed and that you are reluctant to have the building seen by those who pay the bills.

- Anticipate a problem prior to its occurrence. Since you know that attendance and class cutting are national maladies, release information on the current state of things in your school, appealing for cooperation from parents. Such foresight serves to undercut any brewing storm and also causes you to appear to be clear-thinking with a far-reaching outlook—not so much in solving problems *but in preventing their occurrence in the first place.*

- Stay in constant communication with leading citizens of the community. Such people as presidents of Booster Clubs, service clubs of all kinds, clergy, officials on boards and committees, as well as the police department are frequently sources of great support for the schools. Cultivating their friendship as well as their support can be a very profitable enterprise with respect to calling on people to vouchsafe a position in a manufactured crisis.

- Never overreact to a charge; this is the worst way to communicate a guilt which you need not carry. For example, do not put into effect a set of new rules on the heels of an accusation which says you need them. If they are necessary, then they should be put into effect as soon as feasible. But, if at all possible, not in the wake of an hysterical accusation which leads invariably to the school's governance by the political forces which will surely exploit that discovered weakness.

- Label rumor and hysteria for what they are. Never allow yourself to be intimidated by the cascading and crescendoing avalanche of criticism which will surely follow even the weakest charge; because it is charges such as these that the public needs in order to vent its hostility on the culture-at-large.

No one will ever quell rumor entirely. No one will ever stop the Iagos of the world from pumping their collective poisons at gullible listeners. However, illuminating a scene with facts probably punctures the swollen storehouse of malignant, untrue information which periodically seeps into a community, causing it not only to take sides for and against the public schools but also ripping the schools asunder in the process. Many of the rumors about schools, of course, deal with alleged changes in policy and regulatory governance. They presume complete academic collapse in the eyes of the public. It is therefore wise to communicate your knowledge of law as regards requirements for students and the conduct for the schools on a day-to-day basis. Frequently your action relative to "tightening" a situation, or for that matter keeping things in reasonable balance, should have roots in statute either of a court-ordered kind or one that has been promulgated by the state legislature. To communicate a legal situation is an excellent mission which school principals ought to take upon themselves and which, if done properly, will ultimately yield a nondistorted perception of what the requirements are in the schools according to the laws of the state and nation.

THE LAW AND THE STUDENT

Nothing in recent years has come into sharper focus than the legal boundaries of "keeping school." With the decay of dress codes, with the radically altered doctrine of *in loco parentis,* with the dramatic rise of student rights—never has there been a greater need for a school principal to be able to communicate to students and parents alike the nature of the statutory requirements regarding schooling, as well as the full and complete grasp of the legal ramifications of any decision which he might make. It has become insufficient simply to "dabble" in the law. It has become vital not so much to master the laws pertaining to educaiion, but to be fully conversant at a reasonably sophisticated level with what it is the law states, how it applies to students, and what the mechanical applications of that law may be regarding the management of the building.

It is neither feasible nor desirable, at this point, to probe legal technology. Rather, it is important to highlight some of the kinds of communication that might be useful in order to signal, not so much compliance with the law, but managing the institution under court-established umbrellas.

The Business of the Locker Search:

With the advent of radicalism in the late sixties and the full and complete advocacy of privacy of students' lives, public school lockers became the ground over which many legal battles were fought. What arose from varying court decisions regarding the "privacy" of lockers seemed to be the following:

- Any school locker remains public property within certain limits.

- Preemptive locker searches are at best inappropriate and, at worst, illegal.

- Lockers may be searched when principals have reasonable access to information that either something dangerous or contraband has been stored there.

- Indeed, principals not only have the *right* to search lockers for the sake of the general safety of the student body, they have the *obligation*.

  In order to have effective management of the building, however, it is necessary that students be apprised of the institutional obligations and procedures pertaining to the search of lockers when the conditions outlined above exist.

Probably the most appropriate place in which to advertise the school's policy clearly would be in the student handbook, which most prudent administrators distribute at the beginning of each school year.

Lockers and their search are not the only areas of day-to-day school management which require specific outlining in a student handbook, or other forms of conspicuous advertisement. Clearly, there are a number of areas which involve freedom of speech, invasion of privacy, and other legal technicalities which require sensitive treatment by aware school administrators, since the possibility of litigation, which is both costly and embarrassing, always exists.

Probably one of the more explosive areas in which students have expressed an interest and with which there have been some rather fiery concerns, is the matter of distribution of student-written and student-generated literature, much of which is not infrequently critical of the school, its operation, and, more particularly, its administration. Without going through the rather serious number of legal citations concerning the matter of freedom of speech and the rights which accrue to students concerning the writing of less-than-laudatory materials, and furthermore their attempts to distribute these on the school's premises, one can nonetheless formulate a clear set of rules by which students will live and with which the law has concerned itself. It would be wise to advertise policies regarding distribution of literature in the following way in the student handbook, or in other forms of widely circulated documents:

Students have every right to prepare materials for distribution to other students concerning any matters pertaining to their school and the quality of schooling. The usual channel for appropriate communication from student to student is of course the school newspaper or other legitimately sponsored school publication. However, should any student or a group of students decide that they would like to communicate with the balance of the student body in another legitimate form, they may so do under the following guidelines:

- Any material prepared for distribution must first be shown to the principal of the school. While his approval of the content is not necessary, it is reasonable to assume that he must know what is being given to the student body on school property and has the right and obligation to see such material prior to its distribution.

- The principal shall, after seeing the document, determine its appropriateness for distribution and, furthermore, decide whether that distribution will be free of potential strife among the student body, so that students in his charge will remain safe from violence or harassment.

- Material which could cause sufficient incitement to be instructionally disruptive will not be permitted to be distributed.

- Students are required, when they see the principal requesting permission to distribute written materials, to abide by the following conditions:

They must secure points and times of distribution of the materials. Dissemination of written materials will not be permitted on a casual basis. The principal shall assign one or more points from which students may distribute the material which they have prepared.

Under no conditions will students be permitted to distribute material at any time during the school day, but only during the times and hours indicated by the principal.

After distribution has been accomplished, students making that distribution are required to clean the area of all litter or debris which may have been caused by the circulation of materials which they have prepared and circulated.

The principal, and only the principal, shall decide whether the material is appropriate for distribution. For example, subject matter which uses vulgarity, obscenity, or other tasteless methods of calling attention to its substance will not be allowed to be distributed in the school. Should students wish to challenge that decision by the administration, they will have to do so through normal, legal channels.

Students failing to comply with the preceding regulations will be subject to disciplinary action in accordance with policies established by the board of education.

Clearly, when dealing with the law, no student handbook or other manner of publication will cover all the fine points or contingencies of which litigation in our contemporary society has caused people to become aware. The preceding illustrations serve, at best, to provide some models which students of school administration can apply intelligently to other issues which will surely come about as the result of further work in the courts. It is good for every school administrator to remember that surprises and mysteries have no place in the predictable administration of the day-to-day affairs of the public school. It is incumbent upon all principals to be aware of the law, to advertise the prohibitions against certain student behaviors, and to indicate clearly, above all, the consequences for failing to comply with the reasonable requirements as established by policy and school rules.

SENSIBLE APPROACHES TO SUSPENSION AND THE COMMUNITY

Nothing detonates quite so much megatonnage as suspending a student from school for a day or more. Especially incendiary is the practice of suspending students for reasonably lengthy periods of time, such as five days or longer. In the Supreme Court decision of *Goss vs. Lopez,* it was made clear that suspensions of up to ten days were patently legal, provided that circumstances existed to cause such an interruption of a student's education.

The Court made clear that due process was observed if a student transgressed, was called to the office of the principal to explain his version of the situation as it developed, and once it was decided that the student did, indeed, breach school rules, was suspended after he had been heard and his parents notified. Despite the clear support of the courts in the matter of suspensions, school administrators are advised to advertise clearly those circumstances for which suspensions of varying lengths will be enacted. Failure to do so is simply imprudent and will only raise more problems than it solves. A student handbook containing those conditions under which a student will be, suspended from school will serve as a first-rate vehicle for advertising the school's intentions and policies.

Communicating with Parents:

Nothing is as sensitive as informing a parent, in writing, that his son or daughter has been suspended because of a serious infraction of the school's rules. Many parents will accept the issue at hand in a matter of fact fashion. But *most will not,* despite the fact that they will theoretically support so-called "tighter" discipline. Some schools prefer a form letter; others insist that a personal letter describing the events that took place is a better system of letting parents know what occurred. Irrespective of the method with which a principal feels more comfortable, he should draft the device which he will use very carefully, making his language clear and keeping the communication free from as much editorial commentary as possible. Every suspension letter should contain the following elements:

- The date, time, and place on which the occurrence took place.
- A brief description of the transgression.
- A short, but not heavily editorialized comment on the impropriety of what took place.
- The length of the suspension in days, including a time bracket from what date to what inclusive date.
- A date and time for a parental conference. This date should coincide with the day on which the student is permitted to return to school.
- A statement to the effect that the student will not only be allowed but will be *required* to make up all work missed during the time of his enforced absence.
- An appropriate closing.

A sample suspension letter may be of assistance:

Figure 3-1

STAPLETON HIGH SCHOOL
213 Washington Avenue
Macon, Ohio 06314

January 12, 19___

Mr. and Mrs. John T. Warner
5 Maple Street
Macon, Ohio 06314

Dear Mr. and Mrs. Warner:

This morning, at approximately 10 A.M., your son, Leonard, was found smoking in one of the boys' lavatories. As you know, smoking in any area of the school except authorized places, as indicated in our student handbook, is prohibited. Time and again, students have been warned that lavatories are for appropriate use of such facilities, and not for smoking. Since areas for smoking have been provided with authorization from the Board of Education, there is no need for him to smoke in areas other than those provided for that purpose.

When confronted by the teacher, he denied that he was smoking, despite the fact that the teacher had seen a cigarette in his hand and had seen him take a puff on it. He was rude to the teacher and subsequently, in the office of the assistant principal, became rather obstreperous with him as well. In accordance with policy, Len is suspended for a period of *three* days, from *January 12*, through and including *January 14*.

Would you be kind enough to return with him to school on *Thursday morning, January 15, at 8:A.M.* to confer, not only about his conduct, but about his attitude regarding the school's rules. I regret the need to invoke our regulations but, as you know, his conduct leaves us with no other choice. I look forward to seeing you on Thursday morning and, in the meantime, if I can be of any further service, please call the school.

Sincerely yours,

Stanley W. Melbourne
Principal

Some principals may, of course, prefer a form letter in the interest of efficiency. While public relations will tend to suffer, they will suffer only mildly, especially if the school happens to be a rather large one and the number of suspensions is reasonably high. An example of a form letter which will surely serve the purpose of notifying parents appropriately follows:

Figure 3-2

STAPLETON HIGH SCHOOL
213 Washington Avenue
Macon, Ohio 06314

January 12, 19___

Dear_____:

Today, at approximately____, your son/daughter,_____ was involved in the following incident:

As you know, our school rules prohibit this kind of behavior and are very explicit in outlining the consequences for this kind of transgression. It will be necessary for you to accompany your son/daughter to a conference when he/she returns to school on_____after his/her suspension of_____days. While we all regret the necessity for this kind of disciplinary action, we look forward to his/her return to school. All work, of course, will be made up without academic penalty.

Thank you for your cooperation and if you have any further questions, please do not hesitate to call the school.

Sincerely yours,

Stanley W. Melbourne
Principal

In the interests of historical documentation, it is wise that all letters pertaining to disciplinary infractions, especially suspensions, be maintained in a so-called "discipline folder," which should be kept in a file separate from the cumulative record. In the event of any litigation in the courts, or should parents wish to see the disciplinary status of their child, this folder may be produced at a moment's notice in such a way as to document clearly the entire negative history a student may have. Carbon copies of all suspension letters, indeed of all negative communications to the home, should be maintained in this file. Failure to so do could conceivably cause a good deal of embarrassment to the administrator, since he has failed to maintain appropriate records of the disciplinary transactions which occur in the school for which he is responsible.

About the best caution one can exercise in the matter of suspending students from school is to insure careful communication and *fair* administration. One of the favorite accusations which parents will bring to bear at a suspension conference is one of lack of equity. To protect against that charge is probably the most prudent course of action any administrator may take. In no way, however carefully the administration of suspensions is exercised, will this kind of disciplinary action be free from strife. Parental involvement in the public schools is such that, despite near perfect communication, parents will still support with vigor the rights and privileges of their children, even though they may be well aware of their child's guilt in the particular situation. Good communication in this regard, however, helps to prevent the administrator from being intimidated by parents whose sense of logic is superb, but whose protective instincts overwhelm a proper sense of righteousness.

STUDENT HANDBOOKS RIDE AGAIN

Nothing quite so quickly captures the imagination of a student and his parents, and yet is so conspicuously ignored after the first day or two of school, than the item called "The Student Handbook." Many schools produce handsome, attractive little volumes, professionally printed with colorful covers and extraordinarily well laid-out interiors, which are designed to inform students of all the academic and regulatory requirements governing the operation of that school. Some schools, however, produce mimeographed, slipshod, and very amateurish documents. These are not only unattractive, but have nothing especially appealing to draw a student's attention to them and the central issues relative to the functioning of the school. Substantive as well as procedural items vary widely across the nation, as well as from school to school within a particular local system. Administrators are advised to produce handbooks which inform students of what the school expects from them, and which have the following central characteristics:

- They should be professionally printed with a very attractive cover—one designed and colored to attract attention and cause the student not only to read the publication, but perhaps preserve it as a memento.

- With respect to content, the handbook should be as lean as possible, and yet, paradoxically enough, as complete as necessary.

- Handbooks are not to include rhetorical outbursts or long, prose tirades concerning proper conduct. They should state things with snap, color, and linguistic sparseness.

- The handbook should provide as much useable and practical data about the school as possible—answering as many central questions about the school in print as one might be able to anticipate.

- While factors governing the school's mechanical existence ought to be clearly laid out, the book must never appear to parallel a guide for the conduct of inmates in a prison.

- The tone of the publication should always be encouraging, warm, and strive to provide interesting reading.

- Student handbooks should be reviewed annually, not only for inclusion of new items which the school as a whole seems to need as matters of form, but also with respect to extracting those items which have outlived their usefulness. Nothing is as disheartening as reading about activities which have long since been disbanded, simply because no one took the trouble or care to clear the booklet of obsolete material.

Preparation and organization of the student handbook is an excellent project for the Student Council. Its general format, tone, and content also provide excellent means for exchanges among committees, student leadership groups, members of the faculty, and the school's administration. In addition, it provides an excellent pivot around which communication ought to revolve. Handbooks should be prepared with the idea in mind that they do, in a sense, provide the general *legislative tone* of a school, and accordingly will be referred to time and again when issues of friction arise during the course of the school year. If an administrator, faculty member, or student can refer to an item in a handbook with which he is familiar and which, indeed, does govern the situation in which he finds himself, the problem usually dissolves. The customary excuse of "Oh, I didn't know," or "No one ever told me," dissipates if one can point to printed statements in a uniformly distributed, printed booklet.

Principal's Message:

As was the case with yearbooks in the preceding chapter, a principal's message, while not a central ingredient of a student handbook, does give the school's chief administrator the opportunity to express himself intellectually and personally to students with whom he might otherwise not have any face-to-face contact. While messages can be inane and sometimes even scoffed at, this is no reason for excluding them. Administrators have the obligation to express their philosophical stance and to extend their views to the student body through this kind of medium. While messages to the student body should be brief, they should always say something of significance. Exhortations to perform well academically and informing the student that the school does not exist as an "enemy camp," but rather as a warm, hospitable environment, probably form the central themes of messages of this kind.

Clearly, there is no telling what positive influence a well-written message will have when read by large numbers of students, their parents, members of the board of education, as well as any other interested parties. Examples of messages which might be appropriate follow:

WEST ACTON PUBLIC SCHOOLS
West Acton High School

Principal's Message

The years in high school have no substitute; when they are gone they cannot be recalled. Emptiness punctuated by regret serves only to haunt a future tainted by thoughts of what might have been. Take advantage of what is here *now;* recognize that "high school" is a precious, special time, unique in all your lives. In short, understand while *you are young,* the magic in being young.

To the end of creating a sound and pleasant environment, we have prepared this handbook to inform you of the expectations our academic community has, the conditions which surround an institution of high quality, and the activities available for your participation. Your cooperation helps us to help you.

Above all, learn what there is to learn, form lasting friendships, and wring every drop of fondness and togetherness from your days here so that you will never need to "look back in anger." Have a grand and spirited year!

Edward T. Moran
Principal

TROUTBROOK PUBLIC SCHOOLS
Troutbrook High School

Principal's Message

The easiest road to remaining nameless in a large high school is *not* to become involved. Failing to participate in the life of a high school guarantees apathy in the student body and a chronic lack of the zest, sparkle, and enthusiasm which are so essential in developing good feeling, mutual respect, and pride in self and school.

May I encourage you, as we open our new plant for its second year, to seize every moment, to make good things happen, to give of yourself to your school and your companions. In short, to become the person you are capable of becoming—*here, now*. Do not think that you can defer to a later day the act of doing your part for and with those around you; that would be a gross self-deception which would rest with you for all time—for those "tomorrow's" somehow never come.

There is no excuse for abdicating either your responsibilities or the just plain fun of lively years in high school. Do not leave the delightful memories, the priceless moments to others. Let the "others" be you so that when high school is over you will not know the meaning of the word "regret." Have a grand year!

Anthony Starret
Principal

Contents: Variations on the contents of student handbooks are legion, and frequently reflect not so much the school's philosophy but that of its chief administrator. If one senses that a complete document is vital to the administrative image as well as governance of the school, then one will have a book which is a good deal longer and more complicated than others whose philosophies may be riveted to simplicity and flexibility. Whichever view one holds, however, it must be remembered that a handbook is supposed to be a guide and aid to the student, and accordingly should be as complete as the needs of students compel. In secondary schools in particular, student handbooks ought to include at least the following:

- An attractive multicolored cover including the name of the school, whatever symbolic designations stand for it, as well as the academic year which the handbook reflects.

- An alphabetized table of contents which may appear either at the beginning or at the end of the document.

- Photographs of students "in action" on the school scene liberally sprinkled throughout the book, not only to make the publication more attractive, but also to lend a personal touch to what otherwise could conceivably be a desiccated, abstract document.

- An attractive size, one which can fit into a standard jacket pocket. It is always helpful to have two holes punched near the spine of the booklet as well, so that should the student wish he may insert the handbook into one of his ring-notebooks and carry it with him.

- An intelligent organization of the contents of the booklet which reflects all of the school's activities, policies, and guidelines for success as a student in that school. At the very least, the student handbook ought to contain the following:

The educational goals of the school system and that school, particularly if such goals have been formulated.

An articulate message from the head of the school.

A faculty listing reflective of that school's organization either by department, by "house," or by grade in the case of elementary schools.

All calendars relating to the scheduled or anticipated activities for that school year; such as the actual annual calendar as well as an academic calendar reflecting the times and lengths of the marking periods, scheduling of exams, and those kinds of programs with which students ought to have direct familiarity.

Academic guidelines which would be of help to a student in organizing his studies and performing well in them.

Publication of the school's policies which are involved with recent legal decisions pertaining to students' rights and responsibilities, such as the privacy of lockers and the school's obligation to check them where danger exists, drug abuse regulations, requirements governing distribution of literature not officially sanctioned by the school, and the like.

An organized presentation of all the rules, regulations, and requirements which govern the school mechanically. Expectations regarding attendance, arrival to class on time, conduct at assemblies, use of the library, and smoking are all areas which deserve and, indeed, require explanation and commentary in any student handbook worthy of the name.

A map of the school with all rooms appropriately numbered to include a traffic pattern, if one exists.

A complete disciplinary code which would include behavioral expectations for students as well as action to be taken by the school's administration in the event of breaches of that code. This would include a detailed listing of those offenses for which suspension will be required, either by policy of the board of education or the regulations which govern the school.

Full explanations on grading policy, election to the honor societies, as well as the awarding of letters for athletic teams. It is essential to state clearly the requirements for earning any award in the school, since this is usually a point where conflict with both students and parents who feel themselves wronged for one reason or another will arise.

A brief description of all extracurricular activities offered in school, requirements for membership, as well as a partial listing of the kinds of activities in which each of these organizations participates.

A section on the activities of the student council, excerpts of its constitution which are especially pertinent to student governance, as well as the requirements for election to this body and the dates and times when these elections are held.

A full listing of awards and scholarships available if the school happens to be a high school.

Any other pertinent "odds and ends" which might assist the student in adjusting and functioning in the school environment. For example, the provision of a schedule blank which the student may use to complete his weekly program is always helpful.

Student handbooks are not magical solutions to persistent problems in communication. Their absence, however, is a sure-fire symptom that something is wrong with the general level of communication in the building and will cause untold problems to occur because of the lack of codification and prompt and proper communication of requirements and policies. While it is true that student handbooks tend to be frequently ignored, it is also true that they provide a serious base upon which a school's administration and faculty can lean when an accusation as to "Why weren't we told?" is made. Any prudent school administrator will produce as attractive and comprehensive a document as possible, at the same time urging the entire student body to become fully familiar with its contents.

SELLING YOUR COURSES OF STUDY WELL

What is available by way of program is probably one of the more important areas in which school administrators need to relay information to students. Everyone is familiar with so-called "program of study" booklets which describe in college-catalogue fashion the course offerings available in secondary schools throughout a school system. It is not our intent here to replicate a course of studies booklet, or to presume to indicate the generalities of how one might be set up, for it is fairly well standardized throughout the country in secondary schools. On the other hand, perhaps some hints for the general organization of such booklets, as well as introductory material, may be of assistance. As was the case with other publications sponsored by the school, messages from the school's leadership are always useful in setting down and establishing the central reasons for the existence of both the school and its offerings. Perhaps an illustration of a sound message may be of help to practicing school administrators when designing a course of studies booklet and deliberating on what to say in introducing material:

Figure 3-3

INTRODUCTION

Selecting a sound academic program for one's high school years is becoming increasingly complicated. Salem High School offers a modern, comprehensive curriculum designed to prepare *each* student for his current needs, higher education, or entry into the world of work. We cannot stress strongly enough the need for careful and intelligent planning among the student, his parents, and his counselor if sound programs are to be well adapted to individual requirements.

As you examine the large number of course selections in this booklet, please bear in mind not only short-term needs but also long-term goals. Be aware that we have a wide variety of *electives* from which you may choose; on the other hand, we also have a number of *requirements* for graduation which must be kept in mind at all stages of planning.

Please be guided in your choices of program by today's job and college admittance requirements, not by standards which may be obsolete or by fictions which may have been around for years. Where you have a question, please call the school to determine accurate information. We will be more than pleased to assist you by answering any questions which may arise or clarifying situations about which you may have doubt.

Above all, please plan a program which challenges you appropriately, sets realistic goals, and enables you to take advantage of the diversified offerings available here. Always plan course selections with alternatives in mind, since that is the only flexible way to assure a sound education in today's constantly changing environment.

As always, the school is ready to help you in any way it can. Please do not hesitate to call.

Irwin Madden
Principal

Frequently, however, these booklets, while complete in listing courses available, have other kinds of shortcomings which limit their utility. Perhaps some general guidelines in the construction of what ought to be in them may be of help:

- Arrange all departments offering courses in alphabetical order. Nothing is as frustrating to a reader or causes communication to lapse quite as quickly as being unable to *locate* information quickly because of a willy-nilly arrangement.

- Be sure to mark off carefully and print in boldface type all requirements for graduation from that school, whether the level of secondary education is junior high school or middle school or a sophisticated high school.

- Indicate very clearly what the *minimum* class load requirement is for each student. For example, if a school is organized on the Carnegie unit method and requires a student to carry five (5) full credits in addition to physical education, this should be pointed out very clearly, as well as the fact that no exceptions to that load will be made.

- A section on what it takes to *change* a student's program once it has been fixed ought to be clearly laid out for all individuals reading the document. One of the most aggravating things is the phenomenal percentage of changes that take place in student schedules after the school year has begun or, at the very least, after the scheduling procedure has been completed. This counterproductive activity takes hundreds of man-hours away from faculty and especially guidance counselors and administrators. Once that is established and printed in the handbook, the number of disagreements is remarkably reduced when refusals are given to students who want to change courses capriciously. Also, such quarrels take place with a good deal less friction than would otherwise be the case. It is a central ingredient of sound communications to let people know what the institutional requirements are, so that in no way can these established ground rules be considered a surprise or mystery to anyone attending the school. Sections on recommended programs for preparation for college, preparation for work or technical training, advanced placement courses, requirements for early graduation, or such semi-exotic items as dual enrollment programs (where a student attends high school part-time and a nearby college or university for the balance of his schedule) ought to be *conspicuously* advertised in any such handbook. Be sure to list all prerequisites for courses as well as all requirements for course credit (inclusive of any attendance requirements which could conceivably negate credit if the absence factor is too great), and other special programs available such as independent study for credit.

While no program of studies booklet is ever perfect or complete, long-range planning concerning its central intent will do much to produce a document that is tight, coherent, easy to read, and simple to use.

SELF-SCHEDULING MADE EASY

In many schools, the so-called "arena" method of scheduling is either in use or about to be initiated. Students schedule themselves via this method, essentially a college system whereby the student chooses his courses and circulates from table to table selecting computer cards which correspond to the courses in which he has decided to enroll. It is not our intent to describe the method of arena scheduling at this time. But to point out that in order to have an effective process of self-scheduling, the booklet which contains the listing of courses, their times, locations, and instructors ought also to contain specific and precise information about the *procedure* so that students are fully informed on how the system works. The absence of such careful, detailed planning will cause a severe letdown in desirable communications, causing the entire execution of arena scheduling to become muddled, confused, and inaccurate—a self-defeating situation.

Following, the reader will find excerpts from the arena scheduling booklet published in 1974-75 at Trumbull (Connecticut) High School which gives each student the following:

- Procedure for arena scheduling
- A map of stations through which the student is expected to navigate in order to select his courses
- Instructions for completing course selection planning sheets
- Extract of a course selection planning sheet which the student completes

Illustrations follow:

Figure 3-4

TRUMBULL HIGH SCHOOL

Student Procedure for Arena Scheduling

19___ -19___

Students will proceed through arena scheduling by the following method:

Each class president, using the lottery system, will draw homeroom numbers for his class (class of '75, '76, and '77) thus determining scheduling priorities. All vocational students will be scheduled first (based on homeroom lottery) because of their complicated needs and shortened academic day. Following the vocational students, 11th, 10th, and 9th graders (based on the results of that same homeroom lottery) will be scheduled in the arena. Upon being notified, students will report to the gymnasium for scheduling as follows:

1. A department chairman, together with one staff member, will be stationed outside the entrance to the gymnasium at station "A" in order to control the number of students in the gymnasium at any given time.

2. After stopping at control station "A," the student will move to table "B" to pick up a *student identification slip* which will list all courses previously selected. (Vocational students will have slips with special markings.)

3. The student will then proceed to schedule himself by picking up course selections (IBM cards), one per course, for the program he has previously designed. Check station "E" for closed section.

4. If a student discovers a conflict in that he cannot schedule a course listed on his student identification slip, he should report to the *Guidance Conflict Table ("C")* for immediate resolution of the conflict.

5. Upon completing his schedule, the student will proceed to table "F" (student check-out) where his program will be verified and approved. The student leaves all cards, student programs, and identification sheet at this table and leaves the arena to return to class.

6. Once the student has had his courses approved, *there will be no changes of any kind permitted.*

7. In the event that a student is *absent* during his assigned schedule, he should report on the last day which will be set aside for those students who have missed their appointment.

Figure 3-5

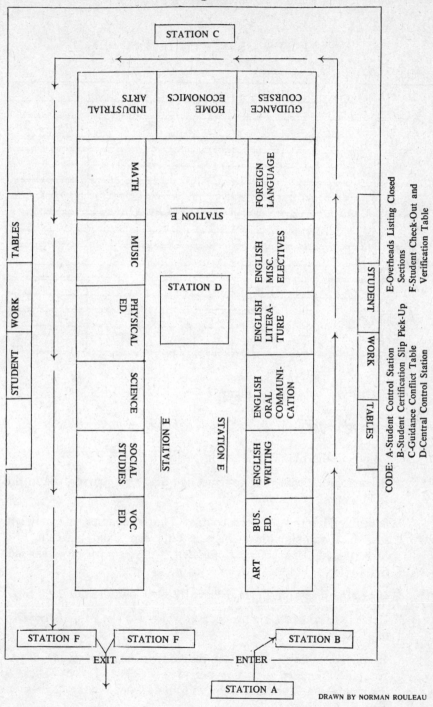

CODE: A-Student Control Station
      B-Student Certification Slip Pick-Up
      C-Guidance Conflict Table
      D-Central Control Station
      E-Overheads Listing Closed
         Sections
      F-Student Check-Out and
         Verification Table

DRAWN BY NORMAN ROULEAU

Course Selection Planning Sheet

1974-1975

FIRST SEMESTER COURSES

Period	Code/Sec.	Subject Titles	Days
1 1 M.P.			
2 M.P.			
2 1 M.P.			
2 M.P.			
3 1 M.P.			
2 M.P.			
4 1 M.P.			
2 M.P.			
5 1 M.P.			
2 M.P.			
6 1 M.P.			
2 M.P.			
7 1 M.P.			
2 M.P.			
8 1 M.P.			
2 M.P.			

Figure 3-6

Instructions for Completing Course Selection Planning Sheet

1. Complete the planning sheet in *pencil.*

2. Be sure to indicate your course *Code/Sec.* and course *Title* in the right *Period* and *Semester.*

3. Schedule *First* the *Singleton* courses. That is, courses with only *one* section. (Example: Since there is only one Band class, it is a *Singleton.*) Then schedule *Doubletons* (courses with only two sections offered, etc.).

4. If a course meets on *All Days,* leave the *Day* column *Blank.*

5. Enter the *Lettered Days* for courses which *Do Not Meet Every Day* (e.g., T., Th.).

6. If you are taking two courses that do not meet everyday, try to schedule them for the same period (e.g., Phys. Ed. on Tues. & Thurs., period 3, and Sociology on Monday and Wednesday—*same period* [3]).

7. If you wish to schedule more than one course during the same period, write them both in the same area, one above the other. (Example: Physical Educ. and science lab.). Enter the *Code* and *Title* of each and indicate the *Lettered Days* each one is to meet.

8. Remember, you must be carrying 5 subjects at *all times, in addition* to Physical Education.

You are to work out your program on the following form based on the student indentification slip and by consulting the master schedule.

NOTE: This must be done *prior* to entering the arena.

One of the major "secrets" of good communications is to publish material which is *complete* and *packed* with necessary *details*. To assume that people understand a practice, a rule, or a procedure is an invalid quantum leap which will only cause disarray and, ultimately, frustration and anger. It is always wise to bear in mind that if you want someone to understand something completely, tell him completely and spare no precision in that narration.

GRADUATION—THE FINAL TOUCH

Aside from good feelings and general satisfaction about a school which may be communicated by students to their parents, nothing is as colorful as the pageantry created by well run, emotionally positive graduation ceremonies. Careful planning is required so that the details and complex arrangements necessary for a satisfying set of commencement exercises are handled with dispatch and efficiency.

In order to establish the proper tone for planning for graduation, it is good to reduce all details to an organized memorandum which reflects the chief administrator's concern with the magnitude of the event. Once such a memorandum is established, all else follows with reasonable ease:

Figure 3-7

Elmwood High School

TO: Administrators
FROM: Dr. Samuel Morris
             Principal
SUBJECT: Graduation, 19

In order to prepare appropriately for graduation, I am dividing the general workload into specific areas of responsibility, I will

work with each of you separately as well as together, both
generally and specifically, in the areas listed below:

Mr. Edward Stone

- Field and stage organization
- Coordination with music dept.
- Organization of processional
- Appointment and placement of Junior Marshals
- Arrangements for security and traffic control

Ms. Leonora Smith

- Preparation of graduation lists
- Printing of program
- Arrangment for caps and gowns
- Printing of diplomas
- Distribution of diplomas to students on "hold" list

Mr. Ralph Carter

- Review "Senior Reflections"
- Appointment of ushers and ticket takers
- Printing of tickets
- Organization of homeroom teachers for distribution of diplomas
- Alternate indoor arrangements in event of inclement weather

Graduation date is not yet set and will be determined once we are
certain when the last day of school will be. If the last school day
falls on June 20, then I will recommend Sunday, June 22, at 2
P.M. for graduation. If it should be necessary for me to
recommend a weeknight, graduation ceremonies will be held
outdoors at 6 P.M.

Many thanks for your help.

SM:mr
cc: Graduation Committee, 19__
     Head Custodian

While the preceding is not a communication with students or to
them, it surely is one *about* them and is worthy of consideration, as it
establishes the fundamental framework and the areas of concentration which are required to plan first-rate ceremonies.

Situation: Despite the fact that all planning for graduation has
been completed and several rehearsals have been held in order to
prepare students for the pomp and ceremony which is to take place on
the day scheduled for the exercises, the telephones continue to ring

Figure 3-8

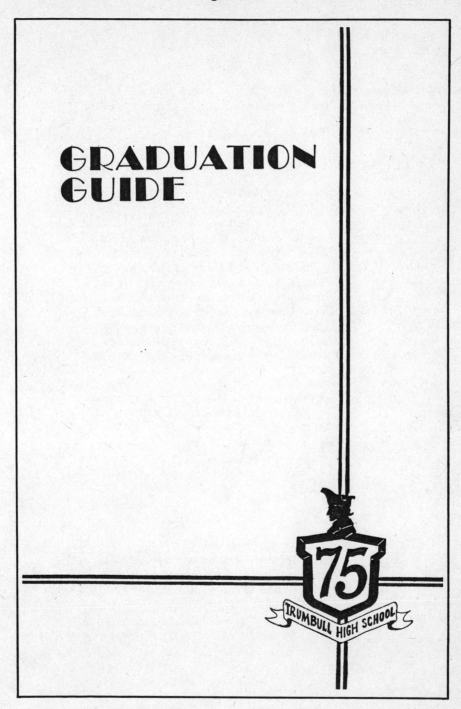

Please follow the brief set of instructions listed below and note especially all dates and times:

Date: Sunday, June 22, 1975

Time: 2 p.m.

Place: Athletic Field - Trumbull High School

Inclement   In the event of inclement weather
Weather: graduation will be held on the same
             date, at the same time (2 p.m.) in the
             gymnasium at Trumbull High School.
             The black and gold tickets (4 of each
             have been distributed to you) will admit
             your family to the indoor graduation in
             the event such scheduling becomes
             necessary. (Decision will be made by
             10 a.m. and announced on WICC and
             WNAB).

Tickets: Each senior receives four (4) regular
             admission tickets--black and white
             (outdoor only) and four (4) black and
             gold tickets good for admission out-
             doors and indoors.

Seniors   Place - Commons (House areas as
Report: marked)
             Time - 1:15 p.m. (no later than)

Special   Ladies - white shoes
Attire: Gentlemen - shirt and ties
             (No high-heeled or tapped shoes if
             graduation is scheduled indoors..PLEASE).

Wearing of Tassel:	1. During processional and <u>through</u> awarding of diplomas - tassel is worn on <u>left</u> side of mortarboard.
	2. On signal only from stage and <u>after</u> all diplomas have been awarded, tassels will be shifted by all graduates to <u>right</u> side of mortarboard.
Streamers:	On <u>signal</u> from stage, black and gold streamers are released after diplomas are awarded.
School Indebtedness:	All money owed to the school <u>must</u> be paid no later than <u>Thursday, June 19, 1975 by 2 p. m.</u> Students owing money subsequently <u>will</u> be permitted to graduate, but <u>will not</u> be issued their diplomas until all indebtedness is cleared.
Return of Caps and Gowns:	After graduation ceremony all caps and gowns are to be returned to the company representative and your homeroom teacher in the area designated by your homeroom number in the Commons. Upon return of the cap and gown, your homeroom teachers will issue your diploma.

GOOD LUCK AND BEST WISHES ALWAYS.

_____
Headmaster

both in the central office and the high school. Questions are asked about what will happen if it rains, what time the ceremony will take place, how long it will last, and the usual kinds of family-riveted concerns, especially since parents are planning to have some sort of reception for their graduating child immediately upon completion of the ceremonies. As principal of Elmwood High School, you are now faced with the problem which seems to be recurring from year to year and about which, historically, very little has been done except to answer the phone calls individually. Is there, perhaps, a better way to accomodate people's concerns prior to such a major event in their lives?

Proposed Solution: Perhaps the easiest way to accomodate the people's need to know is to distribute at the first or last rehearsal for graduation a small, attractively printed document which, for want of a better title, one may wish to call a "Graduation Guide." It answers in crisp form the general questions which are asked repeatedly over the telephones. A sample of a useful graduation guide is shown in Figure 3-8.

Once planning has been completed with administration and staff and students are informed of all contingencies which revolve around the mechanics of graduation, time is left for students to experience the feelings of leaving, for the last time, the place about which they will talk for years to come.

CONCLUSION

Communicating with students does not occur in the proverbial vacuum; it comes about as a result of administrative sensitivity and awareness of problems and potential problems. Sound communications occur when people *plan* for them. They do not occur by happenstance; they are not created magically. Sound thinking, a commitment to communicating well, and the establishment of appropriate machinery for transmitting the information are the prime ingredients for successfully communicating with *all* students.

4

COMMUNICATING EFFECTIVELY WITH THE FACULTY

The nature, content, and form of communications with members of the faculty are complicated, varied, and subject to all kinds of critical review and scrutiny. So diverse are the kinds of transmissions and needs to communicate well that attempts to classify and codify such correspondence yield only sparse results. Nonetheless, the life of a school impels certain "types" of communiqués more than others. With this in mind, certain repetitive categories of written communication deserve added attention.

"GOOD TO HAVE YOU WITH US"

Welcoming new personnel to a faculty warrants attention only insofar that it occurs. Failure to correspond warmly with a new teacher is simply rude, negligent, or both. Such letters need little

99

embellishment; their composition and appropriate dispatch usually are sufficient to make someone new feel that he or she matters and belongs. The following simple communication, however lacking in freshness and spontaneity, will easily do the job:

Figure 4-1

Dear Jack:

I am delighted with your appointment by our Board of Education to teach English at Lowden High School for this coming academic year. Given the competition for professional positions these days, I can well imagine how pleased you must be with your selection.

You know our expectations; I know how conscientiously and ably you will fulfill them.

Welcome to our school and bring our students the highest quality performance of which you are capable. Please call me if you have any questions at all.

Sincerely yours,

Richard Folsom
Principal

To rhapsodize or jargonize in such epistles is most inappropriate. A simple, lucid letter says it all.

DAILY BULLETINS

Much of the communication with the faculty-at-large easily reduces to mechanical announcements. Frequently, however, teachers and administrators, other than the principal himself, need to convey information to colleagues. As was the case with the student body, the most efficacious means of accomplishing this may be through a so-called "Faculty Bulletin" whose mechanics would operate identically to those of the "Student Bulletin." Construction and distribution would parallel those used for students as well. It is, however, poor practice to combine the two, because occasionally "sensitive" material may appear on a faculty sheet which ought not be shared by students.

Security of information should not, however, be a prime consideration on materials whose distribution is fairly wide, since open mailboxes in faculty rooms, the use of student messengers, and the like hardly make for confidentiality. All that aside, separate bulletins for students and faculty add greater maturity and better management to the day-to-day affair of communicating appropriately and well. Two sample entries in a faculty bulletin follow:

ELMWOOD HIGH SCHOOL

Friday, June 18, 19___

Faculty Bulletin

1. I would like to thank all members of the faculty who attended the senior banquet. I was most impressed with your support of this activity, especially since each adult had to pay his own admission. It was most gracious of you.

2. Posted in the faculty dining room and faculty workroom are extra-curricular openings at the middle school.

HERE'S OUR POLICY

"Policy" is a strange, abused word in the lexicon of public education. Technically, only a board of education "makes" policy. Despite this, the word has become generalized and frequently substituted for "regulation," "procedures," or "expected practices." In schools, principals and their "cabinets" tend to generate "policies" applicable to that building only: these are in reality procedures or operational requirements and are, in fact, administrative regulations which govern certain mechanical functions, such as the administration of discipline. By whatever name one chooses to label such expectations, he must at least: (1) communicate his intent very clearly, (2) indicate *precisely* what is expected of the staff member, (3) indicate dates and timelines where appropriate, and (4) indicate to whom all correspondence or questions ought to be addressed. The purpose of policy is to establish working bases and limits; the purpose of regulations is to fulfill policy efficiently. If clarifying information exacerbates a former muddle, it obviously fails spectacularly. A brief policy-guiding memorandum on reimbursement for professional travel may serve as a reasonably precise model to guide faculty toward fiscal prudence and fidelity to policy intentions and expectations:

Figure 4-2

ELMWOOD HIGH SCHOOL

TO: Faculty   October 14, 19___
FROM: Richard Folsom
         Principal

SUBJECT: Professional Conferences

From time to time, many of you will be going to professional conferences which, if approved in this office, will be reimbursed by the school system. So that everyone is clear on what is involved, the following steps should be adhered to closely:

- The pink "Request for Permission to Attend Professional Conference" form must be completed in duplicate *at least two full weeks in advance* of the conference date.

- Once approval is received, arrangements must be made with your unit coordinator for a substitute teacher.

- A careful, *exact* record of expenditures must be kept so that reimbursement may be effected efficiently.

- Mileage, currently reimbursed at 10¢ per mile, and round-trip odometer readings must be kept scrupulously.

- Registration fees and room costs must be vouchered with receipts.

- A summary report of the conference must be submitted with all requests for reimbursement on part "B" of the approved conference form.

- All forms and vouchers must be submitted to Mrs. Johnson upon return from an approved conference so that the exact dollar amounts expended may be logged via our accounting system.

- *Estimates of any kind are unacceptable for reimbursement; only exact vouchered dollar amounts will be reimbursed.*

- Teachers are to *sign* requests for reimbursement beside the "Total Cost" blank on part "B" of both copies of the pink form.

Please keep this memo for your use so that we have no delay in reimbursing you for any appropriate conference expenses. Thank you for your cooperation.

RF:dm   R.F
cc: Business Manager
     Administrators

PRACTICAL GUIDELINES FOR COMMUNICATING WELL WITH FACULTY

Most principals are understandably reluctant to construct vapid, textbook-like guidelines in written form, especially such memoranda which purport to promise "success" if followed. Nonetheless, however embarrassing it may seem, a faculty is owed some guidance on performance expectations.

In planning a communication which could appear to be lacking in maturity and professional worth, especially to cynical, but influential members of the teaching staff, an administrator would do well to be guided by the following:

- Choose the exact topic title with caution (e.g., "Expected Standards of Professional Performance" *not* "Keys to Successful Teaching").

- Never sound omniscient (a matter of tone) or as if the material were extracted from an infallible text.

- Always emphasize the *practical*, the *realistic*, the *"doable."* Theory is best left to theoreticians; practitioners need to deal with immediate, visible problems.

- Be brief, succinct, and avoid jargon.

An abbreviated example of practical guidelines follows:

- Keep careful records of all grades, completed assignments, and pupil attendance.

- Correct examinations in detail and return them promptly (within three [3] school days). Be sure to review their contents with the class.

- Do not begin classes late or dismiss them early without prior approval.

- Call parents *immediately* on class cuts, inappropriate behavior, or chronic problems in failing to do assignments.
- Keep emergency lesson plans available in the event of your absence.

Advice such as this cannot possibly be resented or mocked. In addition, it is especially useful to teachers new to the school system or to teaching altogether.

DO TEACHER HANDBOOKS MATTER?

A mildly cynical view of handbooks may not be unjustified; like course syllabi and teachers' lesson plans they frequently go ignored. Nonetheless, they are necessary items of sound communication without which no well-administered school ought to be. Administrators should never clutter them with useless, seldom used information. A lean, packed with essentials, clearly laid-out volume which "tells all" or nearly all is infinitely preferable to an all-inclusive, forbidding compendium or tome. There should be certain minimal essentials, however, that ought to be clearly stated in such a collection of guidelines. While the list below is not intended to be complete, it should serve to illuminate, to some extent, the recommended scope of coverage of this kind of publication:

- A clearly laid out, alphabetized index
- The school's philosophy, stated succinctly (updated at least every two years)
- A faculty listing with addresses and telephone numbers
- Organization of the school
- Procedures on treatment of disciplinary infractions
- Policy on grading
- Instructional expectations for faculty
- Academic and school calendars
- Procedures for absence of teachers
- Procedures for field trips
- Emergency school closing procedures
- Pupil attendance procedures

To elasticize a faculty handbook beyond its reasonable limits is tantamount to "stuffing" for its own sake or reaching for needless completeness. To be sure, the inclusion of certain policies of the board of education in order to emphasize them properly (e.g., corporal punishment) may be prudent, but such items should be carefully and intelligently selected. Listing skeletal essentials in such a publication appears to be a sensible outlook on its construction.

INTRIGUING METHODS OF COMMUNICATING BOARD POLICY

Except through their representative organizations, teachers have no official way of knowing when new policies are enacted by their board of education. Unless there exists a regularly published, periodic summary sheet on board activities, probably the best way to let people know what has happened in regard to critical policies is for an administrator to send a memorandum to the faculty stating: (1) the exact new policy and regulations, (2) the date it becomes effective, and (3) its implications for the school insofar as reasonable interpretation permits. It is wise to remember that while it is vital to communicate with dispatch, it becomes a futile exercise to do so foolishly and in haste. An illustration follows:

Figure 4-3

Elmwood High School

February 17, 19___

TO: Coaches and Advisors to
           Extracurricular Activities
FROM: Richard Folsom
           Principal
SUBJECT: Appraisal Form—Extracurricular Activities

Attached please find an appraisal form for extracurricular activities for which a stipend is paid. In the future it will be necessary for me to complete that form prior to the stipend being released to the supervisor, upon the completion of his responsibility for that activity. I would suggest that once you have reviewed the forms, you plan your activity in a way which conforms appropriately to the criteria listed.

So that we have minimal delay in the issuance of checks, it would be helpful for you to follow this procedure:

After a season is completed, in the case of coaches, or an activity terminates, the advisor prepares an evaluative summary of that activity for its duration that year or fragment of that year. This summary should be produced in *three copies* to be distributed as follows:

1. Two copies to the principal: one for the high school file and one to be forwarded to the central office along with the appraisal form. One copy will be maintained by the faculty member sponsoring the activity.

2. If there is an inordinate delay in the issuance of a check, please apprise me so that I may communicate with the central office before too much time has elapsed.

3. Upon receipt of the supervisor's summary, I will forward to that advisor a copy of my assessment of that program or activity. If, after one week's time, you have not received my appraisal, please see me right away so that the situation may be remedied.

4. Please be sure to summarize the activity in sufficient detail to give any reader a clear perception of the strengths as well as weaknesses in the program, since we would want to accomodate your needs as well as we can and give the activity an honest evaluation.

5. If a funded activity has a low student participation factor, it would be good to call this to my attention so that we may assess its desirability for continuance.

Thank you for your cooperation.

RF:ap   R.F.
cc: Unit Coordinators
     Enc.

INTRODUCING AND ANALYZING THE COMMUNITY
TO NEW FACULTY

Probably the best way to introduce the community or communities which a school system serves is with an attractive, professionally printed, illustrated brochure. To expect school administrators to write such a pamphlet misplaces emphasis and talent. All towns, cities, and school districts have residing in them talented, artistic, graphics-oriented people who, if asked, would be delighted to construct such a publication. Communicating should not always translate into an administrator's "do-it-yourself" exercise. Frequently, making the proper contacts resolves the problem far better than an amateurish struggle to produce a document of marginal value. The administrator's role in such a project is quickly reduced to: (1) contacting appropriate "committee" people, (2) handling the business aspects of the activity such as bids on printing, (3) suggesting *some* of the contents of the proposed circular, and (4) advising on final touches. After all, who can describe the community with greater pride than its residents, the tendency to overpraise notwithstanding?

Teachers should, of course, see the community mirrored properly—that is with minimal distortions. Furthermore, they should be given full information pertaining to the schools. Some vital elements to be included ought to be:

- Nature of educational level of residents
- Income data (averages)
- Population statistics
- Zoning information
- Grand list, tax, and property assessment rates
- School listings and enrollment figures
- Budget data, including per pupil expenditures
- Distribution of the community's annual budget as well as the educational dollar
- Educational philosophy and aspirations of the community for its young people, including college attendance data
- Civic organizations
- Municipal services, including library data, police, fire, health, and social welfare
- Brief history of the community
- Religious institutions
- Parks and recreational facilities

● Sources of employment within the community and nearby areas

Thoroughness, brevity, and attractiveness are key elements in producing any guide to the community. Such a pamphlet should "say it all" without overstatement or oppressive salesmanship.

LETTERS OF REFERENCE CAN MAKE A DIFFERENCE

A staple of a professional staff member's marketability is the file of reference letters he accumulates during his career. Given even "adequate" performance, most letters tend to be laudatory and supportive, psychologically buttressed by a supervisor's reluctance to say "bad" things about "nice" people. One cannot alter the general perception of praise in the absence of specific blame. Rather, he can distinguish levels of acceptable competence, even excellence, by treating his correspondence with precision and specific, illustrative support of his praising generalities. While letters of reference should say things firmly and concretely, they should neither overpraise nor understate, depending on the worth of an individual's services. Inhibiting praise or inducing inflated judgments both fail as techniques of letter-writing integrity. The following might be an appropriate supporting document for an assistant principal looking for his "own" school. A man whose performance, one might add, has indeed been outstanding.

Figure 4-4

February 19, 19____

Dear Jim:

It was a pleasure speaking with you yesterday about the candidacy of Bob Matts for the high school principalship open in Riverton. As I indicated to you on the phone, Bob and I worked together at Elmtown High School for four years, where he was one of my assistant principals in the old school plant and one of four unit coordinators when we opened the new school in 19   (the title changed to accomodate the "house plan" on which the new building was organized). As the school's principal, I had the pleasure of directing its inception and working with Bob and the other three unit coordinators to guide it through to a ten-year accreditation from the Far West Association of Schools and Colleges. As a matter of fact, I appointed Bob to "chair" that evaluation, and he did a superb technical job of preparing the materials required for this massive accreditation project.

Over the years, I have found Bob to be one of the most conspicuously dedicated people with whom I have ever had the pleasure of working. He is superbly organized, very bright, intellectually curious, and most articulate.

Among his responsibilities during my years with him were the construction of the school's master schedule, full charge of a "house" of some 700 students, and many other school-wide administrative responsibilities—such as the operation of the cafeteria, the supervision of teachers assigned to building duties, and the organization of certain key research-type projects. He is a sound, eminently fair disciplinarian and an expert organizer of people and materials. He has a profoundly strong sense of positive values and a well thought out educational philosophy which blends the best of tradition with the best of modern thinking. He is most supportive of school activities, attending almost all major sporting events home and away every year. It goes without saying that he is present at almost every evening social function at which students appear.

In my judgment, Bob Matts would not be an average principal; he would be an excellent one. He has the capacity to persuade and the courage to direct, when that kind of behavior is necessary. He understands people, relates to them well, and has a clear vision of the directions toward which a public high school, in these days, should move. Having had years of experience in a high school whose enrollment is in excess of 3,000 students (currently I believe it is about 3100), Bob would be eminently well suited to assume the principalship of any size high school.

Bob Matts is one of the most delightful human beings with whom I have ever had the pleasure of associating, and I recommend him to you categorically and enthusiastically for the high school principalship in Riverton with the full confidence that he would do a superb job for you and the students in your school system.

Best personal regards.

Sincerely yours,

Richard Folsom
Principal

RF:dm

CORRESPONDENCE WITH THE "CHIEFS"

Essentially, one communicates with leadership personnel in written form in virtually the same way as with the balance of the faculty. While the substance varies significantly, form and style tend to remain similar—though perhaps a bit less formal at times. The major variance appears to rest in leadership topics. A typical memorandum to building administrators dealing with central administrative matters follows:

Figure 4-5

Elmtown High School

TO: Unit Coordinators
FROM: Richard Folsom
          Principal
SUBJECT: Administrators-in-Charge

In order to maintain effective decision making in the building in the event of my absence, the following designations as administrator-in-charge will be operational:

Month	Administrator-in-Charge
September	A—Mr. King
October	B—Mr. Smith
November	C—Mrs. Madigan
December	A—Mr. King
January	B—Mr. Smith
February	C—Mrs. Madigan
March	A—Mr. King
April	B—Mr. Smith
May	C—Mrs. Madigan
June	A—Mr. King

Any decisions with school-wide implications will be made by the administrator-in-charge should the principal be out of the building for any meeting, inclusive of district meetings. Where I will be able to be reached easily by telephone, please try to contact me first unless it is an emergency in which case the needed decision should be made.

It will be the responsibility of the administrator-in-charge to insure that all student activities scheduled for that month are carried out properly and safely.

RF:dm
cc: Department Chairmen
     Secretaries

NOTE: In the event that two administrators are out of the
        building at any one time and one of them is the designee
        of the month, the next unit coordinator in rotation
        assumes the role of administrator-in-charge.

R.F.

August 8, 19___

REPORTING AND EVALUATING INSTRUCTIONAL DATA

While many data pertaining to the matters of teaching and
learning are elusive, others lend themselves to fairly sound, if at times
laborious interpretation. Such common reports as analyses of class
size, teacher load, and room use are basic to administrative communication. Once an acceptable form for repetitive reports is reached,
these tend to become annual, "fill-in-the-blanks" scenarios. On the
other hand, unique or initiatory projects require the construction of a
form and the selection of content which: (1) defines the problem, (2)
reports available data, (3) assesses these data and draws appropriate
inferences, and (4) recommends further involvement or discon-
tinuance of the project. Cautions on such reports are:

- Do not cloak them with esoteric mystique or fraudulent
  scientism.

- Represent all data in crisp, tabular, easy-to-read form.

- Lead a lay reader through any potential statistical avalanche
  with ease and clarity.

- Make no wild leaps at unjustifiable conclusions.

- Use even, well-modulated language which does not "load the
  dice."

An example of an evaluative report follows:

Figure 4-6

ELMTOWN HIGH SCHOOL

To: Dr. Robert Gregory
           Superintendent of Schools
From: Richard Folsom
           Principal
Subject: General Summary and Evaluation of
           Computer Guidance System
           Academic Year 19__

At the time of installation of the computer terminal we indicated that an evaluation of the project would follow upon its completion. In order to cover some of the major items which would probably be asked in this kind of new project, I thought it would be wise to also include funding and numerical tallies in the guidance experiment.

In general, the project may be summarized as follows:

Purpose: It was our aim at Elmtown High School to provide a quick, low-cost information retrieval system which would assist students in making decisions concerning vocational and/or college placement. To this end the computer system as sponsored by BOLD seemed to provide a readily available answer on the current marketplace.

After obtaining clearance from the Board of Education, letters were sent, with the initial mailing of this academic year, to all juniors and seniors entering Elmtown High School this past September offering this computer service to students at the rate of $4.00 per person per program.

The above illustration merely provides "lead-in" information. Much more data, of course, would be required by a board of education in order for it to understand the full meaning, value, and impact of such a program. A full report might include the following:

- Organizational details which chronicle the establishment of this system

- A general assessment of the value of the program for students as well as counselors

- Financial summary to include costs and methods of payment

- Evaluative commentary of students (usually based on tallied responses to a structured questionnaire)

- Recommendations for continuance and/or alterations to the program

- Appendices of data too detailed to report in the text of the assessment itself

It is good to remember that too much data in a report serve only to confuse, while too little data always leave too much unanswered. Balance and clarity frequently create the proper psychological climate for acceptability.

SURVEY OF COMPUTERIZED GUIDANCE SYSTEM

	No.	Percent

Were you presented with little known information, i.e., information which might otherwise never have occured to you?

	No.	Percent
Yes	85	43.8%
No	103	53.0%
No Response	6	3.1%
	194 total	

Would you recommend this service to others?

Yes	123	63.4%
No	63	32.5%
No Response	8	4.1%
	194 total	

Did you find that student-parent cooperation in preparing for computer time was a useful and desirable "plus" of this service?

Yes	107	55.2%
No	78	40.2%
No Response	9	4.6%
	194 total	

Note: Appreciation is expressed to the Department of Guidance at Trumbull High School for drafting the survey and tallying the data which appear here.

Any suggestions or recommendations? (optional)

  1. _____

  2. _____

  3. _____

Thank You For Your Help in Completing This Questionnaire!

STRUCTURING DEPARTMENTAL AND FACULTY MEETINGS

Meetings of professional staff members are sufficiently numerous *and* sufficiently resented because of historical abuse of the "meeting" format for solving problems. Intelligent administration demands carefully planned and structured sessions in order to assure their acceptance and positive accomplishments accruing from them. No meeting (except those conceived in raw, conspicuous crisis) ought to take place without precise, written, preprepared agenda. Such agenda are usually generated by administrators and involve issues raised by faculty or with which they (administrators) have serious concern. A usually successful alternative technique might embrace a "faculty agenda committee" method of designing the substance to be discussed at such meetings. Successful communications demand crisp format and limited range of issues, given the normal time strictures operating during a standard work day. An example appears below:

Figure 4-7

ELMWOOD HIGH SCHOOL

TO: Chairmen   March 23, 19____
FROM: Richard Folsom
          Principal
SUBJECT: Chairmen's Meeting—Thursday, March 25

There will be a meeting of departmental chairmen on Thursday, March 25, at 2:30 P.M., in my office. The agenda will be as follows:

- discussion of setting objectives for academic year 19___ -___ .

- Status of current budget (Mrs. Flowers).

- Improving communications with faculty.

- Recruitment needs.
- New cycle of departmental meetings with administration.
- Nominations for service as evaluator.
- Other items.

RF:dm   R.F.
cc: Unit Coordinators

WELCOME BACK! IT'S SEPTEMBER AND WE'RE READY!

Nothing strikes the casual observer of the conduct of school with greater dismay than opening a school in September of each year in a vortex of chaos. To avoid this and, further, to burnish the school's image as a well-run, crisply operated institution, "success" in opening the building may be guaranteed by sound planning crowned by sharp, orderly sequences in written communication. Three *vital* pieces of correspondence exercise governance in this regard. They are: (1) a letter to faculty in mid-August (See Figure 4-8), (2) a letter to all entering and returning students in late August (See Figure 4-9), and (3) an all-inclusive "opening day" set of guidelines for faculty distributed in their September packets of procedural materials (See Figure 4-10). Illustrations of models follow:

Figure 4-8

ELMTOWN HIGH SCHOOL

August 14, 19___

Dear Colleague:

Here we go again! Very shortly now school reopens and, as always, there is much planning and other kinds of work which need to be accomplished. Hopefully, you had a pleasant summer.

Below is the schedule for the faculty workday:

Day	Date	Time	Activity	Place
Tues.	Sept. 3	9:00— 9:30 A.M.	Coffee	Commons
		9:30—11:00 A.M.	Full faculty meeting	Music Room
		11:00—12:00 noon	House meetings	A1, B1, C1
		1:00— 4:00 P.M.	Departmental meetings (general preparation for school opening— procedural and academic)	Departmental Areas

All faculty members new to the Elmtown school system are requested to bring the following with them on the very first day (September 3):

1. Teaching certificate(s) (will be photostated and returned to you immediately).

2. Physician's report of physical examination and x-ray results. (Teachers may be examined by their own physicians or early in the school year by the school doctor. The choice rests with the teacher).

3. Recent picture (this is an optional item which we request you bring so that we may release it to the local newspaper for public relations purposes).

These items should be brought directly to Mrs. White, the principal's secretary, in the main high school office.

Teachers new to the Elmtown school system have probably received or will shortly be receiving mail from our central office concerning an orientation session scheduled for Wednesday, August 28, and Thursday morning, August 29.

In the meantime, I would like to point out that the school will be open during the month of August should anyone wish to pick up material or begin preparation of rooms prior to the official onset of the school year.

We very much look forward to your return and hope that you enjoy the rest of the summer.

Sincerely yours,

Richard Folsom
Principal

RF:dm

Figure 4-9

JEFFERSON HIGH SCHOOL
72 Strobel Road
Trumbull, Connecticut

August 26, 19____

Dear Student and Parents:

With summer almost over, we are very much looking forward to your return to school.

Below you will find some information which we feel will be helpful to you as the first day of school approaches.

School Opens:	Wednesday, September 4—7:40 a.m.
School Hours:	Hours at the high school will be 7:40 a.m. to 2 p.m.
School Lunch:	Lunches will be available on opening day and thereafter in our cafeteria.
Homeroom Assignments:	Homeroom assignments for *tenth graders* appear below. Please report to your assigned homeroom no later than 7:40 a.m. *Juniors and seniors report to homeroom of last year.*

(Insert your listing)

Order of Periods:	*First Day—Wednesday Schedule*
	1. Homeroom (begins at 7:40 a.m.).
	2. House assemblies (auditorium).
	3. Academic day (periods 1—8) following house assemblies.
Transportation:	1. Bus stops will be printed in newspaper and posted in the high school.
	2. Students who drive to school are asked to park properly in the spaces designated and in no other area of the campus.
Student Schedules:	Will be distributed during homeroom period on Wednesday, September 4.
Back-to-School Night:	Scheduled for Monday evening, September 23. Please mark your calendars (7:30—9:30 p.m.)
School Map:	Attached you will find a map of our school which will help keep you from "getting lost."

I would like to extend a very special welcome to our entering sophomores and students new to Jefferson High School in all grades. Also, we look forward to seeing all the upperclassmen again and anticipate an outstanding year. As always, we stand ready to help you in any way that we can.

Sincerely yours,

Richard Folsom

RF:dm   Principal

Figure 4-10

JEFFERSON HIGH SCHOOL

To: Faculty
From: Richard Folsom
          Principal
Subject: Opening Day

In order to accommodate as effective an opening day as possible, the following general instructions apply to all faculty:

Bell Schedule: This bell schedule applies to Wednesday, September 4, *only:*

(Insert *Your* Bell Schedule)

Orientation Assemblies: Three orientation assemblies will be held during the first day of school. These will be conducted in the auditorium, by house, in accordance with the following schedule:

(Insert Your Schedule)

All faculty members assigned to a house are expected to attend their house orientation assembly with the students. This also includes special area teachers assigned to a house who may not have a homeroom.

Handbook: Please be sure to distribute the student handbook to all students in your homeroom immediately on the first day of school and ask them to bring these books with them to the orientation assembly in the auditorium. Students of the other houses will remain in an extended homeroom period with their homeroom teacher. Homeroom teachers are asked to discuss key items of policy and practice contained in the student handbook, as well as orient the students in general to school-wide expectations.

General Homeroom
Details 1. Distribute student schedules (please send any student for whom you have *no* schedule at all to "B" House Guidance office immediately, where his counselor will be waiting to program him). *No other students are to be sent from homeroom for changes in schedule until further notice.* Changes in student program will not be permitted except for *administrative* error.

2. Assign lockers in accordance with unit coordinators memoranda. Please make two copies of your homeroom locker list and send one copy to your *house office* immediately upon completion of locker assignments. The following are to be posted on the bulletin board *immediately:* fire evacuation plan (using school map), bell schedule, and academic assistance schedule. Record homeroom student list in grade book, together with his or her bus route, locker number, and locker combination.

3. Please check Mr. King's attendance memo carefully on computer as well as internal data processed attendance.

4. Please be certain to turn in all class count slips at the end of the regular academic day—daily until further notice—to house guidance secretary. Any student on a class list is presumed to be enrolled in that class unless you are notified officially by a counselor that he has been dropped.

5. *Distribute texts and other pertinent materials on first meeting and begin the instructional program on the very first day.*

6. Be sure all texts are stamped, numbered, and covered by students (please note the condition of the

book at issuance so that whatever fines are levied at year's end are fair).

7. Homeroom activities will include the following, in the order as indicated:

1. School-wide announcements (from the main house). This will be organized and maintained by the Student Council.

2. House announcements.

3. Homeroom activities:

   a. Morning exercises to include flag salute and meditation.
   b. Attendance procedures.
   c. Reading of daily bulletin.

Keys: Keys will be available through the house office on a schedule to be announced.

Supplies: Supplies should be drawn on Wednesday, September 4. For additional supplies you may need, please contact your unit coordinator. Further supplies should be requested through the normal requisition sheet system (check teacher packet for proper form).

Classroom Bulletin
Boards: "Back-to-School Night" is scheduled for Monday, September 23, which is rather early. *Classroom bulletin boards should be attractively decorated immediately so as to reflect the instructional setting of that program* (certainly no later than one week after school is open). We would strongly urge faculty members to have *students* develop all bulletin board displays. Furthermore, each class should be responsible for changing displays in accordance with the instructional setting. Resource Center and departmental areas must also be well prepared.

Corridor
Supervision: All teachers are *required* to supervise corridor traffic between periods, prior to homeroom period, and at dismissal time. Your presence is essential in establishing a tone of concern as well as safety. It is especially critical at the beginning of the school year in a plant which is unfamiliar to one-third or more of the student body. (Supervision of lavatory, stairwells, etc., is similarly a fundamental aspect of proper building tone.)

LET THE FIRST DAY BEGIN RIGHT; ALL ELSE SHOULD FOLLOW WELL.

HAVE A NICE SUMMER, BUT BEFORE YOU DO..

As was the case with opening the building, closing the school each June can be politically and managerially explosive if not handled well. Forms for checkout, summer addresses, receipt for final paycheck and similar authentication vary widely from school district to school district, and are easily designed and produced. A brief covering memorandum solidifies and organizes the school's requirements of individual staff members. The following should suffice:

Figure 4-11

ELMWOOD HIGH SCHOOL

TO: Faculty
FROM: Richard Folsom
          Principal
SUBJECT: School Closing Procedures

In order to close the building as effectively as possible and to avoid any needless delay at year's end, please follow the procedures as they are listed below with respect to the items noted:

Faculty Meeting: Faculty will meet on Tuesday, June 20, in the music room at 11:30 A.M.

Grade Completion: Report card grading procedures to be completed no later than 8:15 A.M., Wednesday, June 14.

Student Debts:
1. Attached you will find two "hold" lists—one is to be used in listing *seniors only* who owe money to the school for loss of books, damages, etc. The other is to be used for listing all underclassmen (sophomores and juniors) by house.

2. Please complete these forms, turn them in to your *department chairmen* no later than:
   a. Seniors—June 13.
   b. Underclassmen—June 16.

3. Department chairmen will turn in separate lists (by house) to Mr. Rollins.

4. All money will be collected in the house office and turned in at the end of each day to Mrs. Snow in the main office.

5. Receipts are available from Mrs. Snow and will be issued in the houses.

6. Once a debt has been cleared, the student't name will be striken from the list and that student will be able to have his report card and/or diploma issued. Any student owing money, no matter how small the amount, will have his report card and/or diploma withheld' until such time as his debt is cleared.

Textbooks: Any textbook lost or destroyed will cost the responsible student $3.50, except Advanced Placement texts for which the student will be billed the *exact sale price* of the book.

Classrooms and Desks: All classrooms must be left clean and empty of books, bulletin boards, etc. Teachers must take with them all personal materials for obvious reasons. We would like to avoid loss of valuable personal belongings as much as possible.

Locker Clean-Out: Tuesday morning from 7:45 A.M. to 8:00 A.M. students will be expected to clean out their lockers. Receptacles will be placed at appropriate corners in the building so that debris may be placed in them without littering the building. Homeroom teachers are expected to supervise this activity carefully, and students are *not* to be allowed to leave the homeroom if there is litter in or around the area.

Keys: Keys will be turned in to the secretary in your *house office* prior to your departure for the summer. Please place your name and appropriate room number (homeroom or classroom) on the face of the envelope which will be provided in your mailbox. Also list the rooms for each key which you turn in.

A-V Equipment: Please be certain that all items of A-V equipment are turned in to Mrs. Palmer no later than Tuesday, June 13. This is especially important since it will, of course, be necessary for her to take inventory on those items.

Supplies: Please turn in all unused supplies to Mr. Mann prior to departing for the summer.

Summer Address: Please complete the attached "summer address" form and bring it with you to your *house office* at the time of receiving final pay checks on June 21. This is especially important in the event we need to contact you during the summer on matters of final grades, etc.

End-of-year
  Check Sheet: Attached you will also find an end-of-year check sheet which needs to be initialed and completed by you and the individuals to whom staff members may have responsibility. Please bring this sheet completely *initialed*—indicating that all mechanical requirements for school closing have been complied with.

Miscellaneous: *No equipment will be taken by staff members over the summer months. All school equipment will remain here for service, storage, etc.*

Books to be rebound should be brought, bundled by the department chairman, and stored in Seminar Room No. 3 in the Resource Center.

Many thanks.

RF:dm

June 6, 19____

NEXT YEAR, YOUR ASSIGNMENT IS...

Of central concern to teachers are their teaching assignments for the forthcoming academic year. So serious is this issue that most negotiated contracts stipulate precise dates when such assignments *must* be delivered to everyone. To meet such tight deadlines, all scheduling and distribution of staff loads must be completed sufficiently in advance to accommodate the requirements of the agreement. Probably the most efficacious way of communicating such assignments is with a pre-cut memorandum, a form designed specifically for that purpose:

Figure 4-12

ELMTOWN HIGH SCHOOL

June 1, 19_____

TO: Evelyn Wright
FROM: Richard Folsom
           Principal
SUBJECT: Teaching Assignment—Academic Year 19__-19__

Your assignment for the coming academic year, 19__ - 19____ , consists of the following:

Period		Course
1	Hall Duty	
2		American History
3		American History
4		Lunch
5		European History
6		American History
7		Preparation

Rooms will be assigned during the summer months for distribution upon your return in September. Extracurricular advisorships have been previously communicated. Please see me if you have any questions.

RF:dm   R.F.

Undoubtedly, the teachers' contract will carry the procedures whereby *necessary* changes in this communicated assignment are to be made and under what conditions such alterations are contractually permissible. If the contract is silent on this issue, the form ought to carry a statement on how the school's administration will handle such eventualities.

GOOD FEELINGS THROUGH CONGRATULATORY NOTES

Probably, the single most important item connected with congratulatory notes is to send them; nothing builds morale and sound human relations quicker or better. Everyone needs his work substantively appreciated. It is always wise to try to say things a bit differently, addressing your comments to the event or action for which you are lauding the recipient of the communication. The following example may be useful:

Figure 4-13

December 15, 19____

Mr. Donald Crown
Elmtown High School
Elmtown, Colorado

Dear Don:

You did it again! The Holiday Concert was one of the most imaginative in format that I have ever seen. It was a magnificient piece of musical design and its innovative character was most praiseworthy.

Our musicians performed splendidly and I was very impressed by their training and talent. Please pass on my congratulations to those who participated so ably in this event.

Sincerely yours,

Richard Folsom
RF:dm   Principal

ISSUING INDIVIDUAL AND SCHOOL-WIDE DIRECTIVES

When communicating in writing with individuals on the staff or the faculty-at-large, do so in acceptable memorandum format, never in a loose, casual way. Sparse prose and precision of language are two critical ingredients of well-conceived memoranda. The need for sensitive and unembellished language becomes singularly critical when the substance of a communication is distasteful to the staff. For example, assigning onerous supervisory periods (which vary from school to school) to already overworked professionals might be handled as follows:

Figure 4-14

ELMWOOD HIGH SCHOOL

January 27, 19_____

TO:　　　Supervisors Assigned to Smoking Area
FROM:　　Richard Folsom
　　　　　Principal
SUBJECT: Supervisory Guidelines

So that there is consistency in our supervisory effort to maintain reasonable and appropriate conduct in the smoking area, as well as the hallways immediately surrounding that spot, the following elements of tone are established:

- Students are not permitted to sit in the hallways or loiter in or around the indoor corridor immediately adjacent to the smoking area.

- All indoor traffic in that area is to be kept moving at all times.

- Careful supervision is required on days when snow is on the ground so that no horseplay, snowball throwing, or any other dangerous activity takes place either in the smoking area or adjoining courtyard.

- Students who persist in loitering in the hallways are to be referred *immediately* to the office on the discipline referral (which teachers should keep handy when they are assigned to that duty).

- Students who are insubordinate or who use vulgarity toward a teacher are to be sent immediately to the appropriate unit coordinator for disciplinary action.

　　(Obviously these will vary with local problems)

When a teacher is assigned to supervision of the smoking area, he should plan to arrive prior to the onset of the period assigned to him and should not leave the area until such time as the bell terminating that period has sounded. Clearly, no one is happy with the need to make this supervisory assignment, but students who frequent the area have failed so conspicuously to cooperate and maintain a reasonable environment there that no other option is available to us. Please remain alert to potentially dangerous situations which hopefully will not develop.

Thank you for your cooperation.

RF:dm   R.F.

DELICATE HANDLING OF
REPRIMANDS AND OTHER NEGATIVE CORRESPONDENCE

Chastisement or exhortation to correct what might be deemed to be unacceptable behavior constitutes the ultimate in sensitive communication. Nuances of language, weighing words over and over, and probing examination of connotations characterize such correspondence. Essentially, three major themes emerge upon analysis: (1) the need to be forthright, (2) the need to cite specific evidence of alleged inappropriate behavior, and (3) the need for the writer to be ultracareful and sensitive to the potential feelings of the intended recipient. The following may serve as an illustration:

Figure 4-15

February 18, 19_____

Dear Miss Carson:

I regret the need to correspond with you on what may seem to be items of less-than-major import. Nonetheless, seven (7) latenesses to work since February 1 hardly are trivial. Although we talked on November 4 of this year about the same issue, namely your habitual lateness, and while some improvement seemed to come about, this recent relapse demands your immediate attention and concern.

On February 7, 9, 11, and 12 you were fifteen (15) minutes late on each day, missing your entire homeroom assignment each time. On February 14, 15, and 16 you were twenty (20) minutes late, so that you also missed the beginning of your first period classes.

I am sure you must realize that such chronic abdication of your professional responsibility cannot continue. You are directed to arrive at work at the prescribed time. Failure for you to so do will necessitate a recommendation from me to the superintendent of schools for your dismissal.

Obviously, an occasional lateness for inescapable reasons cannot be avoided; we understand and appreciate that. On the other hand, your pattern is hardly indicative of sporadic, emergency situations.

If you wish to discuss your problem with me again or if you have any questions, please let me know. I trust I can depend on this situation being corrected at once.

RF:dm   Principal
cc: Supt. of Schools
    Personnel Records

GUIDELINES FOR DEVELOPMENT OF BUDGETS

Not enough can be said about proper communication in a school on the complicated matter of developing a recommended budget. The principal should, however, as briefly and as early as possible, establish working guidelines. These should conform to the charge given him by the superintendent, so that subordinate leadership personnel have clear direction on the limits within which they must work in determining their priorities and requests. One such illustrative memorandum follows:

Figure 4-16

ELMWOOD HIGH SCHOOL

To: Chairmen and Special Departmental Representatives
From: Richard Folsom
          Principal
Subject: Guidelines for Budget Preparation, 19___ -___

In general, I would ask that you be guided by the following:

- Plan fully for all *new* programs you have prepared which, after discussion, are found acceptable to the Board of Education.

- Any new staffing requests must consider anticipated increase in enrollment which is *real* and *justifiable* or which is reflected in accepted new programs. Simply "wanting" staff additions is unacceptable.

- Anticipated student enrollments are as follows:

  Grade   19__-__
           Projected Enrollment

  (Insert Your Student Enrollment)

- In courses where grouping exists, be sure to calculate such needs as textbooks in accordance with grouping practices.

- Where there are urgent needs for capital equipment, these should be requested with prices carefully researched, especially in view of recent inflationary trends. It will do no good and only undercut the budgetary process to use outdated catalogues.

- When an item of capital equipment is merely desirable but not vital, *do not budget it*.

- Emphasis in all budget thinking should be on providing books, A-V materials (softwares), and other necessary goods vital to the maintenance and improvement of *existing* programs.

- "Exotic" requests should be disregarded completely; prudence in sorting the *necessary* from the *desirable* should guide your thinking.

- Any new programs should be recommended using the following format—else they will not be considered:

Budget Guidelines
  I. Title of program.

  II. Need for the program

  III. Brief, catalogue-type description of program.

  IV. Anticipated, briefly itemized budget for program (inclusive of personnel—either fractional or full time).

  V. Credit to be granted to program (includes number of meetings per week and course length).

  VI. Method or methods of evaluation of program's success.

OVERCOMING RESISTANCE TO CHANGE

Sound communications always assist measurably in lubricating the machinery of change. Magical solutions do not exist to overcome the natural fear of the new and unknown, the instinct to protect the comfortable and familiar, the drive to preserve a *status quo* which someone may have had a role in formulating, and the reflex reticence to experiment with the untried and untested. Instant or crisis-generated memoranda are seldom convincing or motivating documents. Rather, a consistent administrative leadership pattern of "involve-analyze-communicate-decide" seems to hold out reasonable prospects for reduced friction in the process of altering what has always been. To this end, communications might be guided by the following:

- Involve as many people in planning new projects as possible without impairing efficiency or rupturing communications channels.

- Keep the staff-at-large periodically informed of progress accomplished by all committees and "task forces."

- Solicit suggestions for revisions of program *prior* to problems arising which could cause "forced" curriculum change.

- Share sound ideas from other school systems with a faculty as matters of routine.

- Develop an image of *not* leaping on every bandwagon. Such stature, then, lends credibility and the perception of thoughtful deliberateness to an administrator so that when he does move in a new direction, there is confidence in his judgment.

- Always be able to explain convincingly and without artificial justification why something new is necessary or desirable.

- Guarantee: (1) that all new programs will be well funded or not be offered, (2) that all results will be objectively assessed and evaluated, and (3) that unsuccessful programs, or ones discovered to be needless, will be eliminated without apologetic attempts at perfuming their inadequacies.

"SO LONG—IT'S BEEN GOOD TO KNOW YOU"

In a manner similar to writing a welcoming letter, some expression of appreciation ought to accompany the permanent departure of a faculty member who has performed well. Such letters need not be prose gems; they must, however, be sincere and personal. An example follows:

Figure 4-17

Dear Janice:

I doubt that our department of home economics will ever be the same now that you are leaving—and that's good. When you came to us four years ago, you found it in disarray and with an enrollment hardly worth mentioning. Not only did you organize it sharply, but caused it to grow to triple its previous population. I would compare our curriculum now to the best in the state.

Your students and colleagues, I am sure, share my enthusiasm for your outstanding teaching and contributions to the high school. We will miss you, but know confidently that wherever you go you will bring your dynamism, delightful humor, and conspicuous dedication. Best wishes always and do stay in touch.

Sincerely yours,

Richard Folsom
Principal

Such letters take on significance far beyond mere courtesy and expression of gratitude. A strong farewell endorsement may be shown to potential employers, perhaps yielding the key to new employment and even greater contribution. Such letters go beyond formality; they become administrative obligations to those who by their performances have earned such tribute.

CONCLUSION

Communicating with faculty is not a sometime exercise; rather, it must be a full-time fixation if one is to be true to the concept of a working educational partnership. No set of models can ever be complete or exhaustive; the need to communicate and correspond transcends prefabrication. Instinct, foresight, an orderly system of priorities, and sensitivity mark positive and productive communication with faculty.

5

CONSTRUCTING AND COMMUNICATING SUPERVISORY AND EVALUATIVE SYSTEMS WITH SENSITIVITY AND SKILL

ORGANIZING THE SYSTEM

With litigation on the matter of evaluation of professional services increasing dramatically in recent years, with supersensitivity having always been a part of any judgmental and corrective process, and with expectations of supervisors from the public and teachers alike having increased dramatically, any method of supervising and evaluating people's services needs to be almost beyond reproach in design as well as sophistication, so that its intent has a reasonable chance of being executed successfully.

132

Constructing a highly useable system of supervision and evaluation is one matter; communicating the elements of that system becomes as central an issue with which an administrator can deal. Any organized system needs to have a clearly laid-out set of components which everyone recognizes and which has practical utility in the lives of those who are supervised. The theoretical dictum that "supervision and evaluation are designed primarily to improve instruction" no longer stands up simply because a figure in authority articulates it. Proof of the tangible effectivenss of any such system needs to be given, and frequently reiterated as any system is implemented. If a procedure fails to demonstrate that it assists measurably in improving instruction, it undoubtedly will disappear quickly.

The first step in designing and implementing a specific program of supervision and evaluation of teachers is to construct all the elements of that system clearly. No system is complete without the following elements:

- An introduction which states clearly the purposes of the system and the methods which will be employed to realize those aims.

- A set of assumptions upon which the entire system is to be based.

- Clear description of the central methods which will be employed to judge performance.

- Definitions of adjectival ratings to be assigned.

- Appropriate forms which are to be used in placing the system into effect.

- A calendar which delineates clearly the visits to classrooms which are contemplated and due dates for written materials attesting to quality of performances.

- Expectations held for teachers *as well as* supervisors in executing the elements of the system.

- Information on use and distribution of completed evaluative documents.

- Methods whereby performances which are less-than-satisfactory are treated above and beyond routine supervisory procedures.

- Stated standards of performance expected in a particular school system which justify: (1) renewal of contract, (2) granting of increment, (3) awarding of any merit compensation which may be built into the system, (4) recommendation and approval for tenure, and (5) denial of contract, increment, or tenure.

- Treatment of objectives which teachers are expected to formulate and realize. This should include methods of assessment and dates at which completed projects are due.

- An appeal procedure.

There really should be nothing shatteringly new about the elements in the preceding list, for they are contained in all good supervisory and evaluative procedures. The problem seems to develop in *communicating* this system so that it is clearly understood by both supervisors and members of the faculty. To publish a major document is, of course, a first step in seeing to it that everyone connected with the system understands all its ramifications. However, this, in and of itself, is insufficient. Meetings, discussions, and individual conferences are required in order for the prudent administrator to insure that those individuals for whose supervision he is responsible understand fully and completely not only the magnitude, but the implications of the implementation of such programs. The following is a reasonably detailed excerpt from a sound evaluation system which, in essence, organizes primary structure of a high-quality system of supervision and evaluation:

Figure 5-1

PROCEDURES FOR SUPERVISION AND EVALUATION

So as to effect as efficient a system of supervision and evaluation as possible, the following procedures will guide and govern the operation:

Purpose: The central intention of our supervisory program is the *improvement of instruction*. In addition to improving instruction, however, it is important to understand clearly that *judgment on the quality of performance* of teachers is another critical aspect of the general supervisory program.

Instruments: Attached are three (3) instruments which are to be used in observing teachers, writing evaluative reports, and logging the number of classroom visits made by supervisory personnel:

Observation/Evaluation Report—This form is to be used for written observation reports on *all* faculty members as well as year-end evaluations for the following categories of faculty members.

1. Non-tenured teachers.

2. Teachers on tenure whose performances require additional supervision beyond that which one might expect from experienced personnel.

Evaluation/Experienced Teachers—This instrument is to be used as the central evaluative tool for all teachers on tenure whose performances have been judged historically to be satisfactory or better. It may also be used for teachers who come to our schools having gained tenure previously in another school system.

Monthly Supervisory Report—This instrument is designed to insure adequate frequency of classroom supervision of all teaching personnel. It is to be completed by chairmen, unit coordinators, and other supervisory personnel whose functions demand that they render evaluative judgment in some form to building principals and the central office.

The following is a recapitulation of the forms to be used and for whom:

FORM TO BE USED

	Observation/Evaluation		*Evaluation/Experienced Teacher*	
	For Observation	*For Evaluation*	*For Observation*	*For Evaluation*
Teacher				
1st Year	X	X		
2nd "	X	X		
3rd "	X	X		
Tenure	X			X

Notes:

1. The evaluation form for experienced teachers may also be used to evaluate outstanding teachers *after their first year of service* at the high school. This needs to be decided in a

conference between the chairman and the unit coordinator, both of whom need to concur in that decision.

2. Similarly, a tenured teacher whose performance is weak, will be evaluated on the Observation/Evaluation form rather than on the one designed primarily for experienced teachers (goal-oriented form). This decision (on a tenured teacher) also requires the concurrence of chairman and unit coordinator in order to be effected.

Non-tenured Staff: Non-tenured staff may be either experienced, coming to the schools from another system, or inexperienced altogether with our school system providing a first full-time teaching position. In the case of teachers whose first teaching experience is in our schools, our supervisory methods recognize the need for a special beginning brand of supervision and evaluation. The system recognizes that there are basic dimensions to teaching which need *direction* and *polish* prior to launching a systematic program of further growth in that faculty member. To that end, the following guidelines are established:

Frequency of observation—All non-tenured teachers shall be visited *at least monthly* for periods varying in length (depending on the teacher's needs and the supervisor's perception of those needs). All visits need not be of a formal type (written); many may be informal wherein no written observation report follows. However, *all* visits by *chairmen* or *equivalent supervisors* shall be followed by a conference of some type so that the supervisor, however briefly, renders his perception of the quality of the experience he has witnessed. Prior to writing any full *evaluation,* however, the staff member shall have received *at least three* formal, written observation reports. All results of visits of twenty minutes or longer shall be rendered to the teacher in written form. The supervisor's visits shall be concentrated in the following order of priority:

1. Teachers whose performances historically have been judged as marginal or less than adequate.

2. Teachers in their *third year* in our schools (judgment for tenure). This includes, of course, those teachers who are in their second year in the schools but have attained tenure previously in another school system.

3. First-year teachers.

4. Second-year teachers.

5. Balance of faculty.

All non-tenured faculty will be evaluated *at least annually* or with greater frequency if the qualify of their performance demands such increased supervision.

One of the conspicuous shortcomings appears to be the lack of a set of serious, agreed-upon, intelligent assumptions upon which any durable system of evaluation rests. With court actions being what they are, it would seem wise for the entire mechanism by which such assessments are formulated, communicated, and transmitted to higher administrative authority (especially hiring and terminating by boards of education) to be undergirded by such a series of assumptions. Such a system in some detail follows.

ASSUMPTIONS LAY GROUNDWORK FOR DURABILITY

In order to construct worthwhile managerial systems of any kind, but especially those which purport to improve the performances of teachers as well as determining their future employability and financial compensation, one needs to establish a firm theoretical base which deals not only with the intentions of a program, but also with its anticipated longevity and usefulness over the years to come. Clearly, teachers will be able to relate to the mechanics of supervision and evaluation much easier if they understand the rationale for the formulation of the system in the first place. The following are a set of assumptions which could conceivably form the base for a supervisory system in a realistic, highly acceptable way:

Figure 5-2

CERTAIN ASSUMPTIONS

In order to establish certain agreed-upon bases for a mature, workable, and intelligent supervisory program, one needs to examine certain basic assumptions which practice has shown to be sensible and acceptable in establishing any worthwhile program of assessment given the sensitivities which inhere in this activity.

1. There must be recognition of the central distinctions between the matters of supervision and evaluation.

2. Whatever program of supervision and evaluation needs to be worked out, it has to carry with it the general involvement of the faculty-at-large.

3. So that supervisors and evaluators are fully aware of their responsibilities and all the implications of their positions relative to the supervisory process, it is necessary to provide some reasonable reporting system allowing for clear evidence that supervision is a consistent, predictable experience and not something executed in cavalier fashion.

4. Whatever system of supervision/evaluation is ultimately decided upon, it should be one which is characterized by *durability* and *foresight*. Hence the substance and method of the operation will not be changed haphazardly or capriciously with turnover of administrative and/or board personnel.

5. All supervisory programs have serious elements of *subjectivity* involved in them. In *no way* is it possible to create a program which professes to assess performance in purely objective terms.

6. Any serious evaluation system of faculty must take into account all phases of on-the-job performance—including contributions to the school life, procedural responsibilities, as well as the substance of the teaching process itself.

7. Any supervisory program worthy of the name needs to have *minimal* administrative impediments and *maximal* observable results.

8. The more complex and involved a system of supervision and evaluation is the *less* likely it is to be accepted by those who are supervised. Furthermore, the less likely its chances will be to bring about productive changes in performance.

9. Self-evaluation in *written form* is a vital ingredient of any supervisory/evaluative process. The establishment of clear-cut, crisp, manageable kinds of objectives ought to form at least part of the central core of any supervisory program.

10. All commentary made about members of the faculty in any permanent evaluative form ought to provide for appropriate responses so that each teacher has the opportunity not so much of rebuttal, but of having his point of view properly considered.

11. Distinctions in years of experience among faculty members need to be made in order to tailor a supervisory program to particular needs of individual staff members.

12. *First-year teachers* need a very special, basic kind of supervisory program which takes into account their lack of experience. *Second* and *third* year teachers, prior to gaining tenure, need to have yet another kind of program. Teachers on *tenure* form a special segment of the academic community and require a form of supervision characterized by what one would hope would be a kind of ultimate form in mature supervision.

13. Annual evaluations are workable only if they produce required results or are demanded in statute. Such annual evaluations for pretenure faculty members could form a fundamental basis for the final determination on whether tenure is to be awarded. For teachers on tenure, however, whose performances have been outstanding, the annual evaluation tends to become a *pro forma* exercise and yields very little more than another filed document. It is conceivable that for tenured teachers, whose performances have indeed been outstanding, triennial evaluations of a detailed character might be more appropriate. And simple annual certification, as to adequacy of performance for purposes of granting increment or satisfying statutory requirements, will reduce and streamline administration as well as create a more mature setting in which a workable supervisory program can comfortably exist.

14. All evaluative checklists or narrative forms used in the supervisory process should be simple, clear, and uncluttered by needless information. Judgments must ordinarily be substantiated by factual supporting evidence.

15. All evaluation reports rendered on professional employees ought to contain *sensible, precise suggestions on improvement* of performance. The absence of such recommendatory items undercuts the central purpose of the entire supervisory process. Such evaluations on teachers where performances are marginal or less than adequate, must be followed by "memoranda of concern" which outline specifically and clearly areas of weakness and prescriptive, corrective steps to be taken by the teacher.

16. Any rating system which purports to judge performance in adjectival or numerical fashion must carry with it clear

definitions of word meanings or numerical equivalents—which are mutually agreed upon by the supervisory staff and those who are to be judged in accordance with those terms.

17. All evaluative documents ought to carry with them monetary recommendations with respect to employment status. For example, the matter of granting the so-called annual increment or any other incentive remuneration ought to be referred to directly in any *final* assessment of a teacher's performance.

18. Letters of congratulation as well as letters which may be less than laudatory ought to form serious parts of the evaluative process. Such letters, once sent, obviously become part of the teacher's permanent record and must be weighed when an evaluator is considering final assessment of a teacher's performance at the time such an assessment is due.

Stating assumptions provides a legitimate, intellectual framework for establishing an operation. The absence of such essential moorings fails to give teachers and the public a rationale which is easily understood and acceptable to the various segments of the academic community. Acceptance of assumptions implies an understanding of the intent of the procedures as well as the means whereby such a process is executed successfully.

OBSERVATION REPORTS:
THEIR NATURE, USE, AND FUNCTION

The staple of all supervisory systems in the public schools is the so-called "classroom observation." No one has yet devised a better method of judging a teacher's performance than seeing that teacher work in the classroom. The format, a type of observation report, varies dramatically from school system to school system. Some are weak and fail to improve essential elements of performance while others are overly detailed and tend to bury both the observer and the teacher in an avalanche of useless particularities. Though no perfect format exists for recording the observations and data they may yield, one can distill the essence of performance rather easily without, as the saying goes, "reinventing the wheel." At the same time, a viable system of supervision makes maximal use of time and clerical help available for the production of documents. Familiarity with the devices to be used in such a system is always of help to the observer, the individual being observed, as well as the clerical staff whose work generates the completed written product.

As is true of most concepts, the simpler the arrangements the better the operation and its communication become. It is folly to create a complex network of written work and evaluative scales if they lead only to confusion. Sound communications are gained by having whatever is in use *understood* clearly by all parties involved. Failure to understand, the inclusion of vagueness or ambiguity, and the unintentional confusion that comes about as the result of complex scales only cause misunderstanding, bitterness, strife, and ultimately litigation on supervisory reports which are contested by those about whom they are written.

The observation report which follows is hardly a model of perfection. It is, however, a clear document which touches on the essential elements of a teacher's performance upon which judgment *should* be rendered, and with which most professional staff members could probably agree. Ideally, the formation of a document of this character ought to have been accomplished jointly and cooperatively between supervisors and those who are to be supervised. The most interesting dimension of the model presented is, of course, that not only may it serve as the reporting instrument for judging a teacher's performance in a single class, but the compilation of such reports may easily be translated into that *same document* for a final, annual evaluation.

MAKING "OBJECTIVES" COME ALIVE

When one discusses the establishment of objectives with sophisticated members of the faculty whose experience in public education numbers a great many years, he is on dangerous ground. Teachers have grown tired of the very word "objectives." It has been hammered at them from so many sources, especially those authority figures whose methods of operation many tend to resent. The major problem with discussing objectives is that teachers have wearied of writing them down and never seeing them accomplished, fundamentally because of the absence of sufficient supervisory personnel to lend appropriate assistance to their completion and a conspicuous unwillingness to provide the funds for their execution.

On the other hand, there is no better way of moving a school or school system to a point to which it wishes to go than by stating an

Figure 5-3

OBSERVATION/EVALUATION REPORT

Teacher_____House_____Department_____
Date(s) Observed_____Evaluative Period_____ to _____

INSTRUCTION	Outstanding	Satisfactory	Marginal	Unsatisfactory	COMMENTS ON INSTRUCTION
1. Knowledge of subject	☐	☐	☐	☐	
2. Organization and planning	☐	☐	☐	☐	
3. Appropriate class discipline	☐	☐	☐	☐	
4. Use of appropriate and varied instructional techniques	☐	☐	☐	☐	
5. Participation of students	☐	☐	☐	☐	
6. Provides for attention to individuals	☐	☐	☐	☐	
7. Enthusiasm	☐	☐	☐	☐	
8. Use of language	☐	☐	☐	☐	
9. Evaluative techniques	☐	☐	☐	☐	
10. Teaching objectives realized	☐	☐	☐	☐	

PROCEDURE					COMMENTS ON PROCEDURE
1. Punctuality	☐	☐	☐	☐	
2. Performance of routine and professional obligations as well as assigned duties	☐	☐	☐	☐	
3. Care and safe use of materials and equipment	☐	☐	☐	☐	
4. Attention to building and classroom appearance	☐	☐	☐	☐	

	Outstanding	Satisfactory	Marginal	Unsatisfactory	
HUMAN RELATIONS					**COMMENTS ON HUMAN RELATIONS**
1. Fairness	☐	☐	☐	☐	
2. Rapport with students	☐	☐	☐	☐	
3. Responsiveness to physical, social, and psychological development of students	☐	☐	☐	☐	

CONTRIBUTION TO TOTAL SCHOOL LIFE

COMMENTS ON CONTRIBUTION TO TOTAL SCHOOL LIFE

1. Cite evidence of supporting school activities:

   a)

   b)

   c)

2. Execution of school and
   departmental policy ☐ ☐ ☐ ☐

PROFESSIONAL GROWTH

COMMENTS ON PROFESSIONAL GROWTH

1. Cite evidence of professional growth:

   a)

   b)

   c)

2. Willingness to accept and
   make use of constructive
   criticism ☐ ☐ ☐ ☐

3. Teacher has a positive
   attitude toward the
   profession ☐ ☐ ☐ ☐

ADDITIONAL NARRATIVE AND SUGGESTIONS
FOR IMPROVING PERFORMANCE:

RECOMMENDATION:
☐ Contract be renewed with increment
☐ Contract be renewed—increment denied
☐ Contract not be renewed

    Justification:

_____
_____
_____
_____

☐ Dismissal (Tenured)

Evaluated by: Evaluation approved:
_____   _____
Date:_____   Unit Coordinator,_____House

                                                Date:_____

TEACHER COMMENTS:

Teacher: _____
                    (Signature)

Date: _____

Distribution

Original—Personnel Records (Central Office)

Copies:
      Unit Coordinator
      School File
      Chairman
      Teacher

October 22, 19

WG/dr

Note: This instrument was first published by Croft-NEI Publications in the following monograph: William Goldstein, "Better Evaluation Reports Through Better Methods: A Mini-Manual," (June 1975), pp. 6 and 7.

objective, indicating the methods whereby it may be reached, and designating the personnel and timelines for its attainment.

The trick, of course, rests with: (1) getting agreement from staff that such a system can indeed work for the benefit of students, (2) communicating clearly on *how* objectives are to be written as well as the manner in which they will be assessed, (3) determining ahead of time that failure to attain such objectives will have no financial penalties attached, (4) limiting the annual scope of the use of the so-called "management-by-objectives" method, and (5) causing the evaluator to comment on the inhibitors of performance which may preclude attainment of objectives. One of the best ways of "teaching" members of a faculty the purpose of establishing a system of objectives in the first place, is to have the building's administration clearly lay out its intent for moving the school in a given direction.

In order to create an appropriate climate for setting objectives, one should limit initial experimentation with such a system to people fully qualified and sufficiently mature professionally to deal with it successfully. At the same time, everyone needs adequate motivation and appropriate spurs to perform at a level commensurate with his abilities and sufficient incentive to navigate through the adventure of an untested method. Accordingly, it is wise, if not in the very beginning then certainly as the inauguration of anything new progresses, to tie the setting of objectives to the matter of evaluation of performance. Only in such a way will people who work in the schools realize that establishing aims and determining methods of accomplishing them is worthy of professional energy on a committed basis. Entirely too much professional time has been wasted in the chronic writing of objectives, the end products of which do not seem to matter to staff nor to the administration who assigned the project in the first place. Therefore, linking the process to the matter of the judgment of performance creates an environment of some urgency and adds bite and reality to accomplishing what one says he intends to do.

After determining who shall participate in the setting of objectives and having the results evaluated as part of an annual assessment of performance, the administrator still needs to communicate the essential manner in which objectives shall be set and the degree of mutuality expected at each phase of establishing "doable" ends without a given time-frame. That same supervisory memorandum which lays out in clear detail the performance expectations one holds for a faculty should also include a segment on the method whereby objectives will be set. Perhaps the guidelines which follow will be of value:

- Objectives should be written in *clear, concise* terms and in such a way as to make their anticipated results at least empirically observable, if not measurable.

- Techniques or methods of obtaining each objective shall be listed.

- Ways of determining whether an objective has been reached shall be agreed upon.

- A timeline for completion or partial completion of objectives shall be mutually determined.

Commentary will be made in *narrative* form on the supervisor's perception of the degree to which each objective has been attained.

Quite obviously, working with leadership personnel provides the easiest route for communicating with larger elements of faculty. Probably a simple procedure would be for the head of a school building to write a rather limited, clearly stated set of objectives which he wishes to accomplish for that school within a given time-frame—let us say one year. After working the project through in consultation with selected members of the staff, he is now prepared to reduce these to simple written format. Once this is accomplished within a viable structure, he may submit these to chairmen of departments in order to provide a working model, both for content and form, illustrating the manner in which such objectives may be set down so that they may be easily understood and emulated. Let us see how this might work in a particular situation.

Situation: You have just been appointed principal of an already existing high school. You have been well briefed by the superintendent of schools and members of the board of education on the problems which have plagued the institution for several years. While you were given no detailed charge on particularities the superintendent and board wished you to accomplish, you got the general impression that it was their intent to have you survey the climate, existing systems, and general tone of the establishment, in order to arrive at a point of action which you could implement in the succeeding years to improve the educational situation currently in existence. Essentially, you have been left to your own devices for determining the general state of things which you are about to inherit. Your mission now is to write a limited set of objectives in order to inform yourself and the board of what needs to be done and in what areas concentration of effort needs to be effected. After several months of visiting classrooms, talking with members of the faculty, gaining information from students and members of the community, you have a set of objectives with the timelines as indicated (See Figure 5-4).

There are numerous ways of causing people to think at longer range than they are accustomed. Communicating that is an essential ingredient of setting objectives in the first place. Having it *understood* may very well be the central element with which an administrator needs to deal in order to convince or persuade a group of professionals to cooperate in this kind of project. If one believes that moving a school in an appropriate direction can best be accomplished through stating intentions precisely and thereby causing people to commit themselves to reaching their aims, then all that remains is developing the form whereby such things may best be accomplished. If the delivery system exists and people are committed to that idea, then communicating a school's progress becomes conspicuously more simple.

After a series of objectives has been established by members of a faculty and administration, judgments need to be made on whether an objective has been reached, and if not, to what extent it has not been reached. At the same time, simply judging the end product of a stated objective becomes an exercise in futility if the method fails to contain within it devices for correcting the failure. Assessment on attainment of objectives is, at best, a slippery business, since educational outcomes are frequently imprecise—despite the claims of some that everything can be measured. Let us examine the following situation as a case in point:

Situation: As principal of a large high school, one of your chief responsibilities is to train leadership personnel in supervisory and evaluative techniques. Quite obviously, your assistant principals and your chairmen would be the primary recipients of your instruction. You determine that a prime objective would be to insure that written evaluations are improved in tone, style, and substance by the end of the next academic year. Accordingly, you write the following ob jective:

By June, 19__, every department chairman and assistant prin-cipal will have improved his *writing skill* with particular regard to work in evaluative documents. Special attention will be paid to improvement in the mechanics of language, as well as preparation of mature, insightful prose which adequately reflects a high level of professional performance expected of management personnel.

One should be quick to note that this objective is stated in general terms and is not riddled with percentages of achievement, requires no tallies, and has sufficient elasticity to allow a variety of yardsticks to be placed against it as a matter of judgment. This is not a precisely written objective, but it nonetheless states clearly the intent of the principal in training his subordinate leaders. The question now becomes how will he make his determination?

No sure-fire method exists whereby absolute standards may be applied arithmetically to ascertain degrees to which an objective has been accomplished. On the other hand, intelligent people may sit down and discuss mutually agreeable ways whereby the principal may assess and, to some degree, judge the increase in quality of written evaluations by subordinate leadership personnel in approximately one year's time. A mini-checklist follows which may be of assistance to people whose experience with judging the accomplishment of objectives is limited or which may, because of the pressure of time, go ignored in the annual crush of events which tends to engulf school leadership personnel:

- Determine the most essential items in writing evaluations which will be examined in materials to be submitted by subordinate leadership personnel (items such as quality of sentence structure, coherence, and appropriate coverage of job responsibilities).

- Agree in advance on how many evaluations will be used to determine the nature of the improvements each educational leader has made. For example, three evaluations submitted by each assistant principal and chairman ought to be a sufficient sampling in order to make that determination.

- Have the person being evaluated submit a brief written explanation on the areas in writing evaluations where he has grown and provide illustrative proof of that growth on his own initiative.

- In the critique of accomplishment at the end, insert the requirement that the person being evaluated be able to identify areas of continuing weakness so that he may, for the following year, increase his polish in those areas.

Clearly, a good deal of imagination can be brought to bear in determining criteria whereby accomplishment of objectives may be judged. It is important, however, to recognize from the very beginning that an atmosphere of reasonable "give-and-take" needs to be induced so that the judgment of the evaluator will be, if not fully accepted, certainly regarded with a positive outlook on the part of those being evaluated. No one will ever agree wholly on a final assessment which may be, at least in part, negative. At the same time, recognition of the imperfection of any system of judgment is most essential for positive growth to take place; even though both parties are aware that no one is ever wholly right and no one ever wholly wrong in a situation involving perception. The essence of good communication requires an understanding that it is quite conceivable that agreeing to disagree may very well be a productive contact in and of itself. Such mutual understanding surely creates a favorable climate for synthesizing opposing points of view.

EVALUATING YOUR SECRETARY

Evaluations of performance should hardly be restricted to members of the professional staff. All workers have dignity; all workers perform at given levels of competence; all workers need to know what it is about their performance which pleases an employer, and certainly should be made aware of elements which fail to please. Much as school systems have an entire procedure established for the assessment of teachers' performances, so they should have one for the evaluation of their nonprofessional personnel.

The individual closest to a school administrator is his secretary and, accordingly, she needs to know the elements of her performance upon which she will be judged. Such elements as: (1) stenographic skills, (2) typing ability, (3) sophistication with which telephone calls are screened and referred, (4) handling of appointments, (5) treatment of visitors, (6) relationships with the professional staff, (7) keeping of the administrator's calendar, (8) capacity to produce volumes of work, (9) ability to work without supervision and to use initiative, (10) anticipation of recurring problems, (11) filing, (12) attendance and punctuality, (13) appropriateness of dress, (14) voice and diction, (15) ability to produce attractive, grammatically correct correspondence,

Figure 5-4

SLOANE HIGH SCHOOL

School Objectives

19X5—19X6

In order to establish an intelligent long-range planning system for Sloane High School and to focus on several central school issues well, the following objectives for the academic year 19X5—19X6 are submitted:

Objectives	*Methods of Accomplishment*	*Personnel Responsible*	*Due Dates*
1. To determine the current "managerial" status of internal administrative systems at the high school with a view toward increasing efficiency.	• Meetings with administrators, guidance personnel, secretaries, chairmen, and central office personnel. • Comparisons with other schools needing to accomplish similar ends. • Revision of forms, reporting systems, and methods of planning.	Principal and Unit Coordinators	6/30/X6
2. Review and analyze testing program at the high school with a view toward having it become a more useful teaching and diagnostic tool.	• Determine *current* district testing programs and grade placement needs in the high school. • Meet with district coordinator and department chairmen to determine more suitable system.	Principal, guidance chairman, and district reading coordinator	6/30/X5

Objective	Actions	Responsible	Target Date
3. Revise the supervisory and evaluative system at the high school regarding staff performance within the context of an approved district format.	• Adopt new system. • Establish a series of mutually agreed upon assumptions within which a reasonable system of supervision and evaluation can exist. • Modify system practices and procedures so as to gain maximal growth in teacher performance with minimal clerical input. • Submit all proposals to joint administrative/faculty committee review. • Adopt new system.	Principal	Basic Assumptions 9/15/X5 Full Plan 12/1/X5
4. Assess school tone, socially and academically, with a view toward improving it in each instance.	• Frequent meetings with student leadership groups to sense school climate. • Initiate discipline and control procedures to increase accountability for greater productivity academically and in school activities. • Increase communication between home and school through a variety of methods—the first one being the initiation of a school newsletter designed to inform parents about the school program, climate, and objectives.	Principal and Unit Coordinators	6/30/X5 End of each marking period

5. Assess the school's intellectual climate.

- Discuss with faculty.
- Discuss with students.
- Analysis of academic practices and enriching activities with view toward desirable revision and strengthening.
- Adopt new practices appropriate to findings.

6/30/X5

6. Explore specifically the need(s) for certain kinds of vocational programs, including supporting facilities.

- Survey by Dept. of Guidance.
- Consultation with State Dept. of Education with particular reference to funding.
- Draft preliminary recommendations (short and longer range).

Principal
Unit Coordinators, and
Dept. of Guidance

6/30/X5

Submitted by: W. Goldstein, Principal

(16) ability to supervise subordinate secretarial personnel and organize their workdays, and (17) general fitness to occupy the position. These are the bases upon which a secretary's contribution to the school ought to be assessed.

While checklists tend to be the easiest way to handle a variety of skills relative to judging how well they are performed, they ultimately are inadequate except as instruments of assessment. Seldom are checklists sufficient motivation for growth—the ultimate criterion of improvement of performance. If one uses the approach of setting and assessing the accomplishment of objectives for professional staff, there is no logical reason why this method cannot be used with secretaries whose job requirements are sufficiently complex to warrant it.

Situation: Your secretary has skills which are better than adequate. You notice, however, that as the years go on no growth appears to be occurring. Even though your secretary's performance is significantly better than satisfactory, you feel that there is room for even finer performance. Accordingly, you sit down with her to discuss areas which could conceivably cause larger volumes of work and a better managerial situation in general to take place. After the conference, you set two major objectives. Conceivably they might take the following form:

- The secretary will make a concerted effort to polish her skills so as to raise her functional level of stenography from 90 words per minute to 120 words per minute with no loss of accuracy or efficiency.

- The entire filing system for the high school will be reconstructed so that location of information is quicker and material of an historical character which no longer has value will be removed.

The accomplishment of these objectives will be predicated on sufficient time being made available during the regular workday to see to it that overtime will not be necessitated. This presumes, of course, a general increase in the speed of completing routine assignments so as to create the time necessary for the accomplishment of the objectives.

Quite obviously, such objectives are to some degree trivial. Nonetheless, the institution of this kind of system could conceivably yield less trivial objectives and cause any secretary to become conscious of the need to grow in her position.

In order to communicate your intentions well, however, it is necessary that all evaluations of secretaries not only describe performance, but also prescribe corrective steps which may be taken to plug gaps in performance. An illustration of an appropriately written commentary follows:

> Over the three years in which Mrs. Jarvis has occupied the position of principal's secretary, her performance has been quite good. Her stenography is better than adequate, her typing skills are outstanding, and her ability to handle people, especially in situations which are exacerbated by crisis, are most commendable. She has the capacity to maintain her own equilibrium as well as see through some of the elements which cause friction in the first place.

> On the other hand, while her correspondence is generally well handled, some areas do indeed need polish and refinement. Her sense of punctuation and capitalization is only adequate, and at times this requires that material be retyped. I would suggest that during the next academic year Mrs. Jarvis take a review course in the mechanics of language so that she is more secure and less apt to need corrective action.

An examination of this brief evaluative commentary shows very clearly that the employer is more than satisfied with his secretary's performance, but does see areas where her efficiency could be improved simply by filling a gap in her background.

One could illustrate endlessly ways wherein a perceptive evaluator could establish a set of purposes for his subordinate secretarial personnel. But it is sufficient to say that the establishment of objectives, communicating the purpose of such a system, and then precisely remarking as to the accomplishment of these objectives is as feasible an approach for ameliorating the performances of secretaries as it is for improving the performances of teachers.

EVALUATING SERVICES OF CHAIRMEN AND ADMINISTRATORS

Probably the most sensitive act which an administrator needs to perform is rendering annual assessments on the quality of the work of his colleagues. Unlike teachers who by any "line-staff" arrangement are considered to be subordinate personnel, the concept of administration as a team has fairly well saturated the organizational mind. Elaborate schemes for evaluating leadership and administrative personnel have evolved over the years in which management has had an abiding concern with improving the performances of these categories of workers. As is true of the evaluation of services of the teaching staff, performances have been assessed with numerically and adjectively loaded checklists, simple narratives with elaborate design, as well as narrative reports wherein design was absent almost altogether.

When all is said and done, when all analyses have been made, when all forms have been compared, probably the most substantial reduction of format for the evaluation of leadership personnel in the schools may be summarized as follows:

- In order to improve performances of leadership personnel, some incentives need to be involved. Whether the incentives are monetary or whether they take the simple form of commendatory statements becomes somewhat irrelevant in the public schools.

- Checklists have proven to be inadequate since they are simply descriptive.

- In order to render an effective narrative report on an administrator or chairman, the writer of the document must himself have a full and complete grasp of the dimensions of the role—the services which he is evaluating.

- Articulateness and precision are central ingredients of any decent narrative report which will not embarrass the writer himself.

- The evaluation report should in, and of itself present a model to the subordinate administrator—one which is worthy of imitation or emulation.

Three central ingredients exist in the evaluation of administrative and leadership personnel. To expand a form to yield an evaluation beyond these three elements becomes a useless exercise. The simpler the form the better. Extravagant, labyrinthine, intricate reports simply cause the focus of the document to be diffused and seldom yield much productivity. While an evaluation report is, indeed, an exercise in using language with skill, form must never be confused with content. Its ultimate mission will always be to transmit useful information to its recipients. If a report fails to do that, however admirable its prose, it has failed to yield the substance of the prime directive of evaluation in the first place. The three major ingredients of a narrative evaluation which ought to be rendered on supervisory personnel are the following:

Accomplishment of Objectives: All leadership personnel should be required to articulate a series of "doable," precisely written objectives along with methods which will be used to accomplish these objectives within a given time-frame, let us say, an academic year. The first segment of any written evaluation of leadership personnel ought to include a narrative assessment, objective by objective, as to how well each aim was accomplished. Or, if intentions were not met, the reasons for the failure to consummate that arrangement. This section of the narrative should be precise and should include detailed explanation on the *quality* of work performed and a substantial *description* of the results of that work.

Failure to comment on the completion of objectives makes the writing of them an exercise in futility and undercuts the entire procedure which is designed to facilitate progress and to insure results after adequate planning. For example:

Objective: Write more precise evaluation and observation reports so that teachers understand with clarity the directions in which they need to proceed in order to improve their performances.

Assessment: Mr. Metcalf has worked all year long visiting teachers in classes with a view towards sharpening his powers of observation and translating those perceptions into suitable, precise language. At this time, he is still writing prose of a general, imprecise kind. I do see signs of greater specificity in that his suggestions to teachers are currently buttressed by examples from the classes he has witnessed. This is a sound first step in making concrete such abstractions as, "The teacher realized his objectives." In order to insure that teachers realize their objectives, it is necessary to be able to articulate those objectives and to cite concrete examples showing precisely how such intentions became realities. On the other hand, words such as "interesting" and "rapport" have little meaning unless one attaches to them verbal amplification in one way or another—so as to induce a reader's focus in such a way as to create clarity and sharpness of a *descriptive* as well as *prescriptive* kind.

Description of Job Performance: A second crucial element in assessing the performance of an administrator or chairman rests in delivering a clear, focused description of how well that individual has performed in his "normal" job expectations. In the case of leadership personnel, certain major categories of performance surface rather quickly. Work in supervision and evaluation, budget development, curriculum planning, general administration, and leadership instincts. No evaluation is complete without remarking to the effectiveness an individual shows in each of these categories. To be sure, there are other areas of performance which may also need attention, but one cannot avoid addressing himself to the staples of leadership behavior. Once again, as was the case with the analysis of the degree to which objectives have been attained, it is necessary for the evaluator to remark precisely about the general performance in each category which he chooses to narrate. For example, it is folly to write descriptive prose that says, "Mr. Smith's work in budget development is good." This has little meaning and delivers no degree of satisfaction except as a *pro forma* ritual for the individual receiving the evaluation report. Rather, it is better to say:

> Mr. Smith has sound instincts with respect to the fiscal responsibilities which accrue to his position. Above all, he is sensitive to the financial crunch which has landed on all the schools, and his budgetary requests reflect his grasp of reality in this regard. For example, he has a refined understanding about requesting only those materials which are essential to the survival of programs; although at times he does set a system of priorities which allows a reviewer of his budgetary segment to see his sensings regarding an item which might be desirable to have but which carries with it no sense of immediate urgency.

One can see readily that Mr. Smith, in accordance with the remarks of his evaluator, understands the difference between requesting something that is simply "nice to have" as compared to requisitioning an item which is *essential* for the continuance of a program or the maintenance of effort at that school.

Recommendations for Improvement: The third and last segment of any material evaluation of administrative staff is contained in this category. An evaluator remains essentially uncommunicative if he fails to suggest ways in which a subordinate can improve his performance. Description without prescription is no evaluation at all. Indeed, such a narrative renders a fraternal package which insures the survival of the *status quo* and no more. For each negative remark in the general text of the evaluation preceding the section on recommendations, a precise "curative" statement ought to be made which points a substantial and lucid direction to the individual receiving the evaluation report. Even semi-sophisticated evaluative narratives carry with them some sensing of what a superior considers an important direction in which a subordinate should begin to move. Following you will find a brief series of suggestions which might well be included in this section of an evaluative narrative:

- Since you are having difficulty in meeting deadlines because of an obvious overload in the assignments which have been given you, I would suggest that you begin to work with a written calendar. Such a conscious effort will surely yield not only a sense of priority, but will serve as a constant reminder for when projects are due so that the next level of administration will not find itself shackled because of your failure to provide information.

- In dealing with committees, some of which you head, insist on building timelines into their work schedule. Many times projects atrophy because people lose interest as a result of inordinate numbers of meetings. One way in which to insure job satisfaction for members of that committee is to insist that their work be completed by a given date, and that meetings which are of a counterproductive character be curtailed.

- Letters with your signature have contained an inordinate number of mechanical errors. Either take the time to proofread the letter more carefully, or show it to a colleague whose sense for language and mechanical correctness may perhaps be somewhat in excess of yours. It is no disgrace to seek advice. It is however unwise to fail to seek help when it is obvious that the end product is sufficiently unsatisfactory to cause mild embarrassment.

- Your work in curriculum, while adequate, does need revitalization now and again. I would suggest you draft for yourself a working bibliography of the better-known publications in the field and, in the next year or so, see to it that you become fairly familiar with the best that has been said in recent times about the business of expanding and creating new programs.

- Since you are responsible for the administration and supervision of extracurricular activities, you are well aware of the lack of knowledge class advisors and sponsors of clubs seem to have with respect to their responsibilities at activities promulgated by their organizations and, furthermore, the absence of detailed knowledge on how to handle funds connected with those activities. I would strongly urge you to draft a "Manual for Advisors" which carries with it a detailed explanation on exactly what an advisor's responsibilities are and how he may best execute them.

It is evident that a basic organizational format restricts and guides the evaluator in making his assessments. Furthermore, the more articulate and precise the document the more productive it will be for its recipients.

EVALUATIONS FOR "IN THE MEANTIME, IN BETWEEN TIME"

One of the most neglected areas in the whole business of supervision and evaluation is the power and influence of a so-called "interim" evaluation. Much of the supervisory/evaluative process is riveted to the academic year, which ordinarily culminates in a written evaluation covering the quality of services rendered by an individual for that specific period of time. Not infrequently, people's performances are such that waiting for the termination of an evaluative period has a deleterious effect, in that it allows the individual to perform badly without any corrective action taking place.

Such interim evaluations usually take the form of simple memoranda with specific topics. For example, let us suppose that a teacher chronically fails to complete his report cards on time, arrives at work late, and in general collapses procedurally with respect to the mechanical requirements of his job. Nothing should prevent an alert administrator from commenting on this slipshod performance in writing and sufficiently in advance to prevent further deterioration of that individual's contribution to the school. Such a memorandum might look like this:

Figure 5-5

TO: Joseph Harold
FROM: Allen James
               Principal
SUBJECT: Recent Problems in Procedural Performance

On several occasions now, we have discussed certain procedural malfunctions in your performance. I would remind you at this time that in the last ten working days you have arrived at least 10 minutes late on six of these days. In addition, when report cards were due, yours were two days late, thereby causing undue delay in transmittal of the entire package to our computer installation.

Until now, we have kept our supervisory, exchanges oral, and we agreed that it would not be necessary to reduce these matters to writing. However, since our last conference, I have seen no improvement in your responsiveness to requests or any improvement in your arrival to school on time. I am sure you realize that the situation can no longer go unchecked. Accordingly, I am directing that you begin performing adequately with respect to your procedural commitments.

Failure to respond will necessitate further administrative action and may conceivably result in a recommendation from me which will deny you an annual salary increment, or which would be an initial step in termination of services.

I know that I can count on you to be cooperative and to do the best you can to bring your performance to an acceptable procedural standard. As always, administrators in the building stand ready to assist you in whatever way we can.

cc: Supt. of Schools   /s/ Allen James
    Asst. Principal
    Chairman

Clearly, one becomes apprehensive in the treatment of negative brands of performance. On the other hand, positive performance likewise yields the need for interim evaluative statements. An example of this kind of statement is usually in the form of a letter of appreciation or congratulations, but may be more specific and allude to several items. Just as there are "letters of concern," such as the one previously cited, there are also letters which attest to the outstanding performances of other staff members. An example follows:

Figure 5-6

TO: John Smith
FROM: Allen James
        Principal
SUBJECT: Involvement in Student Activities

All year now, I have indicated to you how pleased I am with the way in which you have been supportive of student activities. You never leave your responsibilities as a teacher at the doorstep of the classroom, and I thought it time now and more than appropriate to affirm my perceptions of your performance in writing.

Not only was I delighted when you accepted the advisorship of the senior class, but I am pleased with the original way in which you have added to the activities of our graduates-to-be. While coaching two sports, I find it rather amazing that you could somehow sift and sort your schedule in such a way so as to find time to advise a graduating class of some 400 students. In addition, your attendance at concerts, as well as athletic events, has not gone unnoticed.

I would make you aware that you have added a profound dimension to your performance with respect to contributing so vastly to the high quality of school life our students are experiencing. Your conspicuous presence and contributions to the school beyond the classroom reflect most appropriately on your equally enthusiastic classroom performance.

cc: Supt. of Schools   A.J.
    Asst. Principal
    Chairman, Dept. of Mathematics

In a sense, self-evaluation is also a kind of "interim" assessment. Any evaluative system which purports to be continuous must make provision for inclusion of this information into the writing process. Following is a sample extract from an evaluative system which reflects the centrality of such additive information:

Figure 5-7

Self-Evaluation: Each faculty member should submit on the appropriate district form (those used to evaluate teachers by supervisors) a self-evaluation of his performance to his immediate supervisor at least *three (3) weeks* prior to the date when the supervisor's evaluation on that teacher is due. At the teacher's discretion, that document (the self-evaluation) shall be stapled to the supervisor's evaluation as further evidence of performance and to insure that maximum objectivity is presented to administrators.

If the teacher chooses not to append his self-evaluation to the final evaluative instrument submitted to the central office, he should so indicate in narrative form in the "Teacher Comments" section of the evaluation instrument.

The notion of "in the meantime, in between time" appears to be a most useful underlying philosophical commitment.

ACCOUNTABILITY FORMS FOR SUPERVISORS

One of the key malfunctions of supervisory processes, especially in large schools, rests with the failure of principals to be kept well informed on the nature of operational supervision, its frequency, and the results of the efforts of subordinate evaluative personnel. Especially when problems occur, this "blindness," induced by the famous (or infamous) "breakdown of communications," can be lethal to making judgments or denial of salary increments, nonrenewal of probationary contracts, or dismissal of personnel. Such short-circuitry of information feeding can be easily avoided by establishing "accountability relationships," advertising them in the document which outlines the entire system, and insisting on the completion (monthly) of a kind of supervisory log. Following are two illustrations. The first shows how to describe relationships of supervisor to individuals supervised and the second presents a model "accountability sheet."

Figure 5-8

Accountability Relationships: The building principal shall be *responsible* for *all* evaluations rendered on all faculty members in the school to which he is assigned. He, along with other supervisory agents (unit coordinators, chairmen, etc.), will observe and, where appropriate, comment on the quality of performance of all teachers on that staff. For the most part, however, in the cases of secondary schools, chairmen will be the chief supervisors within departments having such assigned leadership, and teachers will be directly accountable to that chairman for the quality of their performances. Unit coordinators and chairmen will be directly accountable for the quality of their performances to the building principal. Evaluations will be written along the following lines of accountability:

Individual Supervised	*Evaluation Written by*
Teacher	Chairman—Consultation with Unit Coordinators
Chairman	Principal—Consultation with Unit Coordinators
Unit Coordinators	Principal

In the cases of teachers, each evaluation will contain three (3) signatures: those of the chairmen and unit coordinator, each as *evaluating* agents, and that of the principal *approving* the document. The evaluations of chairmen and unit coordinators will be *written and signed* solely by the principal.

Figure 5-9

Acme High School

Monthly Supervisory Report

DEPARTMENT:
MONTH:

Name of Faculty Member	Observed on: Date(s)	Approximate Length of Observation(s)	Date(s) of Conference	Remarks

Original: Principal
cc: Unit Coordinators

Unit Coordinators

Signature of Chairman
Date:

Note: W. Goldstein, *op. cit.,* p. 5.

ESTABLISHING SUPERVISORY AND ADMINISTRATIVE CALENDARS

One obvious way of communicating the urgency and significance of the entire supervisory/evaluative process is to call attention to the need for completing its cycle by certain times and dates, many of which have their roots in either negotiated contracts or state statutes.

Every process for evaluation should contain a section on deadlines, perhaps not unlike the illustration which follows:

Figure 5-10

Calendar: Evaluative materials will be due in each principal's office in accordance with the following established timelines:

Teacher	*Date Due*
1st year	January—end of 1st school week
2nd year	January—end of 2nd school week
3rd year	January—end of 1st school week
(for tenured)	
Tenured (judged marginal or less than adequate)	Anytime during school year when performance so warrants
Tenured (satis-factory or better) (1/3 of faculty per annum to be derived by alphabetical listing)	May—end of 1st school week

PREPARATION OF MATERIALS FOR NONRENEWAL OF CONTRACT AND DISMISSAL

In order to communicate with the utmost clarity on hyper-sensitive issues, particularly the termination of employment, one must be especially cautious in: (1) eliminating caprice from his correspondence, (2) having written records to which he alludes in memoranda and letters, (3) writing clear, non-inflammatory, objective, even "neutral" prose, and (4) distributing copies of his correspondence in legal and properly informative fashion.

To distinguish communication on termination of professional services, administrators must be aware of state statutes governing such mandatory departures of faculty. Nonrenewal of contract implies termination of the services of probationary or nontenured teacher. Dismissal clearly means separation of a teacher from the staff at a time other than year's end for a nontenured staff member *or* "firing" of a tenured teacher. Each form of "separation" carries with it legal requirements and strict adherence to constitutional due process. Effective communication demands effective procedures—leaving nothing to chance. The written word must be precise, proper, and have fidelity to good historical and legal practice. Some guidelines may be of help, since all correspondence will need to be privately tailored to the particularities of individual situations and cases:

- Be sure to review all statutes and contract requirements prior to putting pen to paper.

- Gather all written supervisory documents, placing them in chronological order, in order to synthesize whatever negative (or positive) patterns may emerge.

- Examine the *magnitude* of the issues in question, since trivial items will surely be disregarded in ensuing legal proceedings.

- Seek competent legal advice on how to proceed and to review the strength and propriety of language to be used in communicating termination notification.

- Be sure all documents have been appropriately *signed* and *dated*.

- In the text of all correspondence, be sure to refer to:

1. Dates of observed work.
2. Assistance offered and suggestions made.
3. *Exact* description of dissatisfaction with performance.
4. Nature of the action being recommended (withholding of increment, termination of services, etc.).
5. Keep the tone emotionally antiseptic. Diatribes or "loaded" language undercuts the whole process.
6. Mark carbon copies properly to all persons who need to be informed thusly.
7. Cause all correspondence to be receipted either via registered mail or by office signature.
8. Prepare full and complete folder of all pertinent materials; such folder to be available for duplication at the proper legal moment. Materials therein should include all written classroom observations, annual evaluations, interim memoranda, letters, summaries of conferences, and the like.
9. Do *not* introduce written material of which the teacher has not received a copy. As a matter of fact, such material should not even exist.

SUMMARIZING SUPERVISORY CONFERENCES

Oral communications are also highly significant in the lives of working people. Once spoken and heard, a word cannot be withdrawn. Negative comments tend to smolder and frequently become exacerbated and distorted with the passage of time. Assessment of the worth of one's services creates at best a tense, strained, and delicate relationship:

Situation: On three separate occasions, you, as principal, have gone to observe the work of a teacher. Your visits were unannounced deliberately, designed to be of a "surprise" character. Each time you have found students busily at work—with no teacher in the room. In the first instance, you conferred with him, ascertained the reasons for his absence, and cautioned him against repetition by outlining all the reasons of prudence, legality, safety, and responsibility which accrue to a teacher in exercising his functions. To give him a "break," however, you did not reduce the occurrence to a written, "warning" memorandum. On the second occasion, however, your patience elasticized beyond "fraternal" limits and you sent him a sharp, critical note after discussing the issue with him again.

At this time, you warned him that further repetition of such negligent behavior would result in additional, punitive administrative action. With the third incident, your communiqué might look like this:

Figure 5-11

TO: Teacher
FROM: Principal
SUBJECT: Unauthorized Absence from Classes

December 10, 19___

In attempting to observe your classroom performance on three separate occasions (Oct. 12, Nov. 2, and Dec. 9) of this academic year, I have found your classroom abandoned except for students properly assigned there. You may recall that on the first occasion, Oct. 12, I conferred with you at the close of school for twenty minutes, outlining orally the precise expectations which I held for a teacher on this staff. While I enumerated reasons for the need for your physical presence at all times in your classes, I decided that I would not reduce the problem or conference to writing at that time.

In the second instance, having passed the stage of mere oral reprimand, I sent you a memorandum of concern dated November 2, 19 , the day of your second infraction, after conferring with you. Here we are faced with a third violation of the same kind—a most serious breach of professional responsibility in every sense.

Apparently, proper supervision and prudent advice, both oral and written, have failed to produce the appropriate change in behavior required of a mature, responsible teacher. As we discussed today, December 9, I am recommending that your salary increment for the coming academic year be withheld and that you be placed on warning that another abdication of your professional responsibilities will yield a recommendation for your immediate dismissal.

If there are special problems which necessitate your departure from class, you must obtain permission from an administrative official prior to leaving. I look forward to full compliance with my directives.

cc: Supt. of Schools   R.W.
    Asst. Principal
    Chairman, Dept. of English

In summarizing conferences, it is always wise to: (1) be precise in alluding to historical precedences, (2) present the case with objectivity, and (3) allow minimal time to elapse between the conference and transmittal of its written summary.

ADMINISTRATIVE AND APPEAL PROCEDURES

Tight, well-synchronized procedures are essential in establishing *predictability,* the base of sound, trustworthy communications. Disagreements on the substance of written evaluations will surely occur. A secure system safeguards against needless anxiety and informs members of the faculty fully of the treatment and disposition of evaluative documents. Excerpts on the above may appear in the supervisory guidelines as follows:

Figure 5-12

Appeal Procedure: Now and again, there may be serious disagreement between a staff member and a supervisor on the final judgment of quality of performance rendered. The following guidelines for such "disagreements" are submitted:

1. Teachers are asked to sign all necessary evaluative documents with full and complete understanding that signature implies merely *receipt* of the document, not necessarily agreement with its contents.

2. Teachers may ask that another evaluation be submitted on their performance within 90 calendar days after the one about which there is disagreement. This evaluation and all procedures connected with it should be accomplished by the use of at least *two* independent observers/evaluators appointed by the superintendent of schools.

3. Both documents, however, will remain a permanent part of the teacher's file.

4. Resolution of all supervisory conflicts shall be made by the superintendent of schools or his designee.

Submitting Evaluations: So that there is mechanical efficiency in the treatment of the entire process of evaluation, the following will serve as guidelines:

1. Department chairmen will observe all teachers in their department as frequently as possible, and for periods of time realistically adjusted to the nature of the lesson and the needs of the teacher.

2. Unit coordinators or other supervisory agents assigned to a building will observe all teachers assigned to their units as frequently as possible.

3. Once an evaluation has been approved by a unit coordinator or other supervisory agent beyond chairman status, it will be typed into final form and signed by both the chairman of the department and the unit coordinator. Subsequently, it will be presented to the teacher for his reaction, commentary, and signature.

4. Unit coordinators will submit evaluations for teachers in their unit on the dates indicated, to the office of the principal. After reviewing evaluations and making commentary to unit coordinators and chairmen on his perceptions and the quality of the written product, the principal will sign the documents and forward *one* copy of each evaluation and substantiating materials to the office of the superintendent.

5. The mechanical configuration and submittal of evaluations applies to guidance and other specialized personnel assigned to a school as well.

Filing of Evaluative Documents: Disposition of all written evaluative materials will be as follows:

Number of Copies	Where Filed
1	Personnel records (central office)
1	School file (principal's office)
1	Department chairman's file
1	Teacher's file (personal)

Justification of Certain Evaluations: Please note that there are four categories of performance on the Observation/Evaluation report. So that the categories continue to have meaning, it will be necessary for each evaluator to justify the granting of either an "outstanding" rating or an "unsatisfactory" rating.

Supervisory Problems: Supervisory problems are to be dealt with efficiently and appropriately. Building administrators are to be advised by chairmen immediately when a situation begins to look as if added help is necessary to improve teaching performance.

CONCLUSION

There can be no believable communication on the ultra-sensitive issues of supervision and evaluation without sound procedures, fidelity to that established system, mutual understanding of the process, and intelligent execution of its requirements. Careful, detailed planning gives rise to precise, written commentary without which the entire process collapses into a vague, embarrassing exercise in futility and frustration. Adherence to common sense, a proper grasp of guiding principles, and intelligent, mature judgment surely form the essence of reciprocally mature and intelligent acceptance of both supervision and evaluation.

6

COMMUNICATIONS THAT WILL HELP YOU COPE WITH THE UNEXPECTED

The "faculty member stands accused" scenario is not an unusual situation. However, as the principal, how you handle the incident does have tremendous ramifications for your total school image. Your leadership style in resolving the accusation directly affects students, staff morale, budgetary support by the community, and, in a very real sense, your job security.

Perhaps a critical analysis of a few live conflicts will serve to emphasize the need for open, tactful, and sensitive communications.

SITUATION

One of your teachers is accused of drinking on the job. You first hear of this via a parent phone call. The phone call complaint is quickly followed by a student complaint. As principal you have several action options:

171

a) You intentionally ignore the complaints.

b) You send a written memo to the accused teacher asking for a response.

c) You observe the teacher and judge for yourself.

d) You share the complaint with the teacher on an informal basis.

Let's consider the possible ramifications for each of your actions:

a) Intentionally ignore the complaints:

If the complaints get lost in the bureaucracy you have survived for another day, realizing that education has taken another degrading step backwards. If the complaints reach the superintendent's office and/or the members of the board of education and your ambiguous leadership is revealed, you are in trouble.

b) Send a written memo asking the teacher to respond:

The teacher may ignore, deny, or admit the charges. In any case, you have a problem on your hands. The teacher may be hostile, file a grievance, demand to know who the accusers are, bring legal action, and, in general, cause a staff morale problem.

c) Observe the teacher and judge for yourself:

Your observations may not be timed properly, thus both students and parents may perceive this as an administrative cover-up and pursue the charges anyway. In fact, they may become irrational and send a distorted letter to the local newspaper. Either way, it means trouble for the principal.

d) Share the information with the teacher:

Reactions may vary according to the maturity level and basic personality of the teacher. But regardless of the reaction, be it ridiculous, shrugged off, denied, or requesting that a face-to-face conference be set up (which you can offer the parents and students), you have taken proper and concrete action.

Mental Gyrations

Suppose you feel the charges are true but the teacher denies them: perhaps he claims he's taking medicine, has stomach trouble, etc.?

Keep in mind that alcoholism, in most states, is considered a sickness.

Intoxication on the job can be grounds for dismissal. How to prove the charges?

Will you suggest that the parents put the complaint in writing as a formal charge?

Are the students liable for their accusation?

Conclusion

The key to a "no-win" situation like this is open, honest communications.

You hope your conference with the teacher has been a sufficient alert.

You must explain the legal implications tactfully and honestly to both parents and students.

You must remain alert to the possibility that the charges will be substantiated over an extended period of time and these documented facts must be brought to the attention of the superintendent of schools for corrective action.

SITUATION

Another real-life conflict with a "no-win" ending can erupt via your cheerleading squad. This is especially true when you are the principal of a large, multiethnic high school.

Your school has a 25% black, 6% Spanish-speaking, and 69% white population representing all levels of the socioeconomic scale. Traditionally, twelve (12) cheerleaders are selected from the 180 who try out. The regulations are basically the same for all sporting activities.

As principal, you want to have a reasonable balance representing the makeup of the school population. However, through a fair-weighted selection procedure you end up with twelve whites on the squad, or you have eleven whites, one black, and no Spanish-speaking students. Spanish students are reluctant to try out. Selected black students want the rules adjusted to meet their own desires. White cheerleaders hold fast to established rules. A crisis is brewing. Your cheerleading advisor makes adjustments, bends rules to avoid trouble with minority students and ballplayers. Any further bending will be viewed as unfair to white cheerleaders. The advisor is accused of being prejudiced, a liar, and a cheat. You and he survive the year. However, selection tryouts for next year are rapidly approaching. What action do you take as principal?

Perhaps an illustration of a procedure that backfired would be useful. Once again the following real-life developments result in a compromise, but can still be considered a "no-win" situation. First the cheerleader's code:

Cheerleader Regulations

The following is a summary of regulations to be fully acknowledged and respected by all members of the High School Varsity Cheerleading Squad:

Section I—Eligibility and Tryouts

A. *Eligibility*

1) A cheerleader must be carrying four units of work and must pass three units in order to be eligible to cheer.

B. *Tryouts*

1) Cheerleading tryouts shall be held at the discretion of the cheerleading coach. All candidates, including those presently on the squad, must try out.

2) The cheerleading advisor shall, with the approval of the principal, notify the feeder schools of the time, place, and procedure to be used in the screening process.

3) The faculty advisor shall forward to the feeder schools parental permission forms and any other needed forms— allowing two weeks before the practice sessions for tryouts.

4) A girl must be in school on the day of tryouts in order to tryout. A girl under suspension may not tryout.

C. *Selection of Candidates*

1) Selection shall be made by the faculty advisor working in cooperation with a committee selected by himself and/or the principal.

2) Notification of selection shall be done as soon as possible following the last tryout session.

Section II—Number of Candidates and Captains

A. *Number of Candidates*

1) There will be twelve (12) girls on the regular squad with two (2) alternates to replace a regular when necessary.

2) From the first twelve, one captain and one assistant captain will be elected by the group—according to parliamentary procedure. The faculty advisor will preside over elections.

B. *Alternates*

1) The two alternates will be present at each practice session.

2) Each alternate is subject to the same rules and regulations as the regulars.

3) The chief purpose of an alternate is to replace a regular member of the squad when the need arises.

Section III—Responsibilities

A. *Attendance*

1) Cheerleaders must attend all scheduled practices and official functions.

a) There will be two practices per week. During the *football* season, practices will be held on Tuesday and Friday. During the *basketball* season, practices will be on Monday and Thursday.

b) Each practice will start at 2:15 P.M. and end at 3:45 P.M.

2) Cheerleaders must be present in school the day of the game to be eligible to cheer in the evening or afternoon contest.

3) Cheerleaders must participate in the practice session prior to the game in order to cheer at the scheduled contest.

a) A cheerleader may be excused from a practice session or *game* only in cases of emergency, illness, or other unusual circumstances.

4) A cheerleader must give notice to the advisor if she is unable to participate at a scheduled contest. A valid excuse for absence may be granted by the advisor, and she will assign an alternate to replace the excused cheerleader. The cheerleader *must* turn over her uniform to the alternate for that game.

5) *A cheerleader who has missed three practice sessions without a valid excuse will be dismissed from the squad. This will be strictly enforced!*

6) There will be *no half absences*. The cheerleader must stay for the entire practice or receive a full cut.

B. *Uniforms*

1) Functional wearing apparel must be worn to all practice sessions (sneakers, shorts).

2) Cheerleading uniforms must be kept clean and in good condition. Uniforms must be returned to the advisor at the end of each season in good condition.

3) Cheerleaders are responsible for any damage done to their uniforms while they are in their possession.

4) Small earrings and class rings are the only jewelry to be worn.

C. *Conduct*

1) Cheerleaders are responsible to the advisor and/or captains for their conduct during all games and practice sessions.

2) *Suspension* (*first offense*): A cheerleader may not participate in practice sessions or contests while under suspension. She may not participate in the contest following her suspension.
Suspension (*second offense*): Immediate suspension from the squad for the remainder of the season, and removal of athletic awards.

3) *Truancy* (*first offense*): A cheerleader may not participate in the contest following a truancy.

   Truancy (*second offense*): Immediate suspension from the squad for the remainder of the season, and removal of athletic awards.

4) A cheerleader may not smoke on school grounds, or while in uniform.

Section IV—Physical Examination and Insurance

A. *School Insurance*

1) Cheerleaders will be covered under the school's accident insurance plan which will be provided by the Board of Education.

B. *Physical Examination*

1) A physical examination shall be given to each cheerleader prior to the first contest. This may be done by the family physician or the school physician.

Section V—Transportation

A. *Home Contests*

1) Cheerleaders shall report to the school at the time set by the faculty advisor.

B. *Local, In-town Contests*

1) This includes any contest within the city limits. Transportation to and from all local, in-town contests shall be provided by the parents of the cheerleaders.

2) Cheerleaders shall report to the specified school at the time designated by the faculty advisor.

C. *Away Contests*

1) Transportation to and from all away contests shall be provided for by the Board of Education. Transportation shall be by bonded carrier.

2) Cheerleaders shall be chaperoned while enroute and during all contests by the faculty advisor or her delegated assistant.

3) A cheerleader may return from an away game with her parents—if they are in attendance at the game and personally make the request of the advisor.

4) There will be no other passengers on the cheerleaders' bus.

Section VI—Season

A. The cheerleading season begins after tryouts and lasts until after the last basketball game. These rules are binding during that time.

B. A cheerleader under suspension for grades will still be bound by this code.

I have read and understand these rules and regulations and pledge to wholeheartedly abide by them.

_____

Cheerleader's Signature

P.S. This signed cheerleader's code is to be returned to the cheerleader's advisor.

Certainly, the preceding rules, regulations, and guidelines are typical, realistic, and for years were considered to be reasonable. Unfortunately in modern times, rules, regulations, and guidelines are challenged to the point where even the most traditional practices are sometimes considered unfair. Thus an attempt was made to be more selective in the tryout stage. The following invitational approach is patterned after the National Honor Society's preliminary screening procedure. It is designed to reward those students who demonstrate the virtues of cooperation, responsibility, and manners.

Figure 6-1

TO: ALL POTENTIAL CHEERLEADERS
FROM: Cheerleading Advisor, Principal
RE: *Tryouts and Selection Criteria*

A. *Announcement*

1) We will be having tryouts for all interested students in the high school gym on_____.

2) We will select a cheerleading squad of _12_ members. There will be no alternates. *All* selected members will be on the regular squad.

3) The complete squad is selected every year. Former cheerleaders must compete like every other candidate.

B. *Understanding*

In view of the tremendous number of girls interested in trying out for the squad, the school authorities want to be sure that all girls understand the selection criteria, the amount of time, commitment, and *positive attitude* required for successfully performing on the cheerleading squad.

C. *Procedure and Characteristics*

1) All potential cheerleaders will sign up as follows:

    8th graders—sign up with your English teacher
    9th graders—see cheerleading advisor
    10th and 11th graders—sign up with the principal
    *All candidates must sign up by*_____

2) We will then list your names by grades and distribute these lists to the faculty for their input and suggestions concerning the following characteristics:

    a) *A positive, cooperative attitude*
    b) Responsible and acceptable conduct
    c) Willingly and pleasantly accepts direction

3) *All* potential cheerleaders *eligible* to tryout *will be given an invitation note* from the advisor to attend the tryout practices.

4) Finalists will perform for a group of six judges with a decision to be announced within five school days after the final performance.

After the completion of the sign-up period, the following bulletin was disseminated.

Figure 6-2

TO: ALL TEACHERS/STAFF MEMBERS
FROM: Cheerleading Advisor
RE: *Cheerleaders*

The following girls have signed up for the cheerleading squad. Their positive participation can be a tremendous plus for the school, the team, the fans, and our school's reputation. Thus, positive characteristics and attitudes are a must. Negative attitudes can cause all of us unnecessary headaches and damage our total school environment. *Your concern and input are vital!*

With the following characteristics in mind, would you, if you were the advisor, want this student to represent the school as one of our cheerleaders?

1) A positive, cooperative attitude
2) Responsible and acceptable conduct
3) Willingly and pleasantly accepts directions

STUDENTS   RECOMMENDATION   YES   NO

Comment if you desire:
Return to Cheerleading Advisor by_____

The results were reviewed and selected cheerleading candidates were issued the following invitation and permission slip:

Figure 6-3

INVITATION

To Cheerleading Candidate_____

You are invited to tryout for the Brownell Cheerleading Squad for the school year 19X6-19X7. You must do the following in order to be eligible to try out on __May 27__ :

1) You must attend three (3) practice sessions at gym on May 24, 25, and 26. The practice sessions will be from 2:15 P.M. until 4:00 P.M.

2) You must bring the enclosed permission slip, signed by your parent or guardian, with you. If you don't bring the permission slip you will not be allowed to try out.

PERMISSION SLIP:

To Cheerleading Candidates:

In order to take part in the practice sessions and tryouts, you must bring to the first practice session this permission slip signed by your parent or guardian.

I give my daughter_____permission to practice and try out for the Brownell Cheerleading Squad for the year 19X6-X7.

                                 _____

                                 Signature of Parent or Guardian

In case of emergency, please call Dr._____
at _____.
            Phone Number

The preceding seemed like a well-organized and fair approach in dealing with all potential cheerleaders. However, as soon as the selections were posted, the following concerns and complaints were voiced by a group of minority parents (memo indicates the proposed resolution):

Figure 6-4

TO: Superintendent
FROM: Principal
RE: *Parent Meeting Concerning Cheerleaders*
PRESENT:Seven parent and organizational representatives

CONCERNS DISCUSSED:

1) Lack of fairness in selecting cheerleaders, specifically the invitational approach.

2) Lack of authority and control of the cheerleading advisor.

3) Question of providing enough uniforms for all cheerleaders and proper distribution of same.

4) Question of *mandated* summer practices.

5) Question of selection of captain and/or cocaptains.

6) Question of being a cheerleader and playing volleyball at the same time.

7) The question of black/white representation with an equal number of both black and white cheerleaders on the squad was discussed.

After a lengthy discussion of the above and all of the ramifications, the following plans were shared with the group:

1) There is to be a new advisor appointed sometime after June 28. This is in keeping with the teacher's contract procedure. The group has been encouraged to provide names of candidates.

2) The new advisor will be given full authority and will spell out in writing the rules which must be obeyed by all. These will be reviewed with all cheerleaders.

3) The Varsity squad will be expanded to 16 members.

4) There will be a Junior Varsity squad of 12 members.

5) Within the first three weeks of school in September, there will be new tryouts for the three expansion positions *and* the 12 Junior Varsity positions. All students will be able to tryout without invitations. We will order cheerleading uniforms so that all 28 members are suited.

6) The question of summer cheerleading practice will be left up to the cheerleaders. However, if they *decide* to practice it will not be mandated nor will it count as being absent from practice for those who do not attend. (These will not be supervised sessions.)

7) Cocaptains will be selected by the advisor or in consultation with the cheerleaders—one for the basketball season and one for the football season.

8) We cannot have a quota system with an equal number of black and white cheerleaders. We do expect and will encourage a fair representation of the best of those that tryout.

9) The question of being a cheerleader and playing volleyball at the same time was resolved. This cannot be the case. The students will have to make a choice.

10) One of the parents has volunteered to count the judges votes in the fall.

The group is hereby invited to volunteer their participation as chaperones, aides, or in any capacity for which there is a need.

Please Note: A copy of these minutes is being sent to all parties present at the meeting.

CONCLUSION

The agreement reached at the June parent meeting did resolve the situation and does pave the way for a better understanding. However, in no way does this imply that all participants were completely satisfied nor does it imply that the soundest solution was reached.

STUDENT PRESS—WHAT THEY SAY AND WRITE ABOUT

A sample position paper can easily project the many problems a school newspaper encompasses. Let's examine one *viewpoint:*

VIEWPOINT

Freedom of the Press and the High School Newspaper. Far be it for the high school newspaper to tell anyone how to do his job, yet some people think that they should tell us how to do ours. The problems that we seem to be having with the school community are those resulting from a communications gap. Most of the communication problems that have arisen with this school seem to have started when the last issue came out, although these types of problems have really been going on for a long time. When the last issue came out, we got a lot of comments from various people—administrators, counselors, teachers, etc. These comments were mixed, good and bad. It seems that some people in this school think that a school newspaper should just contain little notes about what is going on in the school, like who is going on a field trip, sports, awards, etc. Well, as the dedicated reporters and seekers of wisdom and truth that we are, we do try to write about what's going on in the school. That's where the problem comes in. When we go out to find the truth, we sometimes find that there are acutally things in school that are wrong! When we try to gather information on these things we are usually told everything from "no comment" and "none of your business" to "____ you dirty____." So as you can see, doing good journalistic work is not as easy, in this school anyhow, as you would think.

A school newspaper, as any honest teacher or lawyer will tell you, has the exact same rights as any outside, privately owned newspaper and can write whatever it wants as long as it stays within a few bounds. A school newspaper cannot be obscene, libelous, or interfere with the normal running of the school (i.e., inciting riots, etc.). Well, when was the last time you saw a riot due to an article that we wrote? We are not a "gossip" newspaper—we do not tell lies and do not print anything libelous: and depending on what your definiton of obscene is, we try to stay on the legal side of that, too. So, what we have here is a newspaper dedicated to freedom of the press, truth, and justice. We print everything from those cheery little stories that a lot of people want us to write, to emotional editorials, to well-written, investigative reports that make people's eyes pop out when they see that these terrible things actually happen in this teenage kindergarten. We often put in creative works such as poems and we always have our share of excellent satire, although lately some people can't tell satire from the truth and end up crying on the principal's desk. We are definitely an educated newspaper staff and we certainly know what we're doing, although one staff member in this school let it be known that he thinks we do not have the intelligence to carry out a paper of this caliber by printing the material that we do. If we can't print truth in this paper because it might hurt someone's feelings, then where has all the freedom and democracy gone?

So we leave it up to you—the reader. Do you think that this is a decent publication that prints good stories and tries to treat every story fairly, or do you think that it is something that should be used to put the school in a good light for public relations purposes? If you think the latter, then don't waste your 15¢ the next time the paper comes out because we are not about to knuckle under to anyone's demands.— *Student Editors.*—

Let's look at a school newspaper article:

Figure 6-5

GUIDANCE GANG

Reporter's Note: The thing that I have always admired about people is their good sense of humor. It's nice to know that teachers (and counselors) can read an article in good fun.

Ever since I've been here at school all I've heard about the guidance department is that they drink coffee all day and take four hours for lunch. Well, I think this is an unfair jab because they are also very hard to see and can make one feel very uncomfortable.

As a dedicated reporter, I went to see if I could find out more information about our heroes. Well, I did catch Ms. X slurping a quart of coffee quite often and Mr. Y asleep in his office periodically (once a day). I caught Mrs. Z very diligently working at her desk filing her nails. Mrs. W has been practicing with her new curling iron and the construction engineers are installing bleachers in front of Mr. O's office for students waiting to get in. Mr. P. is often sitting in front of the coffee percolator for several hours watching it perk and I caught Mrs. M. walking into her office with her eyes almost open (I don't think she knew where she was).

After much probing, I was invited to the weekly meeting of our distinguished counselors to discuss any questions I might have about the department (what an honor!). Well, I confidently walked into the guidance office and was greeted very nicely by the master of ceremonies who said they were just getting ready for me (one might say I started to get a bit nervous). I then stepped into the conference room and *slam!*—one door, *slam!*—the other door. I knew this was the end—cut off from the outside world and no escape! There were seven regular wooden chairs and one nice, padded, red arm chair. There sat the seven knights around the table and the king's chair was left for me (I checked to make sure there weren't any live wires attached to it). I sure didn't feel like a king. There sat Mr. Y very quietly in the back (I think he was asleep). Smiling, Mr. P seemed to be amused by the whole thing while Mrs. M seemed spaced out. Mrs. W was curling her hair while Mr. A was trying to get serious. Ms. X seemed ready for a kill and Mrs. Z scared me to death, leaning back in her chair, pushing back her white hair and giving me the most contemptuous evil eye that I've ever seen.

Well, they seemed ready, but I wanted to get out. I started asking questions (while they all gave me dirty looks) about the sign-up system and that was all. There was no way I could continue in that environment. They opened the doors and I quickly exited. What I managed to find out from our coffee drinkers was that to see your counselor you may: (A) sign up and make an appointment, or (B) walk in whenever you want. They don't know who signed up because they don't keep the sheet in their office, so it seems like a waste of ink to do that. They seem to like the walk-in method better. I think neither system is working because 25% of the students I surveyed found it difficult to see their counselors when they have made an appointment and 25% don't go to see their counselors at all. Also, 36% said the sign-up sheet doesn't work and 40% don't use it! (I better stop with the percentages—this is embarrassing!)

Since my "conference," a timeclock has been installed in the guidance office. If you go to your counselor and he/she is busy (ha!), you fill out a slip, punch the slip in the timer, and you will be scheduled for an appointment. The confident crew seems to think the clock has solved their problems (and Mr. P is amazed by the toy), but I don't think so. First of all, it would be much better if they would follow the sign-up sheet and forget about the walk-ins. Changing how they help (?) you is the impossible dream, but changing the way one tries to see his or her counselor may be achieved by a competent crew. Maybe when our secure, hard working, and loving gang get their doctorate degrees they will be able to improve the situation. *Good luck gang and good-bye!*

Obviously, there were a flood of complaints following this article. The president of the local teachers' organization wrote an official complaint; the guidance department threatened to sue; the director was upset at what it would do to the public image of guidance; and the principal felt it was an unfair, slanted attack on guidance.

The principal's reaction, sent to the newspaper's faculty advisor, follows:

Figure 6-6

Dear Mrs. Elm:

The school newspaper, technically and creatively, is a fine newspaper. Your leadership and work with the young people involved are appreciated. However, as principal of this high school, I do have an unsubstantiated theory and some substantiated observations.

Unsubstantiated Theory: It seems to me that too many of the students attracted to the journalism class try to use the newspaper as their personal springboard for venting their negative personalities.

Substantiated Observations: (a) There is hardly an issue published that doesn't have an abundance of "poor taste" satire articles; (b) There are few, if any, constructive suggestions made or positive, influential articles written.

REMARKS:

1) I realize your policy on censorship and I agree with the basic philosophy.

2) Satires, sarcasm, and irony all have a place in publishing, but leadership and guidance are important also.

   It seems to me you could provide more positive educational leadership by encouraging your students to be more sensitive to the feelings of your colleagues; by respecting the feelings of our community leaders, by making positive, constructive suggestions; by building a better school spirit rather than knocking it; and by trying to instill some pride, mutual respect, and dignity to promote a more positive image for all of us in the high school community.

   I realize that old-fashioned virtues of being mannerly, pleasant, supportive, positive, honest, hard working, and constructive may not be popular with some elements of our school community. But as principal, I assure you I am ready, willing, and able to promote all of these old fashioned virtues.

Principal

Conclusion

Where does all this lead to? Should you encourage school newspapers? What about libel laws? Who is responsible? These are touchy and serious questions. Some principals have found a way out by not having school newspapers. Some believe in unrestricted freedom of the school press (mostly in big cities). Some believe in school newspapers, but do attempt to influence not the "what" but the attitude and sensitivity of the advisor and staff. In any case, having a school newspaper is a worthy educational endeavor which demonstrates a humane school administration, and is in keeping with our system of providing a climate of participatory democracy within our schools.

Surveying Influential Segments of the Community

Communications too often are a one-way street in a community school. In order to prevent and cope with the unexpected, one should strive to anticipate and know what the concerns and attitudes of various publics are. Obviously, the analysis of such attitudes, opinions, and perceptions is of vital importance for any school administration.

Who should be interested? Who should survey whom? What kind of information is important? What type of questions should be asked? The following are examples which may serve as models:

Situation

The Board of Realtors of Townsville was becoming increasingly aware of the fact that their community was not gaining its share of home sales to executive and middle-management families moving into the county. There was strong evidence to support the belief that negative advice about Townsville was being given to potential home buyers—in some cases affecting sales that had almost been completed.

It was obvious that such advice was being given on a variety of occasions, social and official, by company executives, bankers, Realtors, and other opinion leaders.

At a banker's office: "Now that you ask me, I'd have to say that I wouldn't send *my* children to Townsville schools."

The Board determined that some kind of action was necessary to counteract the apparently unfortunate "image" of Townsville in the minds of influential people in the remainder of the county. This action might presumably take the form of an advertising and public relations campaign, as well as pressure on public officials to correct Townsville's visible deficiencies.

The general outlines of Townsville's most obvious drawbacks as an executive residential community were, of course, well known to members of the Board. But to conduct an effective promotional campaign on behalf of Townsville, it was believed necessary to measure as precisely as possible two important aspects of public opinion:

1. *The actual extent and degree of negative opinion about the city.*

    This information can be a guide to the size and scope of a pro-Townsville campaign. It will answer the question, "How big a job do we have to do?"

2. *The specific elements of the Townsville situation which were contributing to Townsville's negative image, and the relative importance of each.*

    With this information, a promotional campaign can be directed at exactly the right targets, avoiding a waste of money and effort on matters of little importance.

The school or school system must devise and test a questionnaire which is capable of producing the necessary information by mail. In addition, a select group of those responding by mail must be interviewed to determine the precise reasons for their negative opinions.

The target groups of the particular survey must be designated as "opinion leaders." Thus, only those people who might be influential in the selection of residential real estate should be included: (1) bank executives, (2) Realtors, and (3) homeowners with family incomes of $40,000 or more.

Each of the participants should be asked: *Suppose an executive from out-of-town (with school-age children) was being transferred to our county and he asked you in which towns he should look for a house, what would be your advice?*

As a result of the questionnaire the following conclusions may be drawn: (1) Those who know the most about the city are least prejudiced against it; (2) The Townsville School System is certainly not as unsatisfactory as the surveyed population believes. *Indeed, in certain respects, it is superior to all other county systems.*

The second phase of the survey must be conducted by a number of personal interviews. These interviews are designed to probe as deeply as possible into the actual reasons for negative opinions about the city, and to measure the degree to which those interviewed based their reasons on specific information about the school or school system.

One must realize that this sort of research has one drawback: there is no precise way to measure the objective *strength* of an opinion, that is, how strong a person's conviction is about a particular matter. But a certain degree of measurement can be obtained by probing into the *reasons* given for holding a particular point of view. If reasons given are concise and factual, it can be assumed that the opinion is firmly held and would be difficult to change. On the other hand, if reasons given are vague and general, or if *no* reasons are forthcoming, the opinion is probably not a matter of strong conviction and should be relatively easy to change.

A questionnaire can then be prepared to focus on the most often mentioned reasons for antischool opinions in the mailed questionnaires. The respondents can be asked to explain their point of view about each of these subjects—to give their reasons, if any, for believing that Townsville has a poor school system. They may also be asked for suggestions for improvement in some of the categories.

Questionnaire

The following is an example of the approach and actual questionnaire used by the interviewers:

In this case, we are particularly interested in your point of view toward Townsville, which was one of the communities mentioned in the questionnaire.

For instance, the Townsville public school system is sometimes a subject of controversy. In discussing these schools, what would you say about...

Discipline?_____

_____

Adequacy of teaching staff?_____

_____

Physical facilities?_____

_____

College admission performance?_____

_____

Other comments (if any)_____

Conclusions

A relatively large number of those who are interviewed may admit that they did not have factual information to back up their anti-Townsville opinions. Even those who might mention "facts," may often preface their comments with "From what I have heard." This may be particularly true in relation to opinions about the schools and zoning.

It is possible to conclude, therefore, that many anti-Townsville prejudices are not strongly held—that they would indeed be subject to change if the truth about Townsville's positive aspects was presented in a continuing information campaign.

In general terms, the interviews may disclose that there is very little accurate knowledge of Townsville to back up the prejudices expressed. And where information was volunteered, it was often inaccurate.

Surveying Other Publics

In addition to a professionally conducted Realtors' survey, the principal may wish to survey other publics for the purpose of establishing and improving a continuous, systematic, two-way communications flow.

A questionnaire may be prepared and sent to each of the organizational leaders of these publics, based upon the assumption that each is in a position of leadership and could reflect with a high degree of accuracy how he and his constituents feel about each question.

Here are some typical questions:

Question 1. What specifically would you like to know about the total school system?

Question 2. From what source(s) do you feel most of your associates get their information about the school system?

Question 3. Would you and/or one of your associates be interested in participating in a small group, coffee-discussion hour at a particular school(s)?

Question 4. Do you think a profile providing information about the teaching staff of a particular school would be useful; i.e., total number of staff members, professional preparation, publications, honors, etc.?

Question 5. If you are a parent of a school-aged youngster, have you ever:

    a.   Met the principal or assistant principal of your child's school?

    b.   Met the counselors of your child's school?

    c.   Met the teachers of your child's school?

    d.   Visited a class (in session) of your child's school?

    e.   Attended any school function?

    f.   Visited the school for any other reasons?

Question 6. Do you know how Townsville stands in school support compared to its adjacent neighbors; i.e., expenditure per pupil as compared with the surrounding towns?

Question 7. Do you have sufficient knowledge about special opportunities available in your youngster's school? If not, circle those which you would be interested in:

    a.   Learning centers

    b.   Bi lingual/bi cultural programs

    c.   Guidance services

    d.   Psychological testing services

    e.   Music lessons and programs

    f.   Gifted or advanced programs

    g.   Special, tailor-made high school schedules

    h.   High school work-study programs

    i.   Scholarships and financial aid

    j.   Extracurricular activities

    k.   Interscholastic sports activities

    l.   Social worker services

Question 8. Would you and your associates be interested in becoming more involved in school affairs and/or school instruction?

Question 9. In general, from your personal experience, how would you rate the following school personnel regarding their concern for both parents and students as worthwhile individuals? (Responses may be inserted where appropriate.)

		Very Concerned	*Somewhat Concerned*	*Not Concerned*
a.	Superintendent and his central office assistants			
b.	Principals and assistants			
c.	Guidance counselors			
d.	Social workers			
e.	Teachers			
f.	Secretarial clerical staff			

Question 10. What specific aspect of the curriculum would be of most interest to you and your associates? (Please name grade level or school level; i.e., elementary, middle, or high school.)

Conclusion

It is superfluous to state that the results of surveys such as these are the lifeblood of a school-community communications system. Any alert educator should be aware of what business people, Realtors, and chamber of commerce personnel think of his school in particular and how they rate the total school system in general.

Only by surveys of this nature can you take corrective, preventive action to increase the possibilities of projecting a more positive image and preventing the unexpected.

EVALUATING COMMUNICATION ENDEAVORS

Most schools use the open-house technique for communicating with parents. Some schools use a variation of the telephone-communication approach. A great many schools have some type of newsletter or open message. However, it is seldom that educators stop to evaluate their approaches and if necessary to make adjustments according to the discrepancies discovered. Here are three examples for your consideration.

On-Going Evaluation

Throughout the school year the administration should be conducting many formal and informal on-going evaluation assessments. Each time discrepancies are realized adjustments should be made. Obviously, it is impractical, as well as impossible, to evaluate each and every aspect of a "thousand idea" communication program. Thus, this section will feature selected events, questionnaires, comments, and data as examples of the on-going evaluation process which may be useful to any administrator.

Figure 6-8

Back-to-School Night

A principal may conduct the following parent reaction sheet, analyze the results, and make the necessary and applicable adjustments. The results can then be shared with the entire staff and serve as a discussion base for both classroom activities and faculty meetings:

Would you be kind enough to share your honest reactions with us concerning this evening's Open House. Names are optional.

1. Did you consider the musical presentation in the auditorium worthwhile?

2. Did you consider the choral group in the foyer a good idea?

3. Did you follow your youngster's schedule?

4. *In general,* please rate the program:

   a. The instructional program as presented by the teacher was:

   (1) Very informative
   (2) Somewhat informative
   (3) Poorly presented

   b. Did the classroom appearance reflect the instructional program?

   (1) Strongly positive
   (2) Somewhat positive
   (3) Not at all

5. I found the staff:
   Very helpful
   Somewhat helpful
   Not helpful

6. I rate the evening:
   Superior
   Above average
   Average
   Poor

7. Any suggestions or comments?

Figure 6-9

Telephone Conversations

A staff evaluation may be conducted concerning the telephone conversation sheets with the results shared with all concerned:

I am interested in your honest reaction to the new public relations policy of generating an average of 150 telephone calls per day by the personnel of this high school. Please answer the following feedback questionnaire. *I am seeking a 100% return*

1. I have made an average of five calls per week (i.e., one per day). YES_____ NO_____
   If not, how many did you average?

2. The conversations covered the topics of:
   a. Class attendance   _____
   b. School attendance   _____
   c. Happy messages   _____
   d. Other   _____

3. I feel that the time spent on calling was:
   a. Worthwhile   _____
   b. Only routine   _____
   c. Useless   _____

4. The parent reaction was:
   a. Supportive and pleased   _____
   b. Rather neutral   _____
   c. Negative and annoyed   _____

5. I would urge that we:
   a. Keep up the program   _____
   b. Modify it   _____
   c. Discard it   _____

Open Message

In order to ascertain input and feedback concerning the open-message approach, the following evaluation may be conducted among the high school professional staff:

Figure 6-10

1. What percentage of students read Open Messages? None—1 to 5%; Some—6 to 25%; All—50 to 75%

2. What percentage get home? None—1 to 5%; Some—6% to 25%; All—50 to 75%. (The only time high school students bring home an Open Message is when it applies directly to them and their area of interest. To be effective we would have to mail them home.)

3. Do teachers ever use them in class for discussion purposes? Sometimes_____ Never_____Always_____
   (This depends upon the topic, the timeliness of the subject, and what is generated by the students themselves.)

4. In your opinion, do they cover different interest areas for the total school community (parents, staff, community, students)?
   Yes_____ Somewhat_____ Never_____
   (The vast majority expressed a general interest, but, once again, unless it touches their immediate lives or interest there is apathy.)

5. Are there any topics or suggestions you would like to share with me concerning the Open Message?
          Yes_____ No_____

6. Should I continue producing Open Messages?
          Yes_____ No_____

Community Coffee Hour

This phase of an open communications system was received extremely well, as illustrated by the following letter:

Figure 6-11

December 5, 19___

Dear Sir:

Thank you very much for taking the time to give me a tour of your very impressive school. As I told you, I am a product of parochial schools of times passed. Your many varied facilities overwhelmed me.

However, the most impressive and gratifying sight was the obvious friendship and respect in which you are held by the students. This was clearly evident as we walked the halls. That you can remember so many names was equally amazing. I hope that wherever my children attend high school, they are touched by their principal with as much concern.

I cannot end this letter without my congratulations on the ten-year accreditation recommendation you received today. I know how much it must mean to you and all your staff. It is another indication of a job well done.

Though we are not officially connected with your school, if the PTA Council can ever assist you in any way we are at your service.

Thank you again for giving so much of your time to allow me to explore your school.

Sincerely,

Robert F. Truman
President, PTA Council

cc: Superintendent

Bilingual/Bicultural Program

The bilingual/bicultural program produced impressive results in the area of public relations. This is evidenced by the following statistics and community feedback:

1. There has been a 200% improvement in school-related participation by non-English-speaking parents.

2. Having a Spanish-speaking administrator on the staff has facilitated the closing of the communication gap between the school and the Spanish-speaking community.

3. Greater involvement by non-English-speaking parents has significantly contributed to better attendance records for their children.

4. Community leaders of the Spanish-, Greek-, and Italian-speaking communities have praised the high school as a school endeavoring to meet their particular needs.

Communicating with the Parents of Foreign-Born Students

The non-English-speaking parent-school communications component of the public relations program recorded a high degree of success as indicated by:

1. The parent advisory committee achieving better co-ordination of educational programs for the bilingual/bicultural students.

2. The establishment of parent-school councils consisting of parents, school personnel, students, and other neighborhood community leaders.

3. The involvement of parents in discussions concerning bilingual/bicultural education goals.

4. Visits to homes to improve the communications flow and for better understanding of home and school problems.

5. The improvement of school attendance records of students from non-English-speaking families.

Communication Guidelines

The following guiding principles are necessary in the formation of any public relations program for a school system, and the active implementation of these will insure a close community-school development along positive lines:

1. Accurate, prompt reporting is a prerequisite.

2. Good relationships with the news media are essential.

3. A continuous flow of information about the school, its problems, its accomplishments, its strengths, its public image.

4. A commitment for sound public relations involves the total educational family.

5. Two-way communications, with every segment and all organizations within the community, enhance the chances of establishing an effective public relations program.

6. Recognition for doing a good job is more effective when put in the form of an award certificate or written commendation.

7. Selected pictures of student activities are effective in promoting the school image.

8. Constant feedback from all segments of the internal and external community is imperative for a sound public relations program.

9. Projecting an attitude of genuine concern and acceptance of ideas is important in any public relations endeavor.

10. Personal contact provides the foundation for the best public relations program.

11. Personal involvement of teachers, students, administrators, and the community is the cornerstone for improvement of school-community relations.

Conclusion

One cannot foster communications that will cope with the unexpected unless one designs, orchestrates, and opens channels by which findings, readings, and pulse-taking can be analyzed.

This chapter has been written in the hopes of providing the reader with situations that require skill in leadership and awareness about surveys and concerns of the many publics of any given community.

Finally, evaluation examples of typical yearly school endeavors have been used to illustrate the need for continuous feedback, even on such mundane events as back-to-school night, telephone conversations, coffee hours, and open messages. These are events that almost every school in the country engages in but few take time out to evaluate and modify.

7

HOW TO ACCOMPLISH MORE WITH CENTRAL OFFICE COMMUNICATIONS

You have just assumed the position of principal of Westfield High School, Westfield, New York, which has a student population of 2200. The student body represents a wide range of socio-economic backgrounds with a nonwhite population of approximately 30%, an Italian-American population of 30%, an English, Irish, Polish, German combination of 30%, and the usual 10% of "others." Thus, Westfield High is a microscopic representation of the country at large.

During the first eight years the school had three principals and a turnover of nine assistant principals. Its philosophy, curriculum offerings, scheduling pattern, and organizational charts, reflected a typical, traditional high school of the 1930s, forties, and fifties.

The sixties were turbulent years of bomb scares, false alarms, black awareness movements, antiwar demonstrations, emerging individual student rights, rebellion against dress-code regulations, and school-community philosophical conflicts.

You are now asked to analyze the situation and submit short-term objectives, intermediate goals, and long-range plans. Thus, the Management-by-Objectives infatuation becomes reality.

It is vital that your M.B.O. strategies follow a logical, sequential pattern compatible with your analytical goals and objectives. Thus, your first strategy has to be concerned with how you are perceived as principal. The following strategies exemplify this approach:

Strategies:

- Most important! Establish yourself as principal of Westfield High School in a fair but definitely firm manner.

- Expect and demand a major voice in the selection and recruitment of all building personnel.

- Be sure you have solicited full support and backing from the central office staff and board of education in dealing with problems and initiating change.

- Expect and demand adequate clerical assistance, supplies, and equipment to accomplish the task properly.

- Establish sound, practical administrative routines which are designed to foster a climate of learning and professional growth.

- Establish administrative responsibilities to include discipline, supervision, and routine responsibilities for each unit coordinator. Example:

The following suggested format may be modified to your own school's needs, but lines of communication are obviously shortened and confusion is eliminated by providing written guidelines for your staff.

Figure 7-1

Administrators' Responsibilities

Principal

Activity Approval
Activity Calendar
Athletics
Building Schedule

Contracts
Curriculum Development
Department Chairpersons
Field Trips
Graduation In-Service Education
Guest Speakers and Resource People
Public Relations
School Policy
School Newspaper
State Reports
Student Council
Teacher Applications
Teacher Supervision
Visitor Permits
Yearbook

Unit Coordinator—Grade 12

Audio-Visual Education
Curriculum Development
Discipline—Teacher Referrals
Hall Supervision
Master Schedule
Facility Utilization
Teacher Assignments
Student Schedules
Class Lists
Schedule Design

Guide to Subject Offerings
State and Federal Reports
Daily Announcements
Teacher Supervision—Group B
Transportation

Unit Coordinator—Grade 11

Attendance
Cumulative Records
Discipline—Teacher Referrals
Hall Supervision
Extracurricular Activities
Orientation by Grade Level
Promotion

Pupil Assignments
Registration and Withdrawals
Report Cards
Student Schedule Changes
Substitute Teachers
Teacher Supervision—Group C
Transcripts

Unit Coordinator—Grade 10

Budget
Curriculum Development
Custodial Supervision
Discipline—Teacher Referrals
Financial Accounting
Hall Supervision
Insurance
Inventories
Lockers
Plant Maintenance
Teacher Supervision—Group A
Textbooks
Ticket Sales and Supervision
Supplies and Equipment

● Create a morning sign-in sheet for *all* personnel.

MORNING SIGN-IN SHEET

The rationale for such a sheet is simply accountability and coverage. This is especially true in a large school with many types of employees; i.e., full-time staff, part-time staff, shared members, alternate day personnel, half-time personnel, student teachers, volunteers, custodians, clerical staff, counselors, work-study coordinators, and teachers. A morning sign-in sheet allows a person or persons to glance at the sheet and know that all members of the team are accounted for, and, if not, to make immediate coverage arrangements.

SITUTATION

A single, known diabetic teacher, living alone, failed to sign-in or call the school at 7:45 A.M. A call was made to her apartment—no answer. A department chairperson drove to the apartment, got the building superintendent to unlock the door, and found the young lady unconscious on the floor. Immediate medical attention saved her life. Unusual? Yes, but certainly a lifesaver!

SITUATION

You do not have a sign-in sheet and a staff member has car trouble on the way to work. The room is opened and a student gets injured. No supervision, why? No one knew the staff member was going to be tardy. Who is responsible? Is there the possibility of a lawsuit? Sign-in sheets can easily be constructed on a weekly basis. Two samples follow:

Figure 7-2

Noncertified Personnel

Week of_____

	Monday	Tuesday	Wednesday	Thursday	Friday
Name	_____	_____	_____	_____	_____
Name	_____	_____	_____	_____	_____
(Please initial)					

Certified Personnel

Week of_____

Department _____	Monday	Tuesday	Wednesday	Thursday	Friday
Name	_____	_____	_____	_____	_____
Name	_____	_____	_____	_____	_____
(Please initial)					

• Create and disseminate a detailed parent/student handbook.

Figure 7-3

Parent/Student Handbook

Table of contents   **Page**

Absence 6
Academic Requirements & Services 21

Accident Insurance 8
American Field Service (AFS) 15
Annals 15
Assemblies 8
Athletic Awards 21
Athletic Requirements & Services.....................21
Attendance 6
Automobiles 8

Band 16
Bell Schedules 5
Bilingual Club 16
Bowling Club 16
Bus Students 13

Cafeteria 9
Care of School Property & Equipment 12
Cheerleading 16
Chemistry Club 16
Chess Club 16
Class Activities 15
Concert Choir 16
Corridors 10
Course Auditing 23

Dismissal 6
Distributive Education Club 16

Ecology 16
Extracurricular Activities 15

Financial Obligations 10
Fire Drills 14
Floor Plan 3
Foreword 1
French Club 17
Future Business Leaders of America 17
Future Nurses & Medical Corps 17
Future Teachers of America 17

General Behavior 12
German Club 17
Grading System 21
Greenhouse Management 17

Guidance Service 21
Guidance Assignments 24

Highlander 17
High Notes 17
History of School 2
Homework 15
Honor Roll 22

Latin Club 18
Leaders Club 18
Library 9
Library Service Club 18
Lockers 13
Lost & Found 11

Martin Luther King Scholarship Society 18
Multimedia Club 18
Mutual Respect & Dignity 11

National Honor Society 18
Night Coach 19

Orchestra 18
Open End 7
Outrage 19

Parents 1
Parent's Responsibility 7
Pep Rallies 8
Photography Club 19
Printing Club 19
Psychology Club 19

Safety Hazards & Annoyances 7
Schedule Changes 12
Senior Class Play 19
Showtimers 19
Ski Club 19
Smoking 9
Spanish Club 19
Stage Band 19
Storm Emergency Procedure 7
Student Accountability 10
Student's Responsibility 7

Study Habits 14
Study Hall 10
Superintendent's Student Advisory Council 15
Suspensions..11

Tardiness.. 6
Textbook Regulations 13
Time Schedules..................................... 4
Truancy 9
Twirling 20

Varsity Club 20
Visitors 1

Welcome 1
Wind Ensemble 20

In addition to creating a parent/student handbook, a teacher's handbook must also be developed. A typical table of contents would be:

Figure 7-4

Table of Contents

General   *Page*

Introduction & Philosophy 1
Accident Reports 14
Announcements 12
Annex Staff.. 2
Audio-Visual.......................................11
Bell Schedule 3
Custodial Services..................................12
Field Trips...16
Fire Drill 12
Lunch Shifts 6
Nurse 14
Parent Conferences 12
Pupil Physical Restraint.............................15
Public Relations 12
Report Card & Attendance Calendar 36
Storm Emergency Procedures 17

Study Halls 15
Textbook Regulations 17
Visitors 14

Teacher

Absence and Request for Sub 7
Arrival and Departure 7
Duties and Responsibilities 9
First Weeks of School............................... 7
Form Letter Requesting Parents to Call 10
Grade Book 7
Housekeeping 7
Keys 7
Lesson Plans 7
Meetings 7
Reports 7
Special Assignments................................. 5

Guidance

Counselor Assignments 9
Student Schedule Changes 9
Student Enrollment 9
Student Withdrawal 9

Student

Attendance Discrepancies 13
Dress Code 13
Office Referrals 14

Guidelines

Coping with Problems 22
Completing the Mark Book 23
Marking Practices 27

Forms

Attendance Discrepancies 35
Field Trips...32
Guest Speakers 30
Homework Assignment 33
Lesson Plans 34
Request for Personal Day 31
Student Enrollment 28

Student Withdrawal 29

Once the "nitty-gritty" organizational routines have been established, the first priority should be one of survival and stabilization through the development of short-term objectives.

Short-Term Objectives:

- Create an honest, open-door communications procedure for the entire community—including students, parents, staff, and community leaders.

- Create a more humane atmosphere by eliminating detention policies and replacing them with positive, teacher-to-student conference periods designed to resolve problems rather than create hostility and resentment.

- Provide for unscheduled student time options, such as smoking privileges, open-cafeteria snack bar, library services, and auditing contracts.

- Establish a climate of mutual respect and dignity among students, students and teachers, school and administration, and school and community.

- Revise the dress-code policies to bring them in line with the constitutional rights of students and individuals.

- Establish a student-faculty-principal advisory council.

Intermediate Objectives:

- Establish a house plan organization pattern to shorten the lines of communication and provide the student with a feeling of belonging.

- Establish your own identity by removing all outside influences from your building.

- Organize teaching teams so that curricular changes can respond to the needs of students in a more realistic manner.

- Establish department chairmanships to facilitate articulation and cohesiveness on the part of teachers.

- Incorporate minority literature and Negro culture into the mainstream of the school community and establish new courses in these areas.

- Provide for human relations activities via teacher in-service, general assemblies, creating a gospel choir, and writing briefs for classroom activities.

- Establish courses of study in high interest areas; such as ecology, psychology, contemporary issues, and career planning.

- Conduct in-school "rap sessions" and community visits to improve communications and encourage parent-community involvement.

Once you have stabilized and survived, your attention should be directed to formulating those *long-term* goals needed to make a good school an excellent one. Obviously, this is where administrative creativity and flexibility shine forth in providing a quality education. By employing your own sound educational theories and balancing them with what the community wants, you are able to establish such goals.

Long-Term Goals:

- Provide for continued student-parent participation in school affairs by the neighborhood meeting concept, open messages, bilingual/bicultural nights and instruction programs, and listening to the concerns of the community.

- Provide alternative procedures and programs to meet student needs; i.e., early graduation arrangements, auditing programs, independent study contracts, semester and mini-courses, utilizing adult education resources, credit by competency examination, and high school-community college arrangements.

Alternative arrangements can be very effective, as illustrated by the following situation:

Situation

Kevin Jones is an 18-year-old minority group youngster from a background that includes an older brother who was successful as a "street entrepreneur." Kevin was an explosive, hostile, anti-establishment student. He finally quit school and went to the big city to become involved in street activities. During his internship, his brother was shot and killed and Kevin reassessed his life.

During his decision-making period he was counseled by the school guidance counselor. Both the counselor and Kevin arrived at a special arrangement plan and presented it to the principal for his approval. Approval was granted. The results were astonishing. He is now a successful college student.

Example follows:

Sept. 5, 19X5

Kevin has accumulated 10.75 units. He successfully passed three marking periods of General Electricity and two-part Algebra for which he will receive one unit for each subject (12.75). He has earned 1 unit work-study (13.75).

Kevin will be enrolled in Language Arts IV, Language Arts III, United States History, Psychology, and Crafts for 4 units. Since Kevin will come to the high school to continue his course in Language Arts IV after the first semester, he will continue in a work-study program, working full time, for which he can earn 2 units. Kevin should have a total of 19.75 units in June.

Kevin will be immediately withdrawn if there is any infraction of school rules, nonattendance, insolence, defiance of authority, and so on.

Feb. 5, 19X6

Kevin Jones has completed all academic work here except Psychology in Literature. He has a full-time job and will need to earn 1 1/2 units in work-study.

In his third attempt to graduate, Kevin returned to high school in September 19X5. He has shown a great deal of maturity and academic promise since his return. His teachers have expressed "delight" in his classroom performance. He has submitted an application to attend college (summer program). His teacher is willing to give Kevin his Psychology in Literature on an independent study basis.

Provide flexible school hours for both staff and students in order to meet the needs of the student body in cooperation with the community. Continue to emphasize community relations and community involvement in the educational processes through a systematic approach for sound public relations.

HUMAN RELATIONS

Role and Function in the School-Community Public Relations Program

In any community or social group, good human relations are essential for an enjoyable and productive relationship. Nowhere is this more important than in a multi-ethnic and wide-range socioeconomic community.

In an effort, therefore, to ensure a community atmosphere of fairness and respect, the board of education created the office for Human Relations. The primary responsibilities of this office are: (1) to encourage and bring about mutual understanding and respect among all groups in the community, and (2) to concentrate, through educational endeavors, on helping to eliminate prejudice, intolerance, bigotry, and discrimination among all the people within the community.

Workable Public Relations Activities

- Organize a broad based student-teacher-administrator-parent-lay people Central Human Relations Committee.

- Disseminate appropriate resource materials, both internally and externally, which may provide insights into the other groups' problems and concerns.

- Utilize a human relations booklet, i.e., *A Brief Reference for Understanding,* as an in-service source for sharing with the teachers the feelings, vocabulary, moods, fads, habits, and cultural backgrounds of the students.

- Organize leadership workshops and human relations workshops for better communications.

- Use local newspaper articles and events to keep the professionals informed as to appropriate community happenings.

- Use the Human Relations Newsletter as a means for two-way seminars and open forums.

- Encourage schools to create and use bulletin boards and the school newspaper to publicize recent successful graduates, especially among the poor, blacks, and minorities.

- Plan small group, financial aid seminars for the people in their own backyard.

- Cooperate with the Guidance and Special Services department to bring their offerings to the people.

- Be available to community groups, student organizations, and schools as an "in-class" resource speaker.

- Share ideas, classroom suggestions, and lesson plans concerning special days and events with the entire community.

- Be available as a "listening friend" to the people.

- Develop an in-system speakers bureau of school people and topics for community use.

- Encourage students, via the classroom, to write about tradition, fear, apathy, laziness, politics, mutual trust, money, health, housing, courts, responsibility, mutual respect, and so on.

- Give a slide presentation about positive happenings within the school system and the community.

- Provide educational and employment information to the people.

- Encourage participation in teacher-aide training courses and job placement within the school system.

- Disseminate materials and summaries throughout the community, i.e., in recreation areas, city offices, waiting rooms, and banks.

- Know juvenile authorities and judges and invite them to tour the schools.

- Participate in community activites.

- Attend school functions—plays, games, and so forth.

- Use the news media for thirty-second briefs and short notices.

- Provide two-way, self-addressed cards so that the people can ask questions and receive answers.

- Be familiar with federal, state, and foundation sources for support and grants.

- Use the services of outside referral agencies.

FIELD TRIPS AND THEIR LEGAL IMPLICATIONS

Field trips and other out-of-school activities have tremendous appeal for young people and solid parental support. However, the unsuspecting principal can easily find himself in a serious legal jam unless firm administrative guideline policies are established and approved by the board of education.

Certainly, the one-day field trip has been an integral segment of our educational scene. Thus, the arrangements, permission slips, and its supervision are nothing new. However, consider yourself faced with the decision to grant permission for any one of the following:

1. The school-sponsored ski club wants to go to Europe for ten days to attend the winter Olympic games.

2. A science teacher wants to take a group of students to the island of Jamaica during the spring vacation. They will camp out and study marine life.

3. The ecology club wants to plan a six-day camp-out hike to Cape Cod during the school vacation.

4. The school band wants to go to Alabama for a jazz festival.

5. One of the teachers is organizing an Easter vacation trip.

6. The English department is advertising a theatre trip to England.

7. The foreign language department wants to take students to Spain and France.

SITUATION AND QUESTIONS

Your board of education has a regular one-day field trip policy, but nothing is spelled out for out-of-country or overnight excursions. The policy does not distinguish between school-sponsored and nonschool-sponsored trips.

As principal you approve or disapprove such trips. Are you liable? Does the parent have the right to hold you and the school system responsible for such trips? Should school time be used to promote and organize them? Should school materials and equipment be used to promote these trips?

Should teachers be allowed to be compensated by travel agencies for their involvement? Where do you draw the line? Who takes care of insurance? Refunds? Who is responsible for the monies and arrangements if a charter does not show, or a hotel does not recognize the arrangements, or a student is arrested for carrying "pot" or runs away?

As principal you seek advice, but no one at the central office level is willing to put their answers in official written form. What do you do? What protection do you need?

Here's a sample:

Policy Rewrite

A. Our present policy adequately covers the normal one-day field trip. (These trips are a benefit to the educational experience of youngsters and are usually associated with a classroom activity. In addition, every reasonable effort is made to insure that all members of the class or group participate.)

B. A new policy statement must be made concerning the *non-school-sponsored trips*. (These trips are usually taken during vacation periods and have little or no relationship to the educational opportunities associated with the school.)

NONSCHOOL SPONSORED TRIPS

The Board of Education does not accept responsibility for trips not covered by policy; i.e., when a teacher, acting on his own plans, runs a trip which may or may not result in some personal profit to himself.

Nonschool-sponsored trips may not occur on school time, and therefore are not to be planned for on school time. The facilities of the schools may not be used in planning such trips. Letters to parents or other communications may not be duplicated on school equipment or distributed at schools. Teachers planning such trips should look to community agencies or organizations outside the schools for sponsorship.

C. A third policy statement must be published which in effect assumes responsibility for *extended school-sponsored trips*. (These are trips which serve as an adjunct to the students' educational experiences and which the school wishes to promote. Normally, every reasonable effort is made to insure that *all* members of the class or group are able to participate.)

I. *Recommended Administrative Guidelines*
   1. There can be no monetary gain for the teacher-sponsor or school employee involved.
   2. No grades or academic bonus can be involved; conversely, no penalties can be involved for non-participants.
   3. All activities of this nature must come under the auspices of a recognized school club or class.
   4. A fiscal accounting must be provided to the principal or his designee.

II. *Preplanning*
   1. *Before* announcing such a trip, the teacher-sponsor must provide the principal with a written statement indicating the objectives of the trip.
   2. *Before* involving the students, the teacher-sponsor must outline in written form all safety provisions and details for protecting the well-being of the participants.

3. *Before* the trip is organized, a special insurance policy must be written for it.

III. *Organizational Phase*

It is the responsibility of the teacher-sponsor to provide each participant and his/her parent with a written summary of:

1. The purpose of the trip.
2. Hazards involved and safety precautions planned.
3. Transportation arrangements.
4. Cost per participant.
5. Any unusual restrictions (e.g., need for passport, etc.).
6. Emergency procedures for handling nonconforming participants.
7. Permission slips, agreement forms, and deposit receipts.

IV. *Preparation of Students and Parents Prior to Trip*

The teacher-sponsor shall, in a personal group meeting, review with the students and parents the above details and resolve any last minute problems.

STUDENT SUSPENSION POLICIES AND DUE PROCESS

For the last ten years and most assuredly for the immediate future, school people will be faced with the reality of suspension and all its legal ramifications. Communications, interpretations, and firm board of education policies and procedures are therefore a must for every administration.

The following questions are concerned with Public Act 75-609 of Connecticut. However, the philosophy and foundations are applicable to the constitutional rights of public school youngsters. Thus, the sample may serve as a model or at the very least as an alert.

1. *What is suspension?*

2. *Who may suspend?*

3. *What is the limit of time for any one suspension?*

4. *Is a hearing required prior to suspension?*

5. *What constitutes an informal hearing?*

6. *Does the central office need to be involved in suspensions?*

7. *Under what circumstances is the central office staff involved in the suspension process?*

8. *Who at the central office level is authorized to conduct hearings?*

9. *Do minutes need to be taken at an informal hearing?*

10. *Can a single informal hearing at the initiating level be held for more than one student?*

11. *What is the relationship of pupil placement teams to the suspension process?*

DISCIPLINARY PROCEDURES AND THE NEED FOR WELL-DEFINED BOARD POLICIES

A. Definition of Terms (consistent with Public Act 75-609 of the State of Connecticut)

1. *Exclusion* means any denial of public school privileges to a student for disciplinary reasons.

2. *Removal* means an exclusion from a classroom for all or part of a single class period, provided such exclusion shall not extend beyond ninety (90) minutes.

3. *Suspension* means an exclusion from school privileges for no more than ten (10) consecutive school days, provided such suspension shall not extend beyond the end of the school year in which such suspension was imposed.

4. *Expulsion* means an exclusion from school privileges for more than ten (10) consecutive school days and shall be deemed to include, but not limited to, exclusion from the school to which such student was assigned at the time such disciplinary action was taken, and provided such exclusion shall not extend beyond the end of the school year in which such exclusion was imposed.

5. *Emergency* means a situation under which the continued presence of the student in school poses such a danger to persons or property, or such a disruption of the educational process, that a hearing may be delayed until a time as soon after the exclusion of such student as possible.

6. *School* means any school under the direction of the Board of Education.

7. *Informal Hearing* means that the student is to be informed as to the reasons for the proposed suspension and an explanation of the evidence, and given an opportunity to respond.

In the event of an emergency, the informal hearing shall be held as soon after the suspension as possible.

Nothing contained in the above two paragraphs shall deprive the student and/or his parents or guardian from the right to review and appeal as defined in Section D of these regulations.

B. *Removal*

1. A teacher may remove a student from class when such student deliberately causes a serious disruption of the educational process within the classroom, by immediately sending said student to the principal or his designee for an informal hearing, and shall immediately inform the principal or his designee of the name of the student, and the reason therefor.

2. In all other circumstances any employee of the Board who believes disciplinary proceedings are required shall refer the matter to the principal or his designee.

3. Nothing contained herein shall limit the right and responsibility of the employee to prevent continuation of a situation involving immediate danger to persons, damage to property, or disruption of the educational process.

C. *Rules Pertaining to Suspension*

1. The Superintendent, Assistant Superintendents, Principals, Assistant Principals, Unit Coordinators and other administrative personnel as may be delegated by the Superintendent of Schools are authorized to suspend students in accordance with the previous listed definitions.

2. Suspension is to be considered as one administrative procedure to follow to implement effective discipline in the schools and school system. Only those members of the administrative staff who were previously listed, or others delegated by the Superintendent are authorized to suspend students. Suspension is to be used when it is considered by the administrator to represent the best interests of the student and school and when other reasonable methods of adjustment have been tried and have failed.

3. Students may be suspended from school by the administration for not more than ten (10) consecutive school days. No student shall be suspended without an informal

hearing as defined previously in these regulations, except in an emergency situation as hereinafter explained. Further, no student shall be suspended more than ten times, or a total of fifty (50) days in one school year, whichever results in fewer days of exclusion, unless such student is granted a formal hearing as described in the policies of the Board of Education to which these regulations apply. In the event of an emergency, such formal hearing shall be held as soon after the suspension as possible. In the event of a suspension, it shall be the responsibility of the administrator initiating the suspension to notify the parent or guardian within 24 hours of such action. Copies of this notification are to be submitted within this same time period to the Superintendent of Schools or his designee. If possible and practical, the parent or guardian shall be given verbal notification before the suspension of a student is implemented, with written communication as specified heretofore in these regulations, to serve as a follow-up communication. Prior to reinstatement of a student, the suspending officer shall exert every effort to have the student accompanied to school by the parent or guardian.

4. If the suspension becomes effective while the pupil is in attendance at school, every reasonable effort should be made to have the parent, guardian, or representative appear at school to pick up the student. If this is not possible, the student shall be accompanied home by a member of the staff. A responsible adult must be present in the home if the child is dismissed during school hours. This applies to elementary schools.

D. Review and Appeal

1. Any student who has been suspended and wishes a review of said action shall be entitled to an appropriate review (hearing) with the Superintendent of Schools or his designee, and thereafter, if the student desires, with the Board of Education. The review with the Superintendent, unless it is an emergency, shall be held within the ten (10) day period of suspension initiated by the principal or his designee. Any student who has been suspended shall, in the written notice given of the suspension by the principal, be informed of his right to a review.

2. Should the principal, upon suspension of a student, feel that a further hearing is warranted with the Superintendent

or his designee, then such notification shall be given to the student and his parent or guardian. Such a hearing should be held within the ten (10) day period of suspension.

3. In the event the administration feels that the purpose for suspension is of such a nature as to warrant expulsion, the Superintendent shall provide notification to the Board for the purpose of recommending expulsion.

E. *Emergency Reasons for Suspension and/or Expulsion*

In accordance with Public Act No. 75-609, a student may be excluded from school without benefit of a hearing prior to the exclusion, providing such exclusion resulted from an emergency. This refers to both suspension by the administration and expulsion by the Board of Education.

As defined in Public Act No. 75-609, an emergency means a situation under which the continued presence of the student in school poses such a danger to persons or property or such a disruption of the educational process that a hearing may be delayed until a time as soon after the exclusion of such student as possible and practicable.

In the event a student is suspended for an emergency reason, the informal hearing shall be held by the Superintendent or his designee. In notifying the student and the parent or guardian of the hearing, the following information will be given:

Date, time, and location of hearing.
Written specifications of the charges or complaints
Notification that the student is entitled to be represented by counsel, to hear all the evidence against him, and to present evidence on his own behalf.

This notification pertaining to a hearing shall be prepared and transmitted by the Superintendent or his designee.

At the conclusion of the hearing the student shall be informed of his rights for appeal and review before the Board of Education at the earliest possible date.

In the event the issue cannot be resolved at the hearing with the Superintendent or his designee, the Superintendent reserves the right to refer the issue to the Board of Education and to recommend expulsion.

The hearing before the Superintendent or his designee is to be held within five school days subsequent to the initiation of the suspension. The hearing before the Board of Education shall be held at the earliest possible date after the Superintendent's hearing, should either or both parties request such a hearing and appeal.

In all cases of suspension, not deemed to represent an emergency, the responsibility for an informal hearing rests with the principal or his designee as prescribed in Public Act No. 75-609.

F. *Possible Disciplinary Action by School System in Cases Involving Police*

In the event that any student engages in conduct on school property that results in police action, the administrative staff shall investigate the matter and, if the facts indicate that the student's continued presence in the school presents a clear and present danger to himself, or others within the school, the staff may suspend such student. Any such suspension in excess of five (5) days in length shall be brought to the attention of the Board of Education. The Board, upon review, may take such additional action deemed appropriate and consistent with its policies, regulations and the laws of the State of Connecticut.

G. *Notification to Public and Students*

It is the responsibility of the administration, under authorization from the Board of Education to, at least annually, review these disciplinary procedures with the student body and the public. The specific procedures for implementing this rests with the Superintendent of Schools or his designee.

H. *Follow-up Action with Students and Relating to Students in the Event of Expulsion*

In the event a student is expelled, alternative kinds of education shall be attempted and/or provided in accordance with Public Act 75-609. In addition, the Board of Education must notify the parent or guardian of the student, and the student himself upon attaining majority, and the Commissioner of Education, within five days of the effective date thereof. The notification to the Commissioner of Education shall give the following information:

a. The date of the action of the Board
b. The name, age, and grade of the student
c. The name and address of the parent or guardian

    d. The name of the school

    e. The effective date of the expulsion

    f. The period of time for which the student is expelled

    g. The name of the agency or agencies to which the student is referred for further attention

This notification to the Commissioner of Education shall be submitted by the Superintendent of Schools, acting as executive agent of the Board of Education.

NOW YOU SEE THEM NOW YOU DON'T

Since attendance and class cutting is now considered by many educators as the number one high school problem, there is a sense of urgency for establishing and communicating a sound attendance procedure. The following is an example for one high school:

Figure 7-5

RE: *School Attendance Procedures*

    Attendance and class cutting continue to be the major problems facing the nation's secondary schools, and South High School is no exception. Regardless of some parental apathy, we must continue to exercise our professional responsibility of encouraging regular and punctual school and class attendance, along with frequent parental contact and/or notification. Our massive efforts during the school year were generally well received in the community. Thus, we shall renew our time-consuming but necessary task of attacking a growing problem with reasonable and humane procedures all focusing in upon: (1) pupil responsibility, (2) parental obligation, (3) teacher concern, and (4) administrative enforcement.

    Every member of the school staff will become involved in this multipronged attack in the following manner·

1. *First Period Teachers—Coded Attendance Cards*

    All first period teachers will make out coded attendance cards for their first period classes.

2. *Attendance Clerk—Attendance Bulletin*

    A daily attendance bulletin will be published. In addition, the attendance clerk will spend time checking the coded attendance cards, making calls (at least 20), and sending out form letters regarding absenteeism and tardiness. *All calls and form letters will be notated* on the back of the attendance card, with copies of the letters going to the *counselor* and *unit coordinator*.

3. *All Staff—Personal Telephone Conversation Report Form*

This form has been printed on three-part paper so that teachers, counselors, and unit coordinators will be kept fully informed. On the premise that the personal contact is the best way to communicate, a time-consuming but necessary effort will be made to contact parents in the following manner:

a. *Every* classroom teacher (this includes part time, half time, interns, etc.) will make one (1) call per day and speak with a parent *regarding attendance* and any other pertinent matters.

b. Every counselor will make three (3) calls per day and speak with parents *regarding attendance* and any other pertinent matters.

Making a call and getting no answer does not fulfill your obligation. You must make the contact. Teachers unable to reach parents at home must check with counselors and unit coordinators to secure phone numbers of parents at work. Any number which is disconnected or no longer in service must be brought to the attention of the unit coordinator so as to maintain up-to-date records. In all cases of unit coordinator/teacher/counselor phone conversations, a Personal Telephone Conversation Report form must be filled out and copies distributed as indicated.

Thus, if all follow-through on the above procedure, some 140 calls per day will be made. This, in itself, is a positive step which will give immediate and accurate information to parents. (These calls may be made during your prep period, before school, after school, evenings, or at any time you feel appropriate—but they must be made.)

Your tactful handling of these conversations can result in a big public relations bonus for you as a concerned teacher and for the school as an interested partner in improving attendance.

4. *All Staff—Attendance Advisory Letter*

An Attendance Advisory Letter has been devised for staff use to inform parents of *absence from class regardless of the reasons.* This form letter, in four parts (original to parent, yellow to unit coordinator, pink to counselor, and brown retained by sender), will be used by *all* staff to inform parents when a pupil has missed an *excessive number* of classes, and when you have been unable to contact the parent by phone.

This means that each staff member must keep *very accurate attendance records* to ascertain who should get a letter. Mailing will be handled by the individual teacher, with unit coordinators and counselors getting their appropriate copy.

5. *Reinforcement Procedures*

Excessive absenteeism and tardiness will become apparent to the counselors and unit coordinators as they receive the input from first period teachers, classroom teachers, and the attendance clerk. During the build-up from "normal" to "excessive," the teachers will take reasonable action to correct the problem (through parent contact, *counselor contact,* after school conferences, etc.).

In addition, and at the onset of classes, all pupils must be made to understand that marks are *earned* and that regular school and class attendance are primary prerequisites for success. Each teacher will explain and do the following:

a. Daily marks are given for class participation.

b. If a pupil is identified as skipping your class, he should receive an *F* in classroom participation.

c. If a pupil skips your class on an announced quiz or test day, he may *not* make it up. He will receive an *F* for that quiz or test.

Unit coordinators will enter the problem area when staff efforts have failed to produce a reasonable change. They will contact parents and advise them that absenteeism and class cutting could eventually result in suspension.

In addition, unit coordinators will personally continue to check tardy pupils into school—for obvious reasons.

6. *Tracers*

For some pupils, tracers are an excellent means for a short-term solution to an attendance problem. However, the limitations of a tracer are evident and the parent ought to assume the responsibility for its processing.

7.   Interim reports of *selected students* will be mailed home; the rest will continue to receive them in person.

8. *Referral System*

Please inform all students that after all your efforts have failed to correct the attendance situation, an attendance referral will be made to the appropriate unit coordinator. The procedure will be consistent and automatic. Either the teacher or counselor may make the referral.

1st attendance referral—the student will be sent home at the end of the day and not readmitted until a parent contact has been made.

2nd attendance referral—automatic two-day suspension and no readmittance until there is a personal parent-student conference with the unit coordinator.

3rd attendance referral—automatic five-day suspension and no readmittance until there is a principal-parent-student interim hearing.

4th attendance referral—automatic ten-day suspension and a superintendent's hearing.

Conclusion

Communications with the central office administrative staff often revolve around preventing community-school problems and conflicts. This chapter attempted to focus on precisely those issues which have been real problems in the lives of principals.

Assuming the principalship and a "game plan" as to what you are trying to accomplish, constitutes the M.B.O. infatuation category, practical suggestions in terms of team management and open communications are exemplified in the sign-in sheets, administrative responsibilities, and shortening lines of communication.

Team teaching, alternative arrangements, and clearly defined handbooks have been utilized to enhance the educational delivery system and to communicate options to both the central office staff and the community at large.

Finally, positive human relations, a sound field trip policy, and supervision policies and procedures for home-school communications regarding attendance and cutting are must items for every principal. These policies must be clearly understood and steadfastly supported by the central office administrative staff. Thus, your survival as an effective principal may be directly related to your ability to communicate with these segments of the community.

8

SUCCESSFUL COMMUNICATIONS WITH THE PUBLIC AND PRESS: "VOLCANIC PARTNERSHIPS"

At the National School Public Relations Conference held in September 1973 in Boston, Massachusetts, Ned Hubbell, of Hubbell Associates, Port Huron, Michigan, reported: "The general public does not have an overall attitude or opinion toward their school system and is generally uninformed about what goes on in schools." He further stated: "School leaders, generally, tell the public what they think the public wants to know or ought to know. Little is done to find out what the public wants to know."

This, coupled with the educational reporting made by many of the critics of public schools, results in creating a negative mood. This mood or climate has drastic ramifications for the educational community—ramifications which paralyze public educational ventures and sabotage local, state, and national financing programs. Thus, a systematic attempt must be made to involve the external as well as the internal publics of our public school system.

225

Your successful handling of communications with the public and press is obviously vital for the survival of public education. The following are some examples which face every practicing educator:

HANDLING THE ANGRY LETTER

Handling the "angry" letters of parents is always a touchy situation. Firstly, one must respect the fact that the parent is a taxpayer and virtually your employer. Secondly, if he has been moved to the point where he puts his concerns in writing, no matter how biased or misinformed they are, he is potentially a dynamic force of hostility or support for the school. Finally, regardless of how you perceive his intentions, you must assume that he is concerned about the welfare of his youngster. Thus, he is entitled to a sincere, straightforward, and hopefully tactful answer. Obviously, the response does not necessarily have to agree with the parent's complaint or concern.

Typical Parent Letter:

Bypassing the principal's office and going directly to the superintendent of schools seems to be the *modus operandi* of some parents. Perhaps this route is perceived as having the top man put pressure on the principal so that the particular grievance is favorably resolved. Regardless of the intent, many parents do follow this line of communication and the principal must respond.

Figure 8-1

Dear Dr. Jones:

It is my wish to share with you some thoughts on the National Honor Society of 19X5-19X6 which has been appointed recently at Brown High School.

To qualify for admission to the Society a student must have a 3.2 average or better. Thus, all candidates are honor students. The list of nominees is distributed to a representative number of teachers who are asked to vote on the candidates. The teachers rate the students on a scale of 1 through 4. It is assumed that a teacher votes on students familiar to him or her and refrains from voting on a student who is unfamiliar.

The teachers are then asked to return the results to the central committee and they are tallied by computer. The new membership is thus formed, based on the percentage of students designated by the National Honor Society.

Unfortunately, it is possible that not all teachers return their list of candidates to the committee. It is, indeed, a fact that some candidates are rated by as few as three teachers and other candidates are rated by as many as twelve or more. Therefore, the computer may be dividing one student's total by three and that of his peers by twelve. A gross injustice!

The students are being subjected to a popularity contest. The only honor is to be a candidate for the National Honor Society. After that it becomes a farce.

At a time when SAT scores have declined throughout the nation, it is inexcusable for a student who is motivated and qualified to be denied the recognition he or she truly deserves. An immediate reevaluation is necessary to restore justice to this year's National Honor Society.

I shall expect to hear from you at your earliest convenience.

Sincerely,

Horace X. Credits

Figure 8-2

Principal's Response:

TO: Superintendent of Schools
FROM: Frank X. Kelly, Principal
RE: *National Honor Society*

Prior to receiving my copy of Mr. Credits' letter, I had expressed concern about how members are elected to the National Honor Society. The advisor is also concerned and together we are looking into alternatives. Please be advised that we are following the national guidelines which state:

1. That membership be restricted to no more than 10% of the class.
2. A candidate must have a 3.2 average to be eligible.
3. Service to community and school are important factors to be considered.

4. Faculty be included in the selection procedure.

In Mr. Credits' case:

1. I have spoken with him.
2. Miss Hines, the advisor, has spoken with him.
3. Miss Hines talked with his daughter on two separate occasions and even reviewed the faculty ratings and double-checked the mathematical ratings with her.

There is nothing we can do except up the 3.2 scholastic average which would eliminate many worthy students, *or* weight the average so that the higher it is the better the chances for membership. This would lessen the importance of service to school and community. We are looking into alternatives, but any procedure used will have to abide by the above mentioned guidelines.

Figure 8-3

Advisor's Response:

Dear Mr. Credits:

Our principal has forwarded your letter concerning the National Honor Society to me in my capacity as advisor to that group.

I thank you for your interest and assure you that yours were not the only questions which were raised. In fact, I have directed the officers of the Honor Society to review the whole selection procedure before our spring elections and will give your suggestions to them. However, this does not help Sharon.

After reviewing your inquiry, I personally checked on Sharon's ratings to make sure that no errors were made. The selection procedure you stated is, in basic outline, correct. I will be happy to discuss the specifics with either Sharon or you whenever mutually convenient. (They are a bit too lengthy to include in this letter.) My phone extension is 430.

I hope this answers your concerns. Please let me know if I can be of further help.

Sincerely,

Anna L. Hines
Department Head
Language Arts Department

It may also be in the best interest of the school system for the principal to make a personal phone call to the parent, express his concern, and assure him that a fair and reasonable resolution is desired by all concerned.

PRESS CREDIBILITY OR PERISH

One of the major themes in a sound, two-way communications program is credibility. Unless honesty, open communications, and mutual trust exist, there can be no positive public relations program. If any among the many publics of the educational system perceive a leader as speaking with a "forked tongue," confusion will result and an immediate negative backlash will permeate the relationship. This is especially true with members of the press.

Handling interviews with the press can be a tricky business. However, an open, two-way communications system demands that you:

- State your position on the issues, policies, and happenings honestly.

- Inform people of what is happening.

- Tell the people why and how—successes and weaknesses.

- Remember to communicate to all publics—including students, board members, secretaries, custodians, teachers, bus drivers, cafeteria workers, and anyone else associated with the school system.

Almost all authorities agree that the less interested and less well informed a citizen is, the less favorable his attitude toward school and education will be. Thus, the press interview and how the story is told avoids half-truths and misunderstandings.

How To Respond To "Open" Letters In The Press

One of the most threatening and explosive situations may descend upon you via the "open" letter, the paid advertisement, or the billboard attack. The facts may or may not be correct. However, distortions and emphasis may place your academic freedom in jeopardy and certainly cloud your personal job security and professional future.

SITUATION

As principal, you have been asked by a social studies teacher to approve a political action forum to discuss the American political system. Arrangements are as follows:

Time: Last school period
Attendance: Optional for all students
Place: Gym area

Program participants include representatives from:

    a. American Legion
    b. John Birch Society
    c. League of Women Voters
    d. Local college (professor of political science)
    e. Local political parties
    f. Black Panthers

The class advisor will moderate.

The gym is packed to capacity as the representatives take their places. Each has been given his instructions as to the ground rules—a three to five minute presentation (questions will be directed through the moderator from the floor). The discussion becomes heated. The college professor turns out to be extremely radical in his viewpoint. The Black Panther representative uses shock-treatment language. Many students leave before the end of the program but those remaining chant or make proviolence remarks. The program ends without incident but with high feelings.

Within two days, a forty-foot billboard appears downtown; an open letter to the editor hits the local papers, and a paid advertisement splashes across the back page. All have the same theme: "Do You Know What Your Child is Learning in School?" All contain quotes and misquotes from the radical side of the program.

Figure 8-4

Response and reaction:

First, a student message:
TO: ALL STUDENTS AND TEACHERS
FROM: Harvey Haven, Principal
RE: Processes of Education

As your principal, I would feel remiss in my duty if I did not comment in terms of our most recent social-political conflict.

First, may I express my personal opinion as to the processes of getting an education and being able to objectively think through the emotionally packed informational drama of today.

1. *Read* all sources of social-political commentary in newspapers, literature, and magazines. Always be alert to the slanted, highly propagandized viewpoint.
2. *Listen* to all points of view. Be alert to the "hucksters" trying to convince you that something is "this" or "that".
3. *See* the visual information, such as T.V., which usually presents 10 to 30 seconds of a scene. Be alert to the total situation.
4. *Be aware* of the "big lie" approach, the "I was there' approach, the "I have proof" approach, the "statistics" approach. Be alert to the fact that people may be *distorting the facts* for their own reasons, or they might not even realize what they are doing.

Therefore, education is a process of reading, listening, seeing, and judging—always with critical and thought-provoking questions and by always being aware of the slanted point of view.

Ask probing questions!

Listen for the words "in my opinion." Look for the balanced dialogue. Consider all facts, all sources. Observe for yourself. Do not close your eyes. Do not close your mind. Do not be fooled. Do not allow "people," "peers," "groups," to use you.

You are intelligent and can objectively judge the facts for yourself. Be alert!

These are my own opinions and guidelines. I offer them to you for your own consideration. Judge them for yourself.

Second, a principal's policy is outlined and supported by the Board of Education.

Figure 8-5

TO: ALL STUDENTS AND TEACHERS
FROM: Harvey Haven, Principal
RE: *Rallies, Assemblies, and Programs*

IMPORTANT
Please Read and Post

1. As of this date, all rallies, assemblies, and other programs requested by students and generated by current social-political problems will be held with the principal's authorization and attendance will be optional.

2. Each student will be provided with adequate information as to:

    a. The participants
    b. Their organizational representation
    c. The sponsoring group
    d. The general purpose
    e. The topic
    f. Approximate length of program

3. This information will be posted at least three days in advance of the activity and we will call your attention to the program via the school's public address system.

4. These activities will take place in either the auditorium or the gym, depending upon an estimation of the attending audience.

5. *No visitors or outsiders* are allowed unless they receive the permission of the principal or unless they are *listed as participating in the program.*

6. All programs will be arranged on the Pep Assembly schedule so that those interested may attend and those wishing to leave may so do. The option will rest with the individual student.

7. All programs are to be conducted under the motto of *"Mutual Respect and Dignity."*

Copy: Board of Education members

IMPROVING PUBLIC AND PRESS RELATIONS

Again and again we hear from experts in the field that the key public relations man is the principal. But little, if anything, is ever done to provide the principal with funds to attend public relations conferences or for membership in the state or national public relations organizations. In addition, few principals are trained in public relations, since few school systems provide the means for in-service training or university courses in this vital area of communications.

Robert Olds, vice-president of the School Management Institute in Santa Barbara, California, states: "The principal who puts public relations at the bottom of his priority list is shortsighted and should expect his school's eventual breakdown."

Richard Felicetti, principal of Larsen Junior High School in Elgin, Illinois, stresses the need for *internal* communications. "Congratulations," "Keep up the good work," or "You made us proud of you" will make all personnel aware of your concern for them as individuals. A sincere and positive attitude must be projected by making each person feel he is "number one."

Donald Eels, principal of Lance Junior High School, Kenosha, Wisconsin, in his *NASSP* (January 1964) article, "Are Parents Really Partners in Education?" suggests ways of involving parents in a real partnership with the school. Parental involvement, he stresses, is a sure-fire route to good public relations.

Some of the most successful efforts are: (1) school volunteer services (2) parent involvement in school programs (3) communications to parents and (4) communications to school.

Feedback is imperative. A few sample questions to parents might be:

Figure 8-6

1. Which of these do you favor as methods for improving communication between the school and parents concerning student progress?

    _____a. Retaining the present midterm progress reports.

    _____b. Instituting parent-teacher grade conferences to be held each quarter during the school day, with students being dismissed on the day of the conference.

    _____c. Changing the grading system to some form of comprehensive, explanatory grading sheet (rather than the present letter-grade report card).

    _____d. Retaining the present system.

    _____e. Other:_____

2. Which of these methods do you feel would be acceptable as ways of dealing with students who are habitually disruptive in the classroom?

    _____a. Suspension from school for a brief period of time.

    _____b. Expansion of special programs (such as the Educational Support Program) to deal with these students.

_____c. Initiating a "cooling off" room where students may be sent when they become too difficult to handle. Appropriate counseling or discipline would follow.

_____d. Corporal punishment to be administered by the principal after all other means have been exhausted.

_____e. Other:_____

3. What would you list as the school's greatest strength?

4. What would you consider the school's greatest weakness to be?

Today, it is impossible, in any school system to simply ignore the news media. Therefore, the soundest solution is to embark upon a positive program of building good relations with the news media.

Del Harding provides the following advice:

1. The keys to establishing and maintaining good relations with the news media are: honesty, accuracy, and timeliness.

2. What is news?

   a. Is it unusual?
   b. Would it be of interest to the community at large?
   c. Is it timely?
   d. Is it significant?
   e. Is it humorous?
      (Don't assume that the type of story that is news once, will be so every time.)

3. In answering the question on how to write a news story, one must always keep in mind the who, what, when, where, why, and how aspects—but a flair for news writing helps.

4. Avoid jargon that is meaningless to the reader.

5. *If possible,* provide radio and television with separate news releases—short important coverage.

Harding recommends the following communications checklist:

1. Is someone in your school assigned the specific public information-public relations responsibility?

2. Do you have a readily available list of the newsmen with whom you frequently come in contact?

3. Are you personally acquainted with the newsmen on this list?

4. Have you visited your local editor or station manager recently?

5. Do you send copies of all notices (newsletters, etc.) you send home to parents to the local media?

6. Do you personally greet newsmen when they visit your school, or are you "too busy?"

7. Do you return phone calls from newsmen promptly?

8. Do you prepare a master calendar of school events for use by the news media?*

Roy Azarnoff is a community education consultant with P.O.S. Associates in Los Angeles and succinctly states:

> For historical, sociological, and some philosophical reasons, the school, as represented by administrators and teachers, and the community, as represented by parents and sometimes students, frequently find themselves in opposing positions.
>
> When parent participation is legitimized by a council, as opposed to the more controlled P.T.A. style of participation, the initial thrust of the community is often couched in terms of problem solving. The identification of problems by parents is commonly seen by school personnel as a guise for venting hostile feelings toward the school or toward them personally. Teachers and administrators become defensive in response to what they perceive as attacks on their professional and personal efforts, which they believe to be mainly unwarranted. Where attack-defense postures result, the councils usually become immobilized and ineffective.

GETTING PROPER NEWS COVERAGE

It is imperative to realize that the news media will get the "bad news" about a school without even trying. The police radio, the rumor mill, and the telephone will alert them of the "big fight," "the knifing," "the riot," "the tragedy"—all of which are probably distorted or sensationalized. Thus, as principal, you must make an extra effort to get the "good news" to the media for their consideration. The open message, the weekly tip sheet, or the guidance bulletin help. They let the media know about interesting happenings and coming events. A follow-up phone call or a personal invitation to the local reporter adds that "special person" aspect to your relationship and also serves as a reminder.

---

*Del Harding, "How to Capitalize on News Media," *NASSP Bulletin,* January 1974, pp. 43-50.

Obviously, the news media will make the decision about whether or not to cover a story and how to cover it. Your personal wishes may be ignored, but a refusal to cooperate or a withdrawal of information will only lead to a negative backlash.

THREE OFTEN OVERLOOKED GROUPS OF POSITIVE PUBLIC COMMUNICATIONS

These groups are: (1) the food service personnel, (2) the secretarial and clerical staff, and (3) the substitute teacher. What are their roles and functions? How can they be turned into positive communicators? Here are several workable ideas:

Food Services

A. ROLE AND FUNCTION IN THE SCHOOL-COMMUNITY PUBLIC RELATIONS PROGRAM

The director of food services is a very visible and important public relations director. Practically everyone—student, parent, professional and noncertified staff, members of the community—comes in contact with the food services part of the school system.

The responsibilities of the director are, in fact, all closely related to public relations. The hiring of pleasant and clean personnel, the purchasing and accounting of foods and supplies, running the operation on a self-sustaining basis, and providing for a balanced menu—all generate discussion through the community.

B. WORKABLE PUBLIC RELATIONS ACTIVITIES

- Provide recognition for the employee of the month.

- Establish a bulletin board in each school to be utilized by the cafeteria staff.

- Give individual members an opportunity to make suggestions and ask questions via a written questionnaire.

- Invite student tours through the central kitchen and cafeteria facilities.

- Conduct in-service meetings with cafeteria personnel on human relations problems and working with school-aged youngsters.

- Hold periodic luncheons for teachers, parents, community leaders, and students—both during school hours and in the evenings.

- Organize internal evening dinners—using parents, students, and school personnel.

- Send newsletters home to parents concerning lunch programs and request feedback ideas.

- Speak at local P.T.A. meetings and to community groups.

- Develop an on-going news release flow with local news media.

- Utilize National School Lunch Week to publicize the positive aspects of food services.

- Contribute articles to professional journals concerning innovative and/or successful patterns.

- Work with legislative groups for the improvement of school lunch services.

- Strive for government funds and grants to initiate innovative practices.

- Highlight ethnic groups and their contributions throughout the year, with special emphasis being placed on International Lunch Week.

- Conduct in-school contests in conjunction with special holiday menus, such as Thanksgiving and Christmas.

- Work cooperatively with elementary school personnel to encourage a better understanding of nutrition and foods.

- Encourage cafeteria personnel to prepare attractive and wholesome meals.

- Make personnel services available to cafeteria workers throughout the system.

- Be alert to the needs and desires of ethnic groups.

Secretarial And Clerical Staff

A. ROLE AND FUNCTION IN THE SCHOOL-COMMUNITY PUBLIC RELATIONS PROGRAM

The success of a sound school-community public relations program is intertwined and interdependent on the total school family.

Secretaries, aides, and clerks are an essential, integral part of that family. Contact with them, both by telephone and in person, usually provides the first impression that a parent or visitor gets of the shcool. Hence, they must make the best possible impression on those with whom they come in contact. A good secretary is the liaison between the administration, the teacher, the counselor, and the community. Her function and specific responsibilities play a significant role in shaping public opinion. She is in a strategic position to provide efficient, effective, and courteous service to all members of the community. How she looks, how she works, how she acts, what she says, how long it takes to answer a phone or recognize a visitor may make the difference in projecting an image of a friendly, congenial, and efficient school. The role of the secretaries, aides, and clerks cannot be overemphasized in any positive school-community public relations program.

B. WORKABLE PUBLIC RELATIONS ACTIVITIES

- Always be cooperative and courteous in providing needed information and services.
- Be prompt and friendly in recognizing a visitor to the school.
- Be well groomed and appropriately dressed for your position.
- Project a positive attitude even when the parent or visitor may be angry.
- Be professional and businesslike in handling sensitive information.
- Be a positive liaison with the community. Isolated incidents or comments that a secretary makes may damage the school's image.
- Avoid gossip and criticism about other employees.
- Always praise or express confidence in the official policies of the school.
- Avoid making derogatory remarks about the school.
- Recognition and commendations must be given to the secretarial and clerical staff for a job well done.

Substitute Teachers

A. ROLE AND FUNCTION IN THE SCHOOL-COMMUNITY PUBLIC RELATIONS PROGRAM

It is important to understand that school-community public relations is a continuous program of letting people know what the schools are doing and why. The substitute teacher, the teacher aide, and volunteers are also an integral part of school-community relations. What they say, how they act, and the message they carry to the people of the community will result in creating an atmosphere for or against the school. Thus, the key to good public relations lies in satisfying the needs of this group and providing them with the opportunity to become constructive and contributing members of the educational team.

B. WORKABLE PUBLIC RELATIONS ACTIVITIES

- Select positive, capable, and well-qualified substitutes.
- Provide them with avenues for communicating their frustrations, comments, and desires.
- Provide them with an adequate salary.
- Establish a comprehensive handbook for substitutes in each school—providing for:

  a. Adequate lesson plans
  b. A discipline referral system and backing
  c. Seating charts
  d. Class schedule
  e. Directions concerning routines
  f. Lunch schedule
  g. Supply, textbook, and material location
  h. Emergency and daily routine information

- Encourage the substitute to be tactful, courteous, and pleasant toward students and staff members.
- Allow for proper assignment placement.
- Allow for adequate call-up time of the substitute.

BEING AWARE

An awareness of public attitudes, concerns, and questions about education assists the principal in his preventive and corrective communications. A recent Gallup Poll of "Public Attitudes Toward Education" certainly reflects the concerns already expressed throughout our country. Thus, any public relations effort must concern itself with these attitudes. According to the poll, the major problems confronting public schools are:

- Lack of discipline
- Integration/segregation problems
- Lack of proper financial support
- Use of drugs
- Difficulty of getting "good" teachers
- Size of school/classes
- Parents lack of interest
- School board policies
- Poor curriculum
- Lack of proper facilities

Another important Gallup Poll finding helps identify the type of information the general public is interested in knowing more about. The following are listed in priority order of response:

- Curriculum
- Qualifications of teachers
- Current methods
- How schools are administered
- Problem of discipline
- Financial status of the schools
- Extracurricular activities
- Academic ratings of the schools

- Student attitudes toward schools
- More information about my child
- Handling of students with special problems
- Grading practices
- Integration problem
- How parents can become more involved

TWENTY-FIVE TYPICAL QUESTIONS OF CONCERN

The authors conducted a public relations survey as part of a graduate course designed for potential school administrators. Some of the questions which follow may be considered very pointed; others are rather mundane. Nevertheless, the thinking represented here is significant for anyone involved in communicating with the public.

- Who makes sure the high-priced administrators are really earning their money and not wasting time?
- Why do we allow architects to consume so much money when designing a new school? Why can't we use available, basic designs?
- What is really being done to combat waste of supplies and workers?
- Why can't we have an informal luncheon or breakfast with the principal to discuss issues?
- What kind of special education programs are available for my youngster?
- How do our high school students make out in college?
- What are we doing for the gifted student?
- What is our school system doing to involve the teachers in community relations?
- What kind of in-service programs do you provide for your teachers?
- Does the high school curriculum correlate with the employment needs of the community?
- To whom should the formal public relations program be delegated?

- What is the school system's philosophy?

- Is innovation welcome in the school system?

- How can the citizenry help with the learning process in the schools?

- What is being done about the "dead wood" in teaching?

- What is the real story about discipline in our schools?

- Why do teachers always ask for more money?

- Why is there unrest in the schools?

- What is the achievement level of our students?

- What are the major problems of our system?

- What is the average class size at each level?

- In what ways are teachers held accountable for student performance?

- What are they trying to teach our youngsters in our schools?

- How is my youngster doing in school?

- Is my child giving you any trouble, and if so, do you keep me informed?

Conclusion

The previously mentioned community surveys have been presented to illustrate the growing public concern for the educational system, and its effect upon the lives of all concerned.

Even a cursory perusal of the data, the responses, the types of questions asked, and the concerns projected provided the internal educational family with the sense of urgency to do a better job with our school-community public relations efforts.

The authors used these surveys to impress on all the need for more personal attention to public relations and to encourage all segments of the educational family to get involved in this combined effort.

9

MAKING SPEECHES THAT GET RESULTS

PREPARING A PRESENTATION FOR THE BOARD OF EDUCATION

With the "open" environment phenomenon so characteristic of meetings of boards of education, administrators are given countless opportunities to "sell" their academic wares, their philosophies, and their methods. Also, they spend much of their delivery time "defending" the school and the things for which it stands. In order to do this well, the public board meeting provides a necessary, frequently useful forum. Some general guidelines for delivery to boards of education may be helpful, since there are at least two very separate audiences in attendance at such gatherings—the board of education and the public at large. A third and vital audience, the local press, carries with it special concerns. Given such a psychological backdrop, these hints may prove helpful:

- Always prepare data carefully and recheck their accuracy prior to releasing them orally or in visual form. Inaccuracies will surely return to haunt the careless administrator.

- Arrange materials well physically. Such seemingly minor items as seating, public address systems, electrical connections, availability and location of screens, access to preplanned supplementary handouts, and the like carry with them the *minimal* essentials of a well-received delivery.

- Understand the concept of "timing"—when to begin, when to reveal the central themes of your message, how to expose material for maximal impact, when to "detour" from your main topic, when and how to close effectively.

- Be aware of the "instant boredom" which can afflict boards of education—they perhaps have heard it all before. Conscious closure on their parts must be avoided and such verbal or visual pyrotechnics as necessary must be used without turning the delivery into a circus.

- Keep your deliveries free of technical language, hackneyed phraseology, and obnoxious educational jargon. Failure to do this will lose the more educated, frequently supportive elements of the audience and serves largely to obfuscate issues, creating resentment and misunderstanding.

- Maintain an "antiseptic" tone to your remarks. Avalanches of defensive or apologetic remarks heighten whatever inadequacies people perceive in the schools in the first place. On the other hand, never be so confident about your stance that an audience sees you as unapproachable, distant, and arrogant. A fine line exists here, and it is largely personal style which controls and governs that sensitive middle ground.

- If other professional personnel (e.g., a panel of faculty) are to be used in a presentation, be sure they are rehearsed to an extent deemed prudent. Be sure that each member is briefed on timing, political implications, and the potentially incendiary nature of "unwise" commentary.

- Always avoid "preaching" to sophisticated audiences. Diatribes, polemics, or hysterical outbursts are elements of public speaking which smother what might otherwise have been well-received remarks.

- Never become involved in verbal warfare or exchange intellectual artillery fire (even if baited) with board members, reporters, politicians, or citizens at such meetings. Even if you win the intellectual argument, you lose the emotional one. Pyrrhic victories are useless.

- Be sure all visual and handout materials are prepared well in advance, proofread carefully, and that final versions are scrupulously accurate and attractive. Never "settle" for even questionable crispness, let alone marginal sloppiness.

- Compress all presentations in both time and content as much as possible, however charismatic your speaking or journalistic style. Verbal virtuosity has its place; it does not happen to be at board meetings however.

- Keep deliveries *simple, direct, uncluttered,* and, above all, *clear.* Remember, a misunderstood message will always get increasingly distorted, and such inaccuracies and manglings can *never* really be explained away.

- Never mask or attempt to perfume the truth. Do not shock needlessly, but do not euphemize the obvious either.

- Always review your intended remarks with your immediate supervisor prior to making them final, so that an internal "surprise-free" climate exists. Such prudent caution salvages beforehand what might otherwise prove to be a political holocaust from which the school system may find it difficult, if not impossible, to disentangle itself.

Styles of delivery will and should vary considerably. Administrators may not all be gifted orators; they need not be. Their presentations, however, need intelligent planning, recognition of the nature of the audience, and a sound sensing of *what* needs to be said and *how* best to say it.

THE "SERVICE CLUB" DELIVERY

The professional educator remains in our culture somewhat "different;" our society still cannot relate to him as "real." Now and again, administrators are given glittering opportunities to step out of their idealized, almost separatist roles and materialize as genuine parts of the American way of things. Service clubs (Rotary, Kiwanis, veterans' groups, etc.) not infrequently provide such image-altering opportunities.

Situation: As a well-known, frequently photographed, publicly criticized principal of the local high school, and as a veteran of the armed forces of the United States, the Veterans of Foreign Wars ask you to be their main speaker for Veterans Day, an event you know will be colorful, commemorative, and very well attended. You debate with yourself on your topic and reject any connection with public education, since you feel it is important for you to be seen as "flesh and blood" outside the framework of your sensitive job.

You realize you must appeal to a very wide age range in your audience, but should really focus your remarks on the older group whose representatives invited you to speak in the first place. You sense that a nostalgic theme will do justice to the solemnity of the occasion and that a little scholarship will go a long way in winning friends for the school by popular acceptance of your remarks, *irrespective of content*. You realize that an educated delivery carries with it, however subtly, the message of the value of a sound education and a theme revolving around the moral questions of war and peace. Uniting (1) the appeal of the media, (2) the emotional valence of nostalgic allusion, (3) the pulsation of recent history, (4) the sentimental touch of emotional poetry, and (5) the ultimate morality which inheres in contributing to righteous causes irrespective of price, you might construct your delivery for the sake of *universal appeal* and *lasting impact*.

The following guidelines may help in this instance:

- Understand the "special" nature of your audience and appeal directly to their inclinations and backgrounds.

- Do not hesitate to "load" this delivery with appropriate emotion and remembrances.

- Show your preparedness through precise historical references which will trigger memories and turn back the "pages of history."

- Elevate simple gratitude to loftier, more profound heights.

- Keep your delivery moving, direct, terse, and brief.

- Show your *intellectual* substance without smothering your audience in dessicated historical tedium.

Such a speech may be unusual for an educator, but the administrator's verbal stock must be able to accommodate even drastic departures from his technical field. Indeed, not infrequently, he must demonstrate that he is widely versed and well-educated. Oral deliveries give him that opportunity very well.

In more conventional ways, other service clubs really want to hear about the schools and opportunities that exist to present undistorted verbal photographs of the educational institution. Here, an administrator's *humor* and his capacity to *synthesize* complex notions become major tools. Recognizing that service club members are usually professional people, entrepreneurs, or management types, a humorous story along these lines will never fail to "break the ice."

A new principal arrived on the job just as the old one was clearing out. The new man, wanting to do right, asked for a briefing on the general situation. The departing administrator, obviously in a hurry to leave the old scene, responded by saying he had no time, but had left three letters in his top desk drawer for his successor. He advised the new principal to open them one at a time when things began to deteriorate—as surely they would as time went on.

To be sure, three months later, the school began to have serious problems after the so-called "honeymoon" subsided. Opening the first letter (labelled #1), the new principal read "Ask for more time." He did and was politely granted another six months to "straighten the place out."

Six months later, chaos again struck and the principal opened the second letter. It read, "Reorganize!" Dutifully, he complied and changed titles of leadership personnel, shifted responsibilities, and in general, applied sound managerial thinking to the problem. Nightmare subsided—briefly.

Two months later, fireworks again broke out. Rushing to his desk, the harrassed principal opened the last letter which compellingly read, *"Write Three Letters."*

No delivery without some humor is worth much, and source material is legion. Many service clubs want to hear light deliveries about "heavy" problems. If choices are left to the speaker, he might choose from among these examples:

- Status of Discipline in the School
- How Well Your Children Read, Write, and Calculate
- How "Good" is Our High School?
- Comparing Your Values with Those of Your Kids
- What You Can Do to Improve the School
- What's Wrong with Public Schools?
- Is College Still an Answer?

Under no circumstances should an administrator prepare an esoteric speech about arcane methods of in-service education, the writing of objectives, or similar, technical "in-group" kinds of things. Broad kinds of topics with colorful or unique slants form far better bases for sound, easy communications. Indeed, probably the best approach to local organizations is a theme without a "prepared" speech which is "thrown open" to questions and answers from the very beginning. The charm of such a technique rests with its instant involvement of the audience at a genuine level of participation.

ADDRESSING PROFESSIONAL GROUPS

When an administrator is asked by his colleagues to speak to *them,* such would seem to be the height of professional flattery and recognition. However, it also thrusts him into the most unenviable of situations—the prospect of enlightening colleagues all of whom already see themselves as singularly enlightened. The same *caveats* apply to preparing a speech for professional listeners as those illustrated for local audiences, with the possible exception of the political inhibitors advocated earlier. Obviously, some refinements in preparatory and delivery guidelines may also help:

- Your audience must be assumed to be well informed; attempts at overwhelming them with imprecise detail will surely fail.

- Illustrations (slides, visuals, etc.) must be especially clear, attractive, and, above all, appropriate. It is important to remember that your audience is *you*—with a similar background and expertise. They will, however, unconsciously, resent shoddy razzle-dazzle or substanceless cleverness.

- While "sound scholarship" is impressive (and necessary), too much of a good thing induces "audience tedium" and tends to stupefy even the most conscientious listener. Avoid a scholarly avalanche; it becomes quite counterproductive.

- If compression and sound synthesis of complicated loose ends are virtues in public speaking, they are especially vital for super-sophisticated audiences whose memberships earn their livelihoods the same way you do.

- Always write your remarks fully rather than speaking from an outline; the risks of "wandering," becoming too personal, and leaning on catharsis are too great. This should not preclude intelligent, illustrative digressions for they enliven any delivery. Slavish, legalistic adherence to planning is mostly risk-free, but could yield a needlessly dull product.

Obviously, an arresting beginning and a pungent closing frame any delivery, assisting markedly in capturing an audience and causing it to ponder your remarks. Nothing is quite as forgettable as a colorless speech fenced by blandness and pseudo-professional drivel. Hammering out a snappy opening and drilling home a proper termination need not be lengthy projects, merely thoughtful, rhetorically balanced, and, to some extent, flashy.

Beginnings and endings, however, are merely the slices of bread of the sandwich of articulate delivery; the meat gives it body and flavor. Illustrations, heightening and intensifying the content, provide the necessary condiments and spices.

If you were asked to speak on writing better evaluations, your imagination might allow you to "back into" the problem by illustrating how *not* to embarrass yourself with a hollow, tragically inadequate product. A little humor, a bit of cartooning, and a lot of central truth might be shown in the following visual form, discussed systematically, and perhaps remembered for its uniqueness and consummate sterility. Figure 9-1 illustrates how *not* to write an evaluation on a staff member.

Ways to prepare and deliver speeches are legion; doing this well is a bit more uncommon than one might like. The keys rest in planning, knowing what needs to be said, discarding irrelevancies (no matter how beguiling), organizing trenchantly, delivering with verve, and knowing when the audience has had enough.

SO YOU'RE A PANELIST NOW

A panelist in the lexicon of the media may be defined as an expert, part-time at *that* time. He is not a speaker, but a fractional contributor, one element of a larger body. A panelist's success comes not from occupying an undivided spotlight, but rather from well timed, well-spoken, fragmentary contributions. Success on a panel may be prepared for as follows:

- Read current material on the central topic. Never come to the panel unprepared, even though you may have a general familiarity with the subject.

Figure 9-1

Having joined the staff of West Cipher High School approximately six years ago as an English teacher, Marvin Middleclass continues to improve in his rapport with students and teachers alike. His classes are interesting and students really learn in them. Seldom, if ever, does a parent register complaints about his teaching.

Marvin plans his work well, arrives on time, maintains a neat orderly learning environment to which his students readily respond. He is not reluctant to attend student functions, and they (the students) are grateful for his commitment to them.

Enrolled in a graduate course in the writing of behavorial objectives (Ed.9000 - Basic Accountability for the Masses), Marvin is right up-to-date on the latest methods and materials. Marvin resides in town, is active in local affairs, and loves it.

- Never monopolize the oral time of the panel; it defeats its central mission of airing *diverse* views.

- Come prepared with brief, key items as reminders, but never read them; mini-speeches fail as a good panel technique.

- Try not to incessantly repeat your prejudices or predispositions on an issue; it detracts from the progress and positive motion of any discussion and contributes nothing to enlightment.

- Do not attack fellow panelists or attempt to discredit their views or professional standing; it is professionally distasteful and self-humiliating.

- Be as crisp and witty as possible, but not cutting. Style and substance are frequently indistinguishable.

- Remember you are part of a team in a sense, and your gain or loss reflects on the full contribution, or lack of it, of the group's delivery.

- If each panel member is allotted speaking time, do not run over your allocation; that is bad form and in bad taste, irrespective of how important you may perceive your words to be.

- Relax and be as honest and refreshing as your style permits you to be.

Panels are ubiquitous; it is difficult to subordinate strong views to a clock and one's colleagues. Nonetheless, a little selflessness enhances one's image almost magically; it's well worth the investment in self-discipline and properly bridled commentary.

SPEAKING TO STUDENT GROUPS

Speaking styles, once developed, seldom change much with respect to kinds of audiences. Obviously, sophisticated deliveries are hardly appropriate for young people in elementary or middle schools. Given a nonselective population in the American public high school, there are also limitations on how one approaches speaking to these youngsters. Some hints and cautions may be of benefit:

- Vary your remarks with the nature of the group. Talking with chronic truants demands a very different approach from delivering remarks at the induction ceremonies of the National Honor Society.

- Tell as many "stories" (even contemporary parables) as the occasion demands. The yarn with the built-in lesson *by inference* is far better than the "preaching" style of many adults. Young people *simply* do not deal well with moral abstraction.

- Do not overuse humor; silliness and instant collapse of necessary distance between adult and student march disarmingly hand-in-hand.

- Always maintain your dignity in addressing young people without becoming stuffy or haughty about the occasion. Nothing is as destructive as massive distance between a speaker and young people. Similarly, nothing is as shattering as artificial, immature pretense at hollow partnership.

- Be *very* contemporary in your illustrations, drawing from current news, TV programs, and the current culture. Allusions to what people understand instantly and instinctively work and make the proper conscious connections in the minds of young listeners.

- Say what needs saying; do not be overly concerned with "political" consequences. Young people appreciate candor as long as *they* are not humiliated in the process.

- If you have a tendency to intellectualize, allude to readings with which you know your students have current familiarity. Such references add sparkle and meaning to the school's program and give rise to a benign smugness in students that they are "in the know."

- Be very colorful and lively in your presentations because, like it or not, you are competing at an unconscious level with the entertainment phenomenon of television as well as faced with an attention span which is very brief.

Speaking to students should generally be distinguished by brevity, sincerity, a light touch, and an easy manner. Ponderous, cumbersome, and lengthy oral monographs are singularly inappropriate.

WHAT P.T.A.'S, BOOSTERS' CLUBS, AND OTHER PARENT GROUPS WANT TO HEAR

Unlike service clubs, historical societies, or political or quasi-political organizations, these groups have particular concern with and direct connection to the public schools. Therefore, in essence, they know more about the schools' internal operation and infrastructure. Accordingly, what is said to them may not be as startling or revelatory unless one adjusts his message and properly calibrates in their backgrounds.

A major problem for an administrator speaking to such groups may very well be the enveloping sense of *déjà vu* which often accompanies the content of his remarks. Such groups always *need* to hear amplifications and clarifications of negative rumors. Hence, the staples of an oral delivery are frequently riveted to repetitive complaints on recurring problems. It is wise to remember that just as student bodies change annually with graduation ceremonies, so do parents; only the administration and faculty remain relatively constant as a kind of permanent sales force.

These groups, then, generally face the same professional people with the same messages, asking for the same things in frequently the same way. What they really need is not an alteration of purpose, but one of method and style. An administrator's ingenuity, inventiveness, and imagination are often more important than the substance of his message. Parent groups want to hear: (1) what they can do to be supportive, (2) about new sources of funding, (3) what the *real* problems are, (4) alternate methods of solving these problems, (5) priorities for their activities, (6) sources of workers and other means of support upon which they can depend, and (7) new projects of magnitude with which they can identify and become involved.

INTRODUCTORY REMARKS AT SCHOOL FUNCTIONS

Custom and tradition frequently require an administrator to function as a master of ceremonies at parent meetings, concerts, banquets, and assemblies. Fortunately, such a role is becoming increasingly less common as faculty advisors assume larger, more visible and direct roles for such events. Overexposure of a chief administrator attenuates his effectiveness as a public figure of influence. At the same time, total invisibility emasculates the role altogether. Selectivity on routine appearances may be the best guide to a practicing schoolman.

As is always the case, the substance of one's remarks is largely a matter of personal preference. The following guidelines on style, however, may be useful:

- Introductory remarks should always be brief, to the point, and, above all, *set the right tone*—especially if the audience is required to be especially polite and appreciative by the nature of the event.

- Be sure to thank publicly, by name if possible, those who contributed to the anticipated success of the program.

- Do not permit yourself to introduce administrative announcements which are disconnected with the activity at hand. Captive audiences should not be subjected to administrative convenience.

- If you do not wish to make frequent appearances, delegate your role as master of ceremonies to an appropriate faculty member—except in instances of importance such as inductions into the National Honor Society, Back-to-School nights, and similar high exposure high "PR" yield events.

- After your remarks, become as unobtrusive as good control permits.

CONTRIBUTING FROM AN AUDIENCE

Being part of an audience is far more common than speaking to one from behind a podium. Remarking to that audience as though one were part of it takes far more courage than being on the program. At the same time, one must be aware of two pervading tendencies: (1) not to speak at all, and (2) having decided to contribute, to speak at unending length. Each extreme should be avoided. A few hints follow:

- Do not stray from the theme of the meeting.

- Do not harangue about the inadequacies of *other* schools while endlessly extolling the virtues of yours.

- Never turn a question into a speech.

- Do not "attack" the presenters.

- Save highly personal or esoteric questions for the speaker(s) until *after* the session.

SPEAKING TO "PRESSURE" GROUPS

Taxpayers associations, political groups, and other vested-interest groups (promulgating products, values, or simply points of view) require no special set of guidelines except added statesmanship. Subordinating one's outlook to the special interests of a particular group for the sake of expedience and "survival," marks that person as vapid and continually driven by the tradewinds of fashion, convenience, and moral ambiguity. A speaker should say what is on his mind with grace, dealing with whatever controversial fallout results with similar mature detachment. Liquefaction into the prejudices of vested-interest groups, simply because it ruffles no one in that audience, becomes the pinnacle of administrative spinelessness and marks the man speaking as having no core of commitments. While confrontation may be counterproductive, integrity and scruples are not.

PLANNING THE "BIG" SPEECH

All speeches need sound planning for their (1) content, (2) tone, (3) method(s) of delivery, and (4) timing. A clockwork meticulousness to the construction of any oral delivery cannot be overemphasized. To that end, perhaps the guidelines which follow may be of assistance:

- Research factual information from current, unimpeachable sources, using your librarian for assistance where appropriate.

- Write the speech with a verbatim delivery in mind, even though you may very well plan to digress or improvise later.

- Supercheck all mechanical needs—including seating, audio-visual devices, and the like.

- Prepare extra copies of your remarks for the press in attendance or other interested parties.

- Rehearse your speech sufficiently so that you become thoroughly familiar with it.

- Insert illustrative stories, anecdotes, or humorous material at points where they add proper emphasis and color—not simply to entertain.

- Plan for questions at the end, leaving reasonable time to allow you to answer in acceptable detail.

CONCLUSION

Well-delivered oral communication radiates detailed planning, thorough familiarity with the subject, an understanding of the nature of one's audience, a thorough grasp of the power of language and its appropriate use, and a "feel" for enthusiastic delivery. Style and substance ought to blend in a well-woven tapestry of scholarly outlook. Given such ammunition, it is hard to see how an intelligent speaker can miss the target.

10

WRITING FOR PROFESSIONAL JOURNALS—WITH A PURPOSE

WHAT IS THERE REALLY LEFT TO SAY?

Every astute professional educator in a leadership role has in his career produced volumes of literature, position papers, committee reports, and bulletins. In addition, the administrator who has been involved in professional organizations, be they local, state, or national in nature, has from time to time participated in panel discussions, contributed to major conferences, and perhaps been a keynote speaker in the community. Among these materials are many practical kernels of information. Among these reports are vital, worthwhile concerns. Screen them for appropriate solutions, screen them for items you wish you had read before you experienced the problem. They are virtually a gold mine of natural educational resources.

Your next leading source of what is left to say may be found in your national survey reports. What are the educational concerns of people throughout the country? What are the problems facing education in general and your school, your community in particular?

Have you or your community educators taken any action to resolve the declining PSAT/SAT scores? How has it been organized? Cost? Effectiveness? Modifications recommended? Have you or your colleagues come to grips with the high rate of absenteeism? What positions have you taken in career education, bilingual/bicultural approaches? What are your students saying about alternative forms of education? These are still important items. In your drawers, in your files, in your experience, in your head you may have an answer—share it. Publish!

Let's examine:

- An association survey
- Gallup Poll
- Public perception of a "good school"
- Twenty-five questions
- Student concerns

Once you have analyzed the results of any pertinent survey, you can "zero in" on a topic of concern. Thus, you start with material that is of particular interest to a reading audience.

ASSOCIATION SURVEY

In many communities you will find particular organizations or associations concerned with education. An alert school administrator will attempt to contact the organizational leaderships or particularly friendly members to ascertain their perceived concerns. An analysis of a typical questionnaire will pinpoint the type of concerns being expressed.

Figure 10-1

West Association
School Questionnaire

Please indicate the school and grade level attended by each of your children. Example: Blue Run __K & 3_, Ridge__7__, etc.

Blue Run_____Smith_____Ridge_____
Oxford_____Ryle_____Senior High School_____

Please answer the following questions, Yes or No, in the appropriate columns.

If your response to any of the following questions is negative, please explain your reason on the reverse side and identify the question by number. Use additional sheets if necessary.

QUESTIONS	Blue Run	Smith	Ridge	Oxford	Ryle	Senior High School
1. Do you feel that the school admininstrative staff is doing an effective job?						
2. Do you feel that your child is learning what he or she should with respect to subject matter?						
3. Is there any particular subject area where you feel that the school is doing an inferior job?						
4. Do you feel that children in all ranges of learning ability are given proper attention?						
5. Are you satisfied with discipline?						
6. Are you satisfied with parent-school communications?						
7. Do you find the report card system effective?						
8. Are there adequate safety conditions with respect to						

QUESTIONS	Blue Run	Smith	Ridge	Oxford	Ryle	Senior High School
busing and crossing guards?						
9. Do the extracurricular activities offered meet the needs of the children?						
10. Do you approve of heterogeneous grouping (all learning levels in one class)?						
11. Is there good "school spirit" in the schools attended by your children?						
12. Are the counseling services provided by the schools effective?						
13. Is there effective communication between the students and administrative staff?						
14. Do you approve of having the 9th grade grouped in one school?						
15. What is your opinion of the quality of education being provided in the schools attended by your children?						
16. We solicit any additional comments you have pertaining to the school system.						

When one considers communications, it is only natural to turn to such nationally recognized polls as the Gallup Poll. It is sufficient to say that surveys such as these reveal the real "feelings" of the general public. An example may be the 1974 Gallup Poll.

GALLUP POLL

The Gallup Poll of "Public Attitudes Toward Education" certainly reflects the concerns already expressed by the multiple publics throughout our country.

Another important Gallup Poll finding helps identify particular information the general public is interested in knowing more about. The following are listed in priority order of response:

1. Curriculum

2. Qualifications of teachers

3. Current methods

4. How schools are administered

5. Problem of discipline

6. Financial status of the schools

7. Extracurricular activities

8. Academic ratings of the schools

9. Student attitudes toward schools

10. More information about my child

11. Handling of students with special problems

12. Grading practices

13. Integration problem

14. How parents can become more involved

PUBLIC PERCEPTION OF A "GOOD" SCHOOL

If you could send your child to any school in this area, on what bases would you select a "good" school?

1. Teachers who are interested in their work and their students

2. Teachers who make classes interesting

3. Variety in the curriculum

4. Good discipline

5. Respect for authority

6. Good student/teacher relationships

7. Good student to student relationship

8. Modern equipment

9. Small classes

10. Good administration

TWENTY-FIVE TYPICAL QUESTIONS OF CONCERN

Another important source of information may come from graduate courses designed for potential school administrators. An astute administrator may be in a position to have teachers, principals, department chairpersons, or representatives present and tabulate their thinking. Refer to previous chapters for examples of such questions.

STUDENT CONCERNS

One final example of "source" material for publication can be found in student survey reports. In one of these, four-hundred students participated in 16 regional meetings and rated the following as their top concerns:

- A need for meaningful communication between students, administration, parents, and faculty.

- Better counseling services for jobs and college placement.

- More emphasis on lifelong sports and recreation and less emphasis on interscholastic sports.

- Better teaching in basics: reading, grammar, and composition.

It was interesting to note that there were no significant differences in these priorities between urban and rural districts.

GAUGING THE READING AUDIENCE

Here is a critical area for you to think about. Granted you have the experience, the material resources, and the programs, the question is: How do you reach out to the proper audience?

Do a little brainstorming:

- Are you interested in making an educational contribution to a professional journal? (There will be no monetary compensation.)

- Are you interested in writing a pamphlet or short educational brief for one of the many commercially prepared services? (There is usually a small compensation rate.)

- Are you aspiring to write a full-length hard-cover book? (Royalties and contractual agreements are an intricate and somewhat negotiable area for you to consider.)

- Are you determined to have your manuscript published *and* are you willing to invest your own money? If so, there are legitimate publishing houses that will assist you with the technical know-how, layout, art work, and details. (The royalties and arrangements are individually negotiated.)

FINDING OUTLETS FOR YOUR WRITINGS

Let's examine your desires and identify some potential markets.

A. *Professional Education Journals*
    A partial list would include:
American School Board Journal, State National Bank Plaza. Evanston, Ill. 60201
America-National Catholic Weekly Review, American Press, 106 W. 56th St., New York, N.Y. 10019
Audiovisual Instruction, Association for Educational Communications of Technology, 1201 16th St., N.W., Washington, D.C. 20036
Black Scholar, Black World Foundation, Box 908, Sausalito, Calif. 94965
The Bulletin, National Association of Secondary School Principals, 1904 Association Dr., Reston, Va. 22091
Childhood Education, Association for Childhood Education International, 3615 Wisconsin Ave., N.W., Washington, D.C. 20016
English Education, National Council of Teachers of English, 1111 Kenyon Rd., Urbana, Ill. 61801
Harvard Educational Review, 13 Appian Way, Cambridge, Mass. 02138
Industrial Education, 1 Fawcett Pl., Greenwich, Conn. 06830

Journal For Research in Mathematics Education, National Council of Teachers of Mathematics, 1906 Association Dr., Reston, Va. 22091

Journal of Business Education, 4000 Albermarle St., N.W., Washington, D.C. 20016

Language Arts, National Council of Teachers of English, 1111 Kenyon Rd., Urbana, Ill. 61801

Media and Methods, 401 N. Broad St., Philadelphia, Pa. 19108

The Nation, 333 Avenue of the Americas, New York, N.Y. 10014

Science, American Association for the Advancement of Science, 1555 Massachusetts Ave., N.W., Washington, D.C. 20005

Social Work, National Association of Social Workers, 2 Park Ave., Rm. 2305, New York, N.Y. 10016

Today's Education: NEA Journal, NEA, 1201 16th St., N.W., Washington, D.C. 20036

B. *Commercial Service*
    A few of the most active might be:

Croft Educational Services, 24 Rope Ferry Rd., Waterford, Conn. 06386

Xerox Education Publications, 245 Long Hill Rd., Middletown, Conn. 06457

Scholastic Teacher, 50 W. 44th St., New York, N.Y. 10036

Changing Education, 1012 14th St., N.W., Washington, D.C. 20005

Scholastic Coach, 50 W. 44th St., New York, N.Y. 10036

C. *Book Publishers*
    Two excellent and comprehensive sources for this type of information are:

The Writers Market, ed. by Jane Koester and Rose Adkins, Writers Digest, Cincinnati, Ohio 45242

Literary Market Place, R.R. Bowker Co., 1180 Avenue of the Americas, New York, N.Y. 10036.

INTRODUCING YOURSELF TO AN EDITOR

Editors are busy people and probably get inundated with manuscripts to read. Nevertheless, remember that your article or manuscript is their bread and butter. Thus, take a positive approach. The most important thing to keep in mind is also the most obvious consideration—is your manuscript or article well written and on-target for that particular publication? How can you judge?

- Read several samples of what the editor is presently selecting.

- Check on the style being published.

- Check on the length and format being accepted.

- Emulate!

Let's consider: (1) the professional journals, (2) the commercial services, and (3) the textbook publisher.

The Professional Journals

- Select the journal you feel would be most likely to publish your article.

- Write a short introductory letter offering the article for publication.

- Include the article, neatly typed and double-spaced.

- Include a brief résumé or identification statement, e.g.:

  Dr. John M. Slate, Principal, Norwood Public High School, Canton, Ohio (enrollment 2000).

In addition, if you have successfully authored a recent article why not include it as a reference, e.g.:

  Authored "The Rights and Privileges of Students," Professional Journal, May 19X5.

The Commercial Services

- Proper selection of an appropriate service is imperative.

- Well-written, neatly typed, and double-spaced material will help do the selling.

- A pertinent résumé will help identify you.

- Successful publications will enhance your chances but are not mandatory.

- Be sure to state that they are free to publish all or part of your article at their scaled compensation rate.

The Textbook Publisher

For educators, this is the most prestigious form of publication. At certain levels and in specific communities, the concept of "publish or perish" does have its influence. In any event, it is a plus on the résumé of any educator to have authored a textbook. Hopefully, it is also an educational contribution from which his professional colleagues can benefit.

First considerations are not far removed from any publishing probe to an editor:

- The appropriate publisher.

- A well-written, neatly typed, double-spaced *sample chapter* must accompany your inquiry letter.

- A detailed table of contents will provide the editor with a sound idea of what you intend to write about.

- Your résumé.

WHEN SHOULD YOU HEAR FROM THE EDITOR?

Most likely, the editor will send you a short note or card stating that the manuscript inquiry has been received and giving an approximation as to when you will hear from him.

Within three or four weeks you may receive a critical analysis or some constructive suggestions as to how the manuscript may be improved. The editor may like the concepts and ideas, he may want you to elaborate on certain items, he may politely reject the manuscript and suggest a more appropriate publisher, or you may receive a contract.

HOW MUCH SHOULD YOU EXPECT?

The rate of compensation is fairly well set for the noncelebrity writer.

WHAT DOES THE CONTRACT INCLUDE?

A contract may include such items as:

- Monetary agreement—differential payment basis

- An advance against all royalties
- The number of words and chapters included in the completed manuscript
- Rights and copyright cards
- Deadline dates for submitting the completed manuscript
- A statement advising that the company pays for all promotional sales endeavors

WHAT HAPPENS AFTER YOU HAVE COMPLETED THE MANUSCRIPT?

Your typewritten copy is duplicated and sent to two experts in the field for their evaluation and review.

Several weeks later you will receive a copy of their independent comments. You may:

(1) accept their advice and modify the item, sentence, or chapter; or

(2) reject their advice and offer an explanation as to why the item should not be revised.

Next your manuscript is assigned to an editor who will orchestrate and guide it to completion.

Several months later you will receive the galley proofs which you will proofread.

Next you will prepare a draft for the promotion and sales department.

Concurrently you will prepare an updated résumé with a personal photo to be used for the book jacket.

If artwork and/or indexing is needed, a fee may be attached which will be deducted from your first royalty payment. Finally, when the text is about to roll off the press, you will receive a release date, six complimentary copies, and some promotional flyers.

EXAMINATION OF SOME SAMPLE CORRESPONDENCE

The following correspondence may be useful in illustrating how the same material can be submitted in a variety of ways and with a different focus in mind. Also, rejection does not mean that the material is not well-written; the key may be in the selection of the appropriate journal, publisher, or source.

> Warrensville High School
> 4 County Road
> Warrensville, Conn. 06435
> November 25, 19X5

Mr. Allen Vann
Croft-NEI Publications
24 Rope Ferry Road
Waterford, Conn. 06386

Dear Allen:

Enclosed please find a thirty-nine page learning packet about Puerto Rico for secondary school teachers. It is the perfect vehicle for inspiring Spanish-speaking youngsters in our secondary schools today. In addition, it provides all students with insights into the culture and history of the island.

This can easily be expanded by including several more high-interest topics or it can be used in a two-part or three-part series.

I'm positive the market is favorable for this type of learning pack, and we can quickly complete parts II and III. Please advise.

Yours truly,

John B. Vita, Principal

Joseph J. Porce, Unit Coordinator

Marilyn Espen, Social Studies Chairman

Croft-NEI Publications
24 Rope Ferry Road
Waterford, Conn. 06386
December 1, 19X5

Mr. John B. Vita, Principal
Warrensville High School
4 County Road
Warrensville, Connecticut 06435

Dear John:

Thanks for sending the learning packet on Puerto Rico. I'm afraid there's nothing we can do with it, since instructional material itself is not in our line. I notice that one of the cosigners of your covering letter was your social studies chairman, Marilyn Espen. Perhaps Ms. Espen should get in touch with the National Council of Teachers of Social Studies (a division of NEA). They might be able to provide you with a list of likely publishers. Thanks again.

Regards,

Allen Vann
Contributing Editor

AV/sc
Enclosures

Warrensville High School
4 County Road
Warrensville, Connecticut 06435
December 16, 19X5

Mr. Stephen N. Jones, Editor
English Journal
P.O. Box 112
East Lansing, MI 48823

Dear Sir:

Enclosed is an article which might be of interest to some of your readers. I have found it a useful instrument among my teaching staff, and feel that it has possibilities for definite instructional improvement among English teachers who have foreign-speaking students in their classrooms.

I would appreciate your reactions to this proposed article.

Sincerely yours,

Joseph J. Porce

English Journal
P.O. Box 112
East Lansing, MI 48823

May 7, 19X6

Mr. Joseph J. Porce
Warrensville High School
4 County Road
Warrensville, Connecticut 06435

Dear Mr. Porce:

Thank you for submitting a summary of your "Self-Evaluation Checklist" for ESL teachers. We run announcements in the *English Journal* from time to time describing the availability of materials such as these. With your permission, I will hold on to your description and try to use it as a filler during the 19X6-X7 publishing year.

Thank you for your interest in the *English Journal.*

Sincerely,

Stephen N. Jones
Editor

SNJ/jm

Today's Education
1201 16th Street, N.W.
Washington, D.C. 20036
August 18, 19X6 ·

Dear Author:

We appreciate your submitting a manuscript to us recently for our consideration, and we assure you that it has been read carefully by at least two of our editors. Unfortunately, we have decided, for one or more of the following reasons, that we will be unable to publish it:

1. Our space is so severely limited that we must return many excellent manuscripts—yours among them.

2. We have recently published an article on this subject and will not be able to carry another soon.

3. We have already made a commitment for another article on this topic for an upcoming issue

4. We feel your article is better suited for another publication.

We're sorry that we cannot accept your manuscript, and we apologize for not being able to send you a personal letter about it. The fact is that we are now receiving so many unsolicited manuscripts that our small staff is unable to write personal letters to all those who have submitted them. Because of escalating postage costs, it is also impossible for us to return your manuscript (unless it was accompanied by a self-addressed envelope with sufficient postage, as stated on the contents page of *Today's Education*).

However, we assure you that we are grateful to you for preparing the manuscript and submitting it to us, and we sincerely urge you to submit additional material to us in the future. We'll also appreciate your reactions to the magazine and your suggestions for improving it.

To help you in submitting a copy of your manuscript to others, we are enclosing a list of education magazines and their addresses.

Thanks for your continuing interest in *Today's Education*.

Sincerely,

Walter A. Graves
Editor

Warrensville High School
4 County Road
Warrensville, Conn. 06435

December 17, 19X5

Natl. Assn. of Secondary School Principals
1904 Association Drive
Reston, Virginia 22091

Gentlemen:

Attached is an article which might be of interest to some of your readers. I have found both checklists useful instruments in evaluating classes where teachers are providing individualized instruction for the nonnative English-speaking pupil.

As part of a two-year in-service program to train mainstream teachers to receive the ESL (English-as-a-Second-Language) pupil in their classrooms, the writer developed a checklist for Supervisory Observations. This checklist is designed to give the administrator/supervisor some definitive guidelines for evaluating the effectiveness of teachers in their dealings with non-English-speaking pupils.

Also attached is a Self-Evaluation Checklist for mainstream teachers. This is given to them as a guide for instructional planning for the nonnative English speaker.

Thus, by using both checklists, one for teacher self-planning and one for supervisory evaluation, the probability for instructional improvement is greatly increased.

A summary of the entire model in-service program has been prepared by the writer. Anyone interested in implementing or expanding an in-service program to train mainstream teachers to deal more effectively with the non-English-speaking pupil should contact me.

Very truly yours,

Joseph J. Porce
Unit Coordinator

JJP:gb
Enclosures (2)

CHECKLIST FOR SUPERVISORY OBSERVATION
OF ESL AND MAINSTREAM TEACHERS

1. Has established *verbal* communication with all pupils.

2. Uses uncomplicated English syntax.

3. Avoids words with double meanings and *exceptions* to the rules.

4. Avoids *idiomatic* phrases.

5. Proceeds from the simple to the complex in an organized fashion.

6. Deductive and inductive reasoning are used as necessary.

7. Uses visuals to reinforce the audio.

8. Proceeds from hearing, understanding, and speaking to the reading and writing phase.

9. Provides a variety of activities to insure pupil participation.

10. Encourages an *integration* of pupils from various linguistic backgrounds.

11. Makes use of student leaders in small group sessions.

12. Uses grouping techniques with lab facilities to individualize.

13. Has planned out activities to satisfy *short-range* behavioral objectives.

14. Has provided for evaluation of student work.

15. Proceeds from the unknown to the known and from the simple to the complex.

16. Uses English correctly, with normal pace and volume.

17. Displays a sensitivity to the unique problems of the ESL pupil.

18. Uses models and pattern practice as a basis for habituating new concepts.

19. The cultural aspect of language study is interpreted with the linguistic aspect.

20. Pupil linguistic problems are diagnosed and remedial prescriptions are planned.

21. In showing similarities and differences between the pupils' native language and English, similarities are presented *first*.

22. Has provided a way for each pupil to view his own personal progress.

23. Encourages a cultural exchange between/among the various linguistic groups.

JJP:gb
10/18/X4

SELF-EVALUATION CHECKLIST
FOR
MAINSTREAM TEACHERS
OF ESL PUPILS

1. I am aware that ESL pupils substitute known sounds for new sounds.

2. I am aware that these pupils need assistance in *hearing* and *reproducing* new sounds.

3. I know that normal speech patterns should be used in speaking with these students.

4. I know that my voice volume (speaking loudly) does not insure understanding by the ESL pupil.

5. I should provide many opportunities to practice sentence patterns in a systematic way—going from the simple to the complex.

6. I should introduce one concept at a time.

7. I should select examples of the *general* rule and avoid the exceptions until a later time.

8. I should provide examples of patterns and structure to give oral mastery at first.

9. I should design examples to bring about generalizations and insight through inductive reasoning.

10. I should avoid vocabulary word lists which are out of context.

11. I should design lessons around familiar situations and experiences.

12. I should realize that the audio coupled with the visual produces a greater degree of retention than either one alone.

13. I know that habituation of the oral is preferable before going on to writing.

Conclusion

The secret of writing for professional journals and texts rests in your inner self. Write for yourself without worrying what readers are going to think or criticize. Keep your personal prejudices to a minimum. Write about the world of your daily experience in simple, well-worded, concise language. Remember that you are preparing a manuscript or article that may be useful to your colleagues. Do not expect to make a fortune in royalties. Be satisfied with a modest fee, the knowledge that you have contributed to the field, and the self-satisfaction of a job well done.

INDEX

A

Absenteeism, 258
Academic banquets, 27
Academic ratings of schools, 240
Accountability forms for supervisors, 163-164
Accusations, 171
Achievement level, 242
Administrators, services, 156-160 (*see also* Chairmen and administrators)
Administrators' responsibilities, 200-202
Advertisement, paid, 229
Advisory group, 25, 30, 208
After school help, 25
Alcoholism, 173
Announcements, sent home, 22
Appeal procedures, 168-170
Architects, 241
Articles, 26, 28
Art work, 23
Assemblies, 37
Assignment, next year, 123-124
Assignment placement, substitute teacher, 239
Association survey, 258-261
Assumptions, supervisory system, 137-140
Athletic accomplishments, 27
Attendance, 221
Attitudes toward schools, student, 241
Auditing contracts, 208
Awards, 26
Awareness, 240-241
Azarnoff, Roy, 235

B

Back-to-school night, 193-194
Banquets, 27
Bilingual/bicultural program, 196-197, 258
Billboard attack, 229
Black students, 173
Board policy, 105-106
Book publishers. 264, 266
Booster Clubs, 72, 252-253
Budgets, development, 128-129
Building personnel, 200
Bulletin boards, 25, 29, 211
Bulletins, daily, 39-41, 100-101 (*see also* Daily bulletins)

C

Cafeteria, 208
Calendar of events, 23
Calendars, supervisory and administrative, 165
Cards, preaddressed, 20
Career day, 22
Career education, 258
Career information, 28
Career planning, 20
Central office:
    administrative routines, 200
    administrators' responsibilities, 200-202
    advisory council, 208
    attendance and class cutting, 221-224
    building personnel, 200

Central office: (con't)
    clerical assistance, supplies and equip-
        ment, 200
    community visits, 209
    conference periods, 208
    courses in high interest areas, 209
    department chairmanships, 208
    detention policies, 208
    dress-code policies, 208
    field trips, 212-215
    full support and backing, 200
    house plan organization pattern, 208
    human relations, 208, 210-212
    in-school "rap sessions," 209
    long-term goals, 209
    Management-by-Objectives, 200
    minority literature, 208
    more humane atmosphere, 208
    morning sign-in sheet, 202-203
    mutual respect and dignity, 208
    Negro culture, 208
    open-door communications, 208
    parent/student handbook, 203-208
    removing outside influences, 208
    strategies, 200
    suspension, 215-221
    teaching teams, 208
    unscheduled student time options, 208
    written guidelines for staff, 200
Certificate of appreciation, 22
Chairmanships, department, 208
Chairmen and administrators:
    accomplishment of objectives, 157
    assessment, 158
    description of job performance, 158-159
    evaluating services, 156-160
    objective, 157
    recommendations for improvement, 159-
        160
Change, resistance, 130
Chastisement, 127-128
Cheerleading squad, 173-182
Choir, 28
Class cutting, 221
Class offices, 63
Class schedule, 239
Clean-up days, 23
Clergy, 72
Clerical assistance, supplies and equipment,
    200
Clerical staff, 237-238
Closing school, 121-123
Clubs, 28, 63
Coffee hours, 23, 195-196
College day, 28
College placement, 262
College tours, 30

Commercial services, 264, 265
Committee reports, 257
Community:
    advisory group, 25, 30
    after school help, 25
    American Field Service exchange students,
        27
    articles, 26, 28
    athletic accomplishments, 27
    awards, 26
    banquets, 27
    bulletin boards, 25, 29
    calendar of events, 23
    career day, 22
    career information, 28
    choir, 28
    class picnics, 22
    classroom newspapers, 25
    clean-up days, 23
    clubs, 28
    coffee hours, 23, 195-196
    college day programs, 28
    college tours, 30
    Conference Evaluation Sheet, 35-36
    cooperate with community groups, 26
    curriculum revisions, 28
    curriculum trends, 25
    custodians, 30
    day-care centers, 27
    demonstrations by children, 23
    displays of art work, 23
    educational offerings, 24
    elementary school, 20-25
    evening discussions, 25
    extracurricular activities of teachers, 30
    Father's Club, 30
    getting students involved, 27
    Happy Notes for students, 30-31
    home contacts, 25
    home visits, 25
    hospitals, 28
    innovative methodologies, 28
    innovative subject materials, 28
    interclass plays, 28
    interesting activities, 22
    interpreters, 24
    language awareness night, 27-28
    letters of commendation, 30
    listener's team of parents, 25
    local dignitaries, 27
    messages sent home, 23
    mini-courses, 30
    mini-tours, 25
    musicals, 27
    National Honor Society, 27
    new faculty, 106-108
    newsletter, 21, 26

Community: (con't)
    news releases, 21-22, 25, 30
    Open House, 27
    paper problem, 32-33
    parental complaints, 33-36
    parent conference guide, 34-35
    parent discussion groups, 27
    parents witness classes, 23
    performances by children, 23
    plays, 27
    preaddressed cards, 20
    prevent misunderstandings, 20
    professional publications, 27
    profile sheet, 30
    P.T.A. dinners, dances and events, 30
    radio program, 26
    real estate people, 25
    renting school facilities, 30
    resource people, 30
    review of literature, 17
    scholarships, 28
    school handbook, 22
    school newspaper, 26
    school's philosophy and objectives, 30
    secondary schools, 25-33
    secretarial staff, 30
    selective service, 30
    senior citizens, 28
    senior class play, 28
    skits, 28
    slide presentation, 25
    speakers, 22, 27, 30
    special days and events, 30
    special events, 22
    special interest courses, 30
    sporting events, 27
    staff profile, 24
    student accomplishments, 25
    students as school volunteers, 30
    student teachers, 30
    subject matter, 26
    suggestions box, 25
    superintendent of schools, 17
    supportive staff members, 30
    survey publics, 20
    talent shows, 25
    teacher aides, 30
    telephone, 24
    trips, 22
    tutors, 28
    utilize special days, 23
    voter registration, 30
    working papers, 30
Community visits, 209
Compensation, professional journals, 266
Complaints, parental, 33-36
Computerized guidance system, 113-114
Conference guide, 34-35

Conferences, supervisory, 167-168
Conflicts, 171
Congratulatory notes, faculty, 125
Contemporary issues, 209
Contract:
    nonrenewal, 165-167
    professional journals, 266-267
Correspondence, students, 55-61 (see also
        Students)
Counseling services, 262
Courses of study, 86-88
Curriculum:
    employment needs of community, 241
    poor, 240
    revisions, 28
    trends and offerings, 25
Custodians, 30
Cutting class, 221

                                D

Daily bulletins:
    date, time, place, purpose, 40
    deadline times, 39
    faculty, 40, 100-101
    malfunctions, 40
    order of items, 39
    posted on bulletin board, 40
    short, well written, 39
    someone required to read, 40
    special items "run" several days, 40
    sponsor or person to contact, 40
    time to plan participation, 40
Day-care centers, 27
Debating teams, 27
Decisions:
    administration's initial position, 64
    alternative proposed, 64
    communicating, 64-65
    copies, 64
    date of implementation, 64
    final student recommendations, 64
    follow-up activities, 65
    issue, 64
    student press and local press, 64
    tentative trial period, 65
    written and posted, 64
Departmental meetings, 114-115
Department chairmanships, 201, 208
Dignitaries, 27
Directives, 125-127
Discussion groups, 27
Dismissal, 165-167
Distribution of student literature, 74-76
Dress-code policies, 208
Drinking, teacher, 171-173
Drugs, use, 240

E

Ecology, 209
Editor, 264-266
Editor-in-Chief, school paper, 63
Education journals, professional, 263-264
Eels, Donald, 233
Elementary school, 20-25, 28
Emergency information, 239
Employment information, 212
ESL pupils, 274-275
ESL teachers, 273-274
Evaluating, instructional data, 111-113
Evaluating communication endeavors:
    back-to-school night, 193-194
    bilingual/bicultural program, 196-197
    community coffee hour, 195-196
    guidelines, 197-198
    on-going evaluation, 193
    open message, 195
    parents of foreign-born students, 197
    telephone conversations, 194-195
Evaluative systems, 132-170 (*see also*
        Supervision and evaluation)
Exchange students, 27
Exhortation, 127-128
Extracurricular activities:
    general public is interested, 240
    offered in school, 85
    teachers, 30

F

Facilities, lack, 240
Faculty:
    assignment for next year, 123-124
    board policy, 105-106
    budgets, development, 128-129
    closing the school, 121-123
    community, 106-108
    computerized guidance system, 113-114
    congratulatory notes, 125
    correspondence with "chiefs," 110
    daily bulletins, 100-101
    directives, 125-127
    guidelines for communicating, 103-104
    instructional data, 111-113
    letters of reference, 108-109
    meetings, 114-115
    negative correspondence, 127-128
    opening school, 115-121
    permanent departure, 130-131
    policy, 101-103
    reprimands, 127-128
    resistance to change, 130
    teacher handbooks, 104-105
    welcoming new personnel, 99-100
Father's Club, 30
Felicetti, Richard, 233

Field trips, 201, 212-215
Financial aid seminars, 211
Financial status of schools, 240
Financial support, 240
Food services, 236-237
Foreign-born parents, 24
Foreign-born students, 197

G

Gallup Poll, 261
Gifted student, 241
Goals, long-term, 209
Goss vs. Lopez, 76
Grading practices, 241
Graduate courses, 262
Graduation, 93-98
Grants, 212
Guidance system, computerized, 113-114

H

Handbook:
    absence, 85
    academic guidelines, 84
    accusations, 86
    attention-getter, 46
    attractive cover, 81
    awards and scholarships, 85
    calendar, 48-49, 84
    characteristics, 80-81
    conduct and achievement, 48
    contents, 83-85
    cover, 83
    descriptions of activities, 48
    disciplinary code, 85
    distribution of student literature, 75
    expectations of students, 48
    extracurricular activities, 85
    faculty listing, 84
    goals, 84
    grading policy, 85
    ignored, 80
    issues of friction, 81
    lean content, 81
    legislative tone of school, 81
    linguistic sparseness, 81
    locker search, 74
    map of school, 85
    mechanical and organizational guidelines,
        48, 81, 84-85
    not magical solutions, 85
    parent/student, 203-208
    photographs, 84
    policies involved with legal decisions, 84
    practical data, 81
    principal's message, 46-48, 82-83
    professionally printed, 81

Handbook: (con't)
  reviewed annually, 81
  rules and regulations, 48
  schedule blank, 85
  school and community rapport, 22
  school policies, 48
  size, 84
  student council, 81, 85
  suspension, 77
  symbols, 83
  table of contents, 84
  teacher, 104-105
  variations, 46
"Happy Messages," 23
Happy Notes, 30-31
Harding, Del, 234
Home contacts, 25
Hospitals, 28
House plan organization pattern, 208
Hubbell, Ned, 225
Human relations, 208, 210-212
Hysteria, rumor and, 68-73

I

Innovation, 242
Innovative methodologies, 28
In-service programs, 241
Instructional data, 111-113
Integration problems, 240, 241
"Interim" evaluation, 160-163
Internal communications, 233
Interpreters, 24
Interviews, press, 229
Intoxication, 173

J

Jazz groups, 27
Job performance, 158-159
Job placement, 212
Jobs, 262
Journals, professional education, 263-264,
  265
Judges, 212
June, 121-123
Juvenile authorities, 212

L

Language, 27
Law, 73-76 (*see also* Student)
Leadership:
  personnel, 110-111
  students, 63-65
Lesson plans, 239
Letters:
  angry, from parents, 226-229
  "open," in press, 229-230

Letters: (con't)
  recommendation, 49-55
  reference, 108-109
Library services, 208
Listener's team, 25
Literature:
  minority, 208
  student-written, distribution, 74-76
Locker search, 73-74
Long-term goals, 209
Lunch schedule, 239

M

Mainstream teachers, 273-274, 274-275
Manuscripts, professional journals, 267
Marching bands, 27
Material location, 239
Media, 69, 234
Meetings, departmental and faculty, 114-115
Methods, current, 240
Mini-courses, 30
Mini-tours, 25
Minority literature, 208
Minority students, 173
Monthly supervisory report, 135
Morning sign-in sheet, 202-203
Musicals, 27

N

National Honor Society, 27
National School Public Relations Confer-
  ence, 225
Negro culture, 208
News coverage, 235-236
Newsletter, 21, 26, 192
News media, 197, 234-235
Newspapers:
  classroom, 25
  local, 26
  school, 26, 41-43, 63, 182-187
    accuracy, 43
    administrator and, 41-42
    appointed advisor, 43
    attack on individual, 43
    censorship, 43
    complaints, 182-187
    criticisms of rules, 43
    Editor-in-Chief, 63
    freedom, 41, 42
    good taste and propriety, 43
    libel, 43
    loyal opposition, 41
    maturity of students, 43
    obscenity, 43
    policy, 42-43
News releases, 21-22, 25, 30
Nonrenewal of contract, 165-167
Non-tenured staff, 136

O

Objectives:
    making them come alive, 146-153
    school, 30
Observation, frequency, 136-137
Observation/evaluation report, 135
Observation reports, 140-146
Officers, class, 63
Officials, boards and committees, 72
Olds, Robert, 233
Open-door communications, 208
Open House, 27, 193-194
Opening school, 115-121
"Open" letters in press, 229-230
Open messages, 192, 195
Organization, school, 63
"Outstanding" rating, 170

P

Paid advertisement, 229
Panel discussions, 257
Panelist, 249-251
Paper problem, 32-33
Parental complaints, 33-36
Parent discussion groups, 27
Parent groups, addressing, 252-253
Parents:
    back-to-school night, 193-194
    bilingual/bicultural program, 196-197
    coffee hour, 23, 195-196
    foreign-born students, 197
    handling the angry letter, 226-229
        advisor's response, 228
        principal's response, 227-228
        typical parent letter, 226-227
    lack of interest, 240
    telephone conversations, 194-195
Parent/student handbook, 203-208
Personnel:
    building, 200
    leadership, 110-111
    new, 99-100, 106-108
Petitions:
    age-old method, 65
    brief, 66
    copies to superintendent of schools, 66
    courses of action, 66
    covering memorandum, 67
    cranks or fringe groups, 67-68
    ignoring, 66
    interim solution, 67
    meeting, 67
    releases to press, 67
    serious implications, 68
    stop-gap measures, 67
    student anger and resentment, 68
    superintendent of schools, 66, 67

Petitions: (con't)
    usual route, 67
    who delivered, 66
    who initiated, 66
Philosophy, school, 30, 242
Picnics, 22
Plays, 27, 28
Police department, 72
Policy, 101-103, 105-106
Political groups, 254
Position papers, 257
Preaddressed card system, 20
Predictability, 168
Prejudices, 251
Presidents, club, 63
Press:
    communicate to all publics, 229
    credibility, 229-232
    getting proper news coverage, 235-236
    handling interviews with, 229
    honesty and mutual trust, 229
    inform people of happenings, 229
    open letters, 229-230
    public relations, 232-235
    state your position, 229
    student, 182-187 (see also Newspaper)
    tell people why and how, 229
Pressure groups, 254-255
Principal, 200-201 (see also Central office)
Professional groups, addressing, 248-249
Professional journals:
    advance against royalties, 267
    after completing manuscript, 267
    artwork, 267
    association survey, 258-261
    better teaching in basics, 262
    book publishers, 264
    commercial service, 264
    compensation, rate, 266
    contract, 266-267
    counseling services, 262
    deadline dates, 267
    finding outlets for writings, 263-264
    Gallup Poll, 261
    gauging reading audience, 262-263
    graduate courses, 262
    hearing from editor, 266
    indexing, 267
    introducing yourself to editor, 264-266
        commercial services, 265
        positive approach, 264
        professional journals, 265
        textbook publisher, 266
    lifelong sports and recreation, 262
    meaningful communication, 262
    monetary agreement, 266
    professional education journals, 263-264
    promotional sales endeavors, 267
    public perception of "good" school, 261-
        262

Professional journals: (con't)
  questions of concern, 262
  release date, 267
  rights and copyright cards, 267
  sample correspondence, 267-272
  student concerns, 262
  what to say, 257-258
    alternative forms of education, 258
    bilingual/bicultural approaches, 258
    bulletins, 257
    career education, 258
    committee reports, 257
    declining PSAT/SAT scores, 258
    drawers and files, 258
    educational concerns, 257
    experience, 258
    high rate of absenteeism, 258
    national survey reports, 257
    panel discussions, 257
    position papers, 257
    problems facing education, 257
  words and chapters in manuscript, 267
Professional publications, 27
Profile sheet, 24, 30
Promotional sales endeavors, 267
PSAT/SAT scores, 258
Psychology, 209
P.T.A.:
  addressing, 252-253
  participation, 30
Public address system, 38-39
Publications, professional, 27
Public relations:
  angry letter from parents, 226-227
    advisor's response, 228
    example, 226-227
    principal's response, 227-228
    principal telephones parents, 229
  back-to-school night, 193-194
  being aware, 240-241
  bilingual/bicultural program, 196-197
  billboard attack, 229
  communication guidelines, 197-198
  communications to parents, 233
  communications to school, 233
  community coffee hour, 195-196
  food services, 236-237
  honesty and mutual trust, 229
  internal communications, 233
  interviews, 229
  news coverage, 235-236
  "open" letter in press, 229
  open message, 195
  paid advertisement, 229
  parents involved in school programs, 233
  parents of foreign-born students, 197
  parents partners with school, 233
  press credibility, 229-232
  public and press relations, 232-235

Public relations: (con't)
  school volunteer services, 233
  secretarial and clerical staff, 237-238
  substitute teachers, 239
  telephone conversations, 194-195
  typical questions, 241-242
Publics, 20, 229

R

Rap sessions, 209
Real estate people, 25
Realtors, 187-192
Recommendation, letters, 49-55
Recreation, 262
Reference, letters, 108-109
Referral agencies, 212
Referral system, 224
Renting school facilities, 30
Reporting, instructional data, 111-113
Reprimands, 127-128
Resource people, 30, 211
Rotary, 245
Royalties, 267
Rumor, 68-73

S

Schedule, class, 239
Scheduling, self-, 88-93
Scholarships, 28
School board policies, 240
School Management Institute, 233
Seating charts, 239
Secondary schools, 25-33
Secretarial staff, 30, 237
Secretary, evaluating, 154-156
Segregation problems, 240
Selective service, 30
Self-scheduling, 88-93
Senior citizens, 28
September, 115-121
"Service club" delivery, 245-248
Service clubs, 72
Sign-in sheet, 202-203
Size:
  classes, 240, 242
  school, 240
Skits, 28
Slide presentation, 25, 212
Smoking privileges, 208
Snack bar, 208
Socioeconomic scale, 173
Spanish-speaking students, 173
Speakers, 22, 30, 211
Special education, 241
Special interest courses, 30
Speeches:
  "big" speech, 255

Speeches. (con't)
    board of education, 243-245
        "antiseptic" tone, 244
        audiences, 243
        avoid "preaching," 244
        compress, 245
        educational jargon, 244
        electrical connections, 244
        hackneyed phraseology, 244
        inaccuracies, 243
        "instant boredom," 244
        local press, 243
        political implications, 244
        professional personnel, 244
        public address system, 244
        public at large, 243
        review with immediate supervisor, 245
        screens, 244
        seating, 244
        simple, direct, uncluttered, clear, 245
        supplementary handouts, 244
        technical language, 244
        timing, 244
        truth, 245
        "unwise" commentary, 244
        verbal warfare, 244
        visual materials, 245
    boosters' club, 252-253
    contributing from audience, 254
    panelist, 249-251
        airing *diverse* views, 251
        allotted speaking time, 251
        crisp and witty, 251
        do not attack, 251
        do not discredit, 251
        honest and refreshing, 251
        key items as reminders, 251
        never monopolize, 251
        not cutting, 251
        part of team, 251
        prejudices or predispositions, 251
        read on central topic, 249
        relax, 251
        style and substance, 251
    parent groups, 252-253
    "pressure" groups, 254-255
    professional groups, 248-249
        beginning and closing, 249
        compression, 248
        delivering with verve, 249
        digressions, 249
        discarding irrelevancies, 249
        humor, 249
        illustrations, 248, 249
        knowing what needs to be said, 249
        organizing, 249
        planning, 249
        "sound scholarship," 248
        synthesis of complicated loose ends,
            248

Speeches: (con't)
        well informed audience, 248
        when audience has had enough, 249
        write remarks fully, 248
    P.T.A., 252
    "service club" delivery, 245-248
        age range in audience, 246
        appeal of media, 246
        educated delivery, 246
        emotion, 246
        gratitude, 246
        heavy problems, 247
        humor, 247
        lasting impact, 246
        moving, direct, terse, brief, 246
        no "in-group" things, 248
        nostalgic theme, 246
        older group, 246
        open to questions and answers, 248
        precise historical references, 246
        recent history, 246
        synthesize complex notions, 247
        theme without prepared speech, 248
        topics, 247-248
        universal appeal, 246
        value of sound education, 246
        war and peace, 246
    student groups, 251-252
Sporting events, 27
Sports, 262
Sports banquets, 27
Staff profile sheet, 24
Stationery, 61
Student Bulletin, 100
Student Council, 63
Student groups, addressing, 251-252
Student press, 182-187 (*see also* Newspaper)
Students:
    assemblies, 37
    correspondence, 55-61
        bland, 61
        don't "overwrite," 60
        first names, 60
        groups, 55
        immediately after event, 61
        letter perfect, 61
        local press, 61
        mail to pupils' homes, 60
        meaningless words, 60
        recognition for accomplishments, 55
        samples, 56-60
        sign personally, 60
        stationery, 61
        unique, 60
    courses of study, 86-88
    daily bulletins, 39-41
    graduation, 93-98
    handbooks, 46-49, 80-86 (*see also* Hand-
        books)
    "instant" communications, 37-41

Students: (con't)
   involving leadership, 63-65
      communicating decisions, 64-65
      exploration of issues, 64
      issue, 64
      "mini-congress," 63
      process, 64
      who leaders are, 63-64
      work-study programs, 64
   law, 73-76
      distribution of literature, 74-76
      locker search, 73-74
   letters of recommendation, 49-55
   petitions, 65-68 (see also Petitions)
   public address system, 38-39
   rumor and hysteria, 68-73
      adult community is afraid, 68
      guidelines, 71-72
      media, 69
      typical situation, 69-71
   school paper, 41-43
      administration, 41-42
      policy, 42-43
   self-scheduling, 88-93
   suspension, 76-80 (see also Suspension)
   yearbooks, 43-46
Student teachers, 30
Study, courses of, 86-88
Subject matter, 26, 28
Substitute teachers, 239
Suggestions box, 25
Superintendent of schools, 17
Supervision and evaluation:
   accountability forms, 163-164
   administrative and appeal procedures,
      168-170
      appeal procedure, 169
      filing of evaluative documents, 170
      justification of certain evaluations, 170
      submitting evaluations, 169-170
      supervisory problems, 170
   assumptions, 137-140
   calendars, 165
   chairmen and administrators, 156-160
      accomplishment of objectives, 157
      assessment, 158
      description of job performance, 158-
        159
      description of results of work, 157
      objective, 157
      quality of work, 157
      recommendations for improvement,
        159-160
   "interim" evaluation, 160-163
   nonrenewal of contract and dismissal,
      165-167
   objectives, 146-153
   observation reports, 140-146
   organizing system, 132-134

Supervision and evaluation: (con't)
   procedures, 134-137
      evaluation/experienced teachers, 135
      forms to be used, 135-136
      frequency of observation, 136-137
      improvement of instruction, 134
      instruments, 135
      judgment on quality of performance,
        134
      monthly supervisory report, 135
      non-tenured staff, 136
      observation/evaluation report, 135
      purpose, 134
   secretary, 154-156
   summarizing supervisory conferences,
      167-168
Supply location, 239
Support, 212
Surveys, 187-192, 257, 258-261
Suspension:
   careful communication, 80
   discipline folder, 79
   fair administration, 80
   five days or longer, 76
   lack of equity, 80
   letter to parents, 77-80
   litigation, 79
   parents notified, 76
   policies and due process, 215-221
   student heard, 76
   support of courts, 76
   varying lengths, 77

               T

Talent shows, 25
Taxpayer associations, 254
Teacher aides, 30
Teacher-aide training courses, 212
Teacher handbooks, 104-105
Teaching assignments, 123-124
Teams, teaching, 208
Telephone communications, 26, 192
Telephone conversation report form, 222
Telephone conversation sheets, 194-195
Textbook location, 239
Textbook publisher, 266
Tours:
   college, 30
   mini-, 25
Tracers, 223
Tutors, 28

               U

Unexpected situations:
   cheerleading squad, 173-182
   student press, 182-187

Unexpected situations: (con't)
    teacher asscused of drinking on job, 171-
        173
Unit coordinators, 169, 170, 201-202
"Unsatisfactory" rating, 170

                    V

Vested-interest groups, 254
Veterans' groups, 245
Volunteers, 30
Voter registration, 30

                    W

Waste, supplies and workers, 241
White students, 173
Working papers, 30
Work-study programs, 64
Writing for professional journals, 257-275
        (*see also* Professional journals)

                    Y

Yearbooks, 43-46